100 YEARS OF FLIGHT

BILL SWEETMAN

Publications International, Ltd.

Front cover: **Keith Ferris Collection/United States Air Force Art Collection.**

Back cover: **John Batchelor** (top left); **Eric Dumigan Photography** (right center); **Northrop Grumman Corporation** (bottom left).

Aces High Photography: Contents, 59 (top), 69 (top), 70 (top); **Airbus Industrie:** 137; **AP/Wide World Photos:** Contents, 11 (left), 12 (top), 13, 14 (bottom), 15 (top, center & bottom left), 17 (center), 20 (top), 23 (right), 25 (top), 26 (bottom), 27 (bottom), 29 (right & bottom), 30 (top), 35, 40 (top right & bottom), 42 (top), 43 (bottom), 44 (bottom), 45, 46 (bottom), 47 (bottom), 50 (right), 51 (top), 52 (left), 55 (bottom), 56 (top), 57 (bottom), 58 (bottom), 59 (bottom), 64 (top & center), 65 (top), 67 (center & bottom), 68, 69 (bottom), 70 (center & bottom), 71 (center), 72 (top), 73 (left), 75 (bottom left), 76 (bottom left & bottom right), 78 (top), 83 (top), 86 (bottom), 88 (center), 89 (top), 90 (bottom), 91 (top center, bottom center & bottom), 92 (bottom), 94 (top), 95, 99 (top), 100 (center), 101 (top), 102 (bottom center), 104 (bottom), 105 (bottom), 107 (top), 108 (top right), 115 (center), 116 (bottom left), 117 (bottom), 122, 129 (center), 131 (top), 134 (top & bottom), 135 (center), 136 (top & bottom), 141 (top & bottom), 143 (left, right & bottom); **John Batchelor:** 8 (bottom); **Bell Helicopter Textron:** 124 (left); **Boeing:** 75 (center), 90 (top); **Peter M. Bowers Collection:** 17 (right), 28 (top), 34 (top), 47 (right center & bottom center), 65 (center & bottom), 71 (bottom), 86 (center), 94 (center), 102 (top & top center), 109 (top); **Corbis:** 16 (top), 28 (bottom), 30 (bottom), 32 (bottom), 37, 46 (top), 50 (left), 52 (top right), 56 (bottom), 61 (bottom), 67 (top), 71 (top), 73 (right), 74 (left & right), 79, 89 (bottom), 115 (left), 116 (left center), 117 (top), 138, 140 (top), 142 (left); John H. Clark: 126 (top); George Hall: 93 (top), 97, 104 (top), 135 (top); Randy Jolly: 133; Roger Rossmeyer: 116 (right center); Richard Hamilton Smith: 53 (top); **Cradle of Aviation Museum:** 28 (top), 77 (top); **Douglas/San Diego Aerospace Museum:** 29 (left); **Eric Dumigan Photography:** 19, 39, 44 (center), 57 (top); **Getty Images:** David M. Doody/FPG International: 53 (bottom); Hulton Archive: 17 (left), 48, 49 (left & center); **Jim Koepnick/Experimental Aircraft Association:** 143 (top); **Courtesy Lockheed Martin Corp.:** 52 (bottom), 54; **Courtesy McDonnell Douglas Corp.:** 4, 5 (top left & top right), 42 (bottom), 102 (bottom), 123 (top), 131 (bottom); Harry Gann: 41, 43 (left); **NASA:** 109 (bottom), 113 (bottom), 115 (bottom), 116 (top & bottom right), 118 (center), 119 (top), 129 (bottom); **National Air and Space Museum, Smithsonian Institution:** 5 Photo No. A14756, 85-18307 (top left & top right), 17 Photo No. A44401-C (bottom); 20 Photo No. 75-6979, 80-2381 (center & bottom), 21 Photo No. 122253, 22 Photo No. A-510, 24 Photo No. 91-17325, 26 Photo No. 80-2384, 75-15531 (left & right), 27 Photo No. 91-17324 (top), 33 Photo No. 91-17358, 34 Photo No. 89-16884 (bottom), 43 Photo No. 1A39065 (right), 44 Photo No. 122257A.C (top), 47 Photo No. 88-16383 (top), 51 Photo No. 80-11041 (bottom), 55 Photo No. 40756A.C, 80-13000 (top & center), 60 Photo No. A38634E (center), 61 Photo No. 76-13683 (top), 85 Photo No. AKS325 (top), 108 Photo No. 97-15029, 97-15169 (top left & center), 140 Photo No. 97-15166 (center); **Naval Photographic Center:** 36 (top), 64 (bottom); **Photri Inc.:** Contents, 5 (bottom), 24 (bottom), 60 (top), 75 (top), 76 (top & center), 81, 83 (bottom), 85 (bottom), 91 (top), 93 (bottom), 94 (bottom), 98, 100 (bottom), 103, 106 (center), 107 (bottom), 112, 113 (left, right & center), 114 (left), 115 (right), 117 (center), 118 (top & bottom), 127 (left), 140 (bottom), 142 (center); Ed Boettcher: 123 (center); Dassauit: 130 (top); Bill Marsh: 106 (top); **Dennis Plummer:** 125 (top); **James P. Rowan:** 88 (top); **Saab-Scania:** 78 (bottom); **SuperStock:** 10 (bottom), 11 (top), 12 (bottom), 31, 32 (top), 36 (bottom), 60 (bottom), 63, 66, 74 (top), 75 (bottom right), 85 (center), 86 (top), 87, 92 (top), 99 (bottom), 100 (top), 101 (bottom), 105 (top), 111, 114 (right), 119 (right), 121, 124 (right), 128, 139, 142 (right); **United States Air Force Museum:** 23 (left), 88 (bottom), 125 (bottom); **U.S. Department of Defense:** 127 (right & bottom), 130 (bottom); **U.S. Naval Historical Center:** 15 (bottom right); **U.S. Navy:** 77 (bottom), 126 (bottom); **Philip Wallick/International Stock:** 129 (top); **Joseph H. Wherry Collection:** 25 (bottom), 40 (left & right center), 49 (right), 84 (top); U.S. Air Force: 72 (bottom); **Wright State University:** 7, 8 (top), 9, 10 (top), 11 (bottom right), 14 (top & center).

Writer **Bill Sweetman** is an experienced aviation journalist, having written more than 30 books in the field, including *Aircraft 2000, High-Speed Flight,* and *Stealth Bombers: The B-2 Spirits.* He was awarded the Aviation/Space Writers Association Award of Excellence in 1990 and 1992. Mr. Sweetman also served as Consulting Editor on *Jane's International Defense Review.*

Consultant **Walter J. Boyne** is a retired colonel in the United States Air Force and a prominent military and aviation consultant and author. Mr. Boyne is a former director of the National Air and Space Museum and the author of *The Smithsonian Book of Flight, The Leading Edge,* and a host of other military and aviation titles.

Louis Weber, CEO
Publications International, Ltd.
7373 North Cicero Avenue
Lincolnwood, Illinois 60712

Permission is never granted for commercial purposes.

Manufactured in China.

8 7 6 5 4 3 2 1

ISBN: 0-7853-6324-6

Library of Congress Control Number: 2002104422

CONTENTS

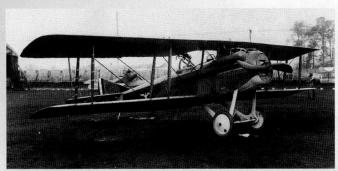

INTRODUCTION

Celebrating a Century of Conquering the Air

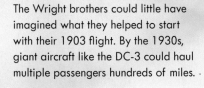

The Wright brothers could little have imagined what they helped to start with their 1903 flight. By the 1930s, giant aircraft like the DC-3 could haul multiple passengers hundreds of miles.

The quest for flight was not new to the Wright brothers and their turn-of-the-century peers; it was a fantasy for many since almost the beginning of time. For thousands of years, people looked to the skies and dreamed of soaring through the clouds like a bird. The lure of the wind beckoned powerfully.

The literature of several ancient peoples tell the stories of each culture's fascination with flying and their longing to take to the skies. Greek mythology offers the tragic tale of Daedalus and his son Icarus, who made wings from wax and feathers to help them escape from prison. Unfortunately, Icarus's waxen wings melted when he flew too close to the sun, and he fell to his death. The Persians told stories of King Kai Kawus, a great ruler who yoked four eagles to his throne and flew all the way to China.

Outside of the realm of fiction, history is dotted with forward-thinkers who speculated about flight and early scientists who worked to find ways for people to fly. The Chinese invented the kite in the 4th century B.C. and learned how to harness the wind's power. Franciscan monk and scientist Roger Bacon theorized in 1260 about "an engine for flying" with "a man sitting in the midst thereof" and a "large hollow globe...filled with ethereal air [that]...would float as a ship on water." Even one of the world's greatest thinkers and artists, Leonardo da Vinci, pondered the possibility of human flight and sketched many designs for flying machines.

Still, despite all of the fascination and all of the dreams—and despite the attempts at creating ways to fly—no one had been able to solve the puzzle of flight.

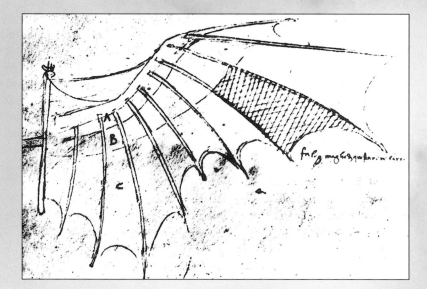

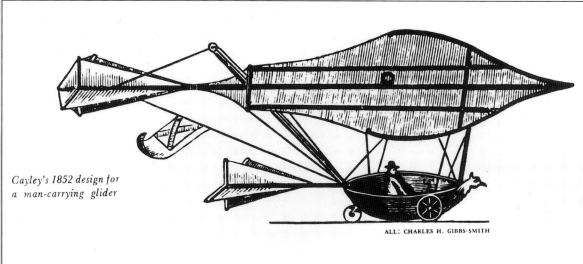

Cayley's 1852 design for a man-carrying glider

ALL: CHARLES H. GIBBS-SMITH

Our fascination with flight and efforts to attain it hadn't been completely unsuccessful, though. There were fits and starts of hopeful periods as small triumphs were made here and there. In 1783, two French papermakers named Joseph and Etienne Montgolfier had discovered that hot air could fill a spherical balloon and cause it to rise. At the same time, French physicist Jacques Charles began experimenting with hydrogen-filled balloons. The French watched with delight as these balloons took to the skies. News of the amazing feats spread around the globe, and others began experimenting with the thrilling new aircraft.

By 1900, Count Ferdinand von Zeppelin and Alberto Santos-Dumont (among others) had designed steerable balloons that could fly safely for miles. While these were exciting developments, the unpredictable crafts were slow and largely uncontrollable.

Heavier-than-air crafts also had their minor victories. Sir George Cayley managed to build a full-size glider that was able to carry his coachman in 1853. Inventor Clément Ader created a bat-like powered craft that achieved an extended hop that took him about eight inches off the ground in 1890.

There were many more failures than successes, however. And then, just as some of the turn of the century's greatest scientists had given up hope of ever solving the enigma of powered flight...just as it seemed that the quest would forever go unfulfilled...the Wright brothers' Flyer victoriously took wing on a December morning in the North Carolina sand dunes in 1903.

While the Wrights were certainly ecstatic about their success, not even they could imagine the amazing new era that their 59-second flight had opened. In that minute or so, the brothers had managed to realize the hopes of thousands of years of dreamers. They also set off an adventurous new period of experimentation and development.

December 17, 2003, marks the 100th anniversary of that first powered flight—a century in which not only an industry has grown, but the world has changed. *100 Years of Flight* celebrates this remarkable century filled with engineering innovations and historic landmarks. From the Wrights' simple (yet technologically spectacular) Flyer to the complexity of the to-the-stars-and-back-again Space Shuttle, *100 Years of Flight* chronicles the aircraft, personalities, and events of the past century of aviation as well as looks ahead to flight's exciting future.

Left: One of Leonardo da Vinci's ideas for a flying machine included wings with flapping tips. The wings were powered by the movement of the pilot's arms and legs.

Right: Some of Sir George Cayley's designs were for "flying boat" styles of crafts. Others showed sleek gliders with one set of wings. All displayed a remarkable understanding of aerodynamics.

Below: In one of the first examples of military use of aircraft, Thaddeus Lowe used hydrogen balloons to provide airborne observation posts for the Union army at the start of the Civil War.

CHAPTER ONE

Experimentation Takes Flight

THE WRIGHT BROTHERS' HISTORIC DECEMBER 17, 1903,

FLIGHT SENDS THE YOUNG FIELD OF AVIATION

SOARING TO NEW HEIGHTS.

A biting north wind raked the massive sand dunes of North Carolina's Outer Banks. Orville and Wilbur Wright had taken to sleeping in their overcoats under five blankets each, but they still managed to shave and don celluloid collars and ties before setting to each day's work.  The Wrights were attempting a task at which one of the nation's most eminent scientists had just failed. Nine days earlier, on December 8, 1903, pilot and engineer Charles Manly had narrowly escaped drowning after his four-winged Aerodrome—designed by Smithsonian Institution secretary Samuel Pierpont Langley—plummeted into the Potomac.

Right: The camera captures a priceless moment in time as Orville Wright navigates at the moment of takeoff on December 17, 1903. Wilbur stands, almost unbelieving, to the right.

The prone position of the pilot was used on the Wright Flyer to lessen resistance. Here it is shown shortly after a false start. Getting airborne depended upon wind, engine power, and luck.

After assembling a 60-foot launch rail on a downward slope, the Wrights moved their delicate machine into position. Orville and Wilbur walked to the rear of the machine, one on each side, and swung the big two-blade propellers. The engine fired. Orville took his place on the lower wing, resting his hips in a sliding cradle that was linked by wires to the flexible outer wings and the rear-mounted rudder. A left-hand control was linked to the forward elevator.

At 10:35 A.M., Orville moved the right-hand control lever, releasing the cable that held the machine in place. Wilbur held the wingtip to steady it as the craft rolled slowly forward into the wind. After a 40-foot run, the machine lifted off its rail and flew for 12 seconds and 120 feet.

The brothers made three more flights that day. Around noon, Wilbur flew for 852 feet and 59 seconds—a sustained, powered, and controlled flight. They would have made longer flights but for a gust of wind that upended the machine and wrecked it. The Wrights had little doubt about their accomplishment. "Success" read their telegram to their hometown of Dayton. "Four flights Thursday morning...level with engine power alone."

SHOWING THE WRIGHT STUFF

The Wright Flyer used a tail-first, or canard, arrangement, with the elevator in front of the wing. It provided the pilot with positive control over the airplane but wasn't as good for stability. The brothers preferred warping wings to hinged ailerons, which later became standard.

On early Wright airplanes, the rudder and wing-warping controls were interconnected; they could not be moved independently. Later designers provided separate controls. Another feature unique to the Flyer was the centrally mounted engine, which drove two propellers through chains.

The restored Wright Flyer was not exhibited in the United States until 1947. The Smithsonian Institution, in charge of the nation's historic aircraft collection, maintained for decades that Samuel Pierpont Langley had produced the first flyable airplane. Until the Wright brothers' work was recognized in the United States, Orville Wright only allowed the Flyer to be exhibited in the Science Museum in London.

The Quest for Flight

During the 19th century, transportation and communication had changed almost beyond the scope of modern imagination. Land travel had progressed from the stagecoach, which covered as much as 12 miles per hour on a good day, to the railroad networks, which allowed trains to travel at speeds sometimes nearing 100 miles per hour. Oceanic sea travel had changed from a risky adventure to a luxurious stay in a floating palace. Still, humanity had not learned how to fly.

People had left the ground, though—even as far back as the 18th century. In 1783, the Montgolfier brothers, the papermakers who

---

A.D. 62
Greek philosopher and mathematician Hero's "Aeolipile" steam-driven sphere illustrates reactive propulsion.

400
A Chinese rotary-wing top is flown. It is the first human-created object of any kind flown under power.

850
The Chinese invent gunpowder.

1232
Rockets are used by the Chinese against the Mongols.

1242
Englishman Roger Bacon produces gunpowder.

1325
A Flemish manuscript shows a string-powered helicopter. It's the first known illustration of a helicopter.

1483
Leonardo da Vinci produces his "Helix," the design sketch of a helicopter.

1687
Sir Isaac Newton formulates the Laws of Motion, which include the third law "for every action there is an equal and opposite reaction."

1780
Indian ruler Hyder Ali, Prince of Mysore, inaugurates the use of large rockets against the British.

August 27, 1783
The first hydrogen balloon is launched from Paris, only to be "killed" by nervous peasants upon landing.

September 19, 1783
The Montgolfier brothers launch a

balloon carrying a sheep, a cock, and a duck at Versailles.

November 21, 1783
The Marquis d'Arlandes and Jean Pilatre de Rozier make the first human free flight in a balloon.

1784
Mikhail V. Lomonosov flies a spring-powered lifting air-screw model, called "Aerodynamic"; in Paris,

helped to create balloon flight, had built a balloon that carried its own burner aloft. Jean Pilatre de Rozier and the Marquis d'Arlandes made the first free flight in a balloon by humans on November 21, 1783.

The Montgolfier hot-air balloon and a competing hydrogen-filled balloon quickly captured the imagination of the scientific community. A basic problem with ballooning became obvious almost

Above: The Wrights used gliders to learn how to pilot an aircraft. This is their 1902 glider, which was a radical redesign of their 1901 model. Note the twin rudders are turning to coordinate the bank.

Left: Orville watches Wilbur test the speed of the wind, always a critical element of any flight.

Launoy and Bienvenu demonstrate a two-bladed, contra-rotating model.

January 7, 1785
Jean Pierre Blanchard and Dr. John Jeffries cross the English Channel in a hydrogen balloon.

1796
Sir George Cayley improves on the Launoy/Bienvenu model.

October 22, 1797
Andre Garnerin makes the first successful parachute descent.

1804
Sir William Congreve begins work on British rockets.

1806
Congreve rockets are used in Napoleonic wars.

1809
Sir George Cayley flies a fixed-wing model glider.

1810
Sir George Cayley publishes "On Aerial Navigation."

1814
The British use Congreve rockets against Fort McHenry in Baltimore, inspiring the words to "The Star-Spangled Banner."

1840
William Hale creates spin-stabilized rockets by placing curved metal vanes in rocket exhaust.

1848
John Stringfellow flies a steam-powered, fixed-wing model airplane.

1849
Sir George Cayley (according to legend) tests the first glider to carry a person.

September 24, 1852
Henri Giffard flies an experimental steam-powered airship.

1857
Konstantin Eduardovich Tsiolkovsky—the Father of Cosmonautics during the days of the USSR—is born.

1861–65
Hydrogen balloons are used experimentally for observation in the U.S. Civil War.

GLIDING INTO AVIATION HISTORY

Sir George Cayley, a 32-year-old gentleman scientist from Yorkshire, England, exploded the belief that a machine should fly like a bird, by flapping its wings. After building his first glider, Sir George Cayley devoted the rest of his life to studies of lift and drag. According to legend, Sir George built a glider in 1849 and found a young boy to fly it. Cayley's sketches of such an aircraft survive, but there is no solid record of such a flight.

as quickly: The balloon could either be tethered to the ground, or it could go exactly where the wind went; there was no third option. Most attempts to develop a dirigible, or *steerable balloon,* failed.

This didn't stop a German cavalry officer from pushing forward with his own experimentation. Count Ferdinand von Zeppelin's airship had an aluminum frame covered in fabric and separate gasbags. By 1900, Zeppelin had built a flying giant, a 420-foot-long airship. It was marginally successful, and Zeppelin became convinced that a practical vehicle for military and commercial use was within reach.

Nineteenth-century engineers had also been working on developing what seemed to be the impossible: a heavier-than-air aircraft. If the development of a steerable balloon was proving difficult, the creation of an airplane-style craft was fraught with peril. The century had started well with Sir George Cayley's 1809 successful small, fixed-wing glider, but further experimentation with the crafts had brought little success.

John Stringfellow—a follower of Cayley—fitted a steam engine to a model aircraft in 1848. Other experimenters followed: In 1890, Clement Ader managed a few short hops in his *Eole,* which was powered by a steam engine and had batlike wings. Samuel

Above: The Wrights were unable to get an engine light and powerful enough from a commercial manufacturer, so they built their own. They were aided by Charles Taylor, an employee at their bicycle shop.

Right: Otto Lilienthal was perhaps the most successful of those who attempted to solve the mystery of flight before the Wrights. He died in his attempts, but he passed on both inspiration and information to those who followed.

Opposite: The Montgolfier brothers startled the world with their 1783 balloon-flying success (illustrated here) and were soon followed by a host of other aeronauts.

1865
Jules Verne's *From the Earth to the Moon* forecasts future space travel.

1870
Edward Everett Hale proposes a habitable satellite 200 feet in diameter to be used for communication, weather, and navigation purposes.

1878
Enrico Forliano builds a small, steam-

powered helicopter model that flies to a height of 30 to 40 feet.

1883
Konstantin Eduardovich Tsiolkovsky proposes that a rocket will work in the vacuum of space.

1884
The French Army airship *La France* makes a closed-circuit flight on electric power.

1890
Clement Ader of France makes short flights in the bat-winged *Eole.*

1895
Thomas Edison declares that "the possibilities of the aeroplane have been exhausted."

August 8, 1896
German engineer Otto Lilienthal is killed while gliding near Berlin.

September 30, 1899
British pioneer Percy Pilcher dies in a gliding accident.

1900
Orville and Wilbur Wright begin their experiments in flight.

July 2, 1900
Count Ferdinand von Zeppelin launches his first rigid airship.

1902
The Wright brothers test their first successful glider.

1903
Konstantin Eduardovich Tsiolkovsky advocates the use of liquid propellants for spaceships.

December 8, 1903
▶ Samuel Pierpont Langley's Aerodrome crashes in the Potomac River during a flight attempt.

December 17, 1903
▶ Orville and Wilbur Wright achieve powered, controlled flight at Kitty Hawk.

September 20, 1904
Orville Wright makes a successful closed-circuit flight.

1905
The Wrights create the first practical airplane.

October 5, 1905
Wilbur Wright makes a 40-minute flight.

January 1906
The first Aero Show is held in New York.

October 9, 1906
The first military dirigible, the Zeppelin LZ 3, flies and becomes the German Army LZ 1.

October 23, 1906
Alberto Santos-Dumont makes the first powered flight in Europe. He covers 200 feet.

August 1, 1907
The Aeronautical Division of the U.S. Army's Signal Corps is formed.

September 27, 1907
Louis Breguet flies *Gyroplane # 1* in tethered flight. He gets two feet above

Opposite: Orville Wright gave splendid demonstrations of the Military Flyer at Fort Myer in both 1908 and 1909. Most flights by the Wrights were made at relatively low altitudes, often no more than 50 feet off the ground.

Pierpont Langley flew a steam-powered scale model of his Aerodrome in 1896 for 90 seconds.

Despite these minor successes, Thomas Edison declared in 1895 that "the possibilities of the aeroplane have been exhausted." At the end of 1901, a dispirited Wilbur Wright was seconding Edison's opinion, remarking to his brother that the goal of manned, powered flight would not be realized soon, "not within a thousand years."

Conquering the Air

Flight presented two difficulties. The first was that the problems of lift, air resistance, stability, control, and propulsion were all intimately related and all had to be solved before a practical manned airplane could be built.

The second problem was that flying was dangerous. German engineer Otto Lilienthal set out in the late 1880s to investigate the problems of lift, stability, and control. Between 1891 and 1896, Lilienthal made more than 2,000 flights in what would today be called hang gliders; they were foot-launched and controlled and

The French love affair with the automobile had given them an early lead in the business of making aircraft, but they lagged, as did all the world, behind the Wrights when it came to propellers. Still, though, Alberto Santos-Dumont (left) got much acclaim when he was able to sustain a short flight in 1906.

stabilized by movements of the pilot's body. In 1896, Lilienthal was mortally wounded in a crash. The same fate overtook British aviation pioneer Percy Pilcher in 1899.

Octave Chanute, a French-born American, was more cautious. Almost 60 years old when he started his investigations, he enlisted assistants to fly his aircraft and discouraged them from flying too high. He studied lessons learned by other aviators and shared his knowledge with others, including the bicycle-making brothers from Dayton, Ohio, Wilbur and Orville Wright. The Wrights were more than just bicycle-builders; they were good scientists and good engineers who knew how to experiment efficiently.

After gliders based on Lilienthal's work proved unsatisfactory, the Wrights built a wind tunnel that let them test and design better airfoil sections. It was basic to the design of their 1902 glider, but so was another insight derived from their love of bicycles.

A bicycle is an unstable vehicle that stays upright only when it is moving, and it can turn only if it leans to one side. While Professor Langley was trying to build an airplane that would be steered like a boat, the Wrights designed a craft that the pilot could steer easily in pitch (up and down), yaw (left and right), and side-to-side roll, with a front elevator control, warping wingtips for roll control, and a rudder. After testing three-axis control on their 1902 glider, the Wrights returned to Kitty Hawk, North Carolina, in 1903 with their Flyer, which was powered by a hand-built piston engine.

The Wrights' success met with more jealousy than congratulations. Press accounts of the Wrights' incredible achievement were distorted or nonexistent. This public disregard continued in 1904 as they tested a more powerful airplane at Huffman Prairie, near Dayton. Amos Root, who ran a local beekeeping supply company, saw Orville's historic flight of September 20, 1904. Orville made a 95-second, 4,080-foot circuit of the Prairie. The Wrights

the ground for a minute, but the aircraft lacks control.

November 13, 1907
Paul Cornu makes a short free flight in an experimental helicopter. He gets one foot above the ground.

November 16, 1907
Wilbur Wright negotiates purchase agreements in Great Britain, France, Italy, and Germany.

January 13, 1908
Henry Farman makes the first European circular flight of more than one kilometer.

February 10, 1908
The Wright brothers sign a contract for the Wright Model A.

July 4, 1908
Glenn Curtiss makes his first flight in *June Bug* at Hammondsport, New York.

August 1908
The Wrights make their first demonstration flights in France and Fort Myer, Virginia.

September 17, 1908
Lieutenant Thomas Selfridge is killed in the crash of a Wright aircraft.

October 5, 1908
Samuel F. Cody makes his first official powered flight in Britain.

October 16, 1908
Samuel F. Cody flies the British Army *Aeroplane # 1* at Farnborough.

1909
Robert E. Goddard concludes that liquid oxygen and liquid hydrogen would be an excellent propellant.

July 25, 1909
▶ Louis Bleriot flies across the English Channel from Calais, France, to Dover, England.

The 1908 demonstration of the Wright Flyer was marred by the accident that killed Lieutenant Thomas Selfridge, the first man to die in a powered aircraft accident. A propeller malfunction clipped a wire supporting the rudder, causing the aircraft to crash.

FROM BICYCLE–MAKERS TO AVIATION PIONEERS

Mythology has cast Orville and Wilbur Wright as "simple bicycle-makers," but the characterization could not be further from the truth. They combined a strong grasp of scientific method with practical mechanical skills—a bicycle, after all, was a mechanical system where the ratio of strength to weight was critical. They were cautious and reserved without a hint of showiness.

A scientific nature led them to study the work of others and to work first with kites and then with gliders to understand the fundamentals of flight. Their engineering background had them build a wind tunnel (shown above) to measure the lift and drag of their glider designs. The Wrights barely began to look at propulsion until they had mastered the art of gliding.

made longer flights throughout 1905, culminating in Wilbur's 38-minute, 24-mile-plus circuit of the field in October. Through it all, Root described their experiments in newsletters to his customers. Readers of *Scientific American* and the national press heard nothing of the Wrights, but the readers of *Gleanings in Bee Culture* knew that the air had been conquered.

No other aviator in the world was within sight of matching the Wrights. In France, Alberto Santos-Dumont made a hop in November 1906, covering less distance than the Wrights had done in 1903. The secretary of the Aero Club of America called the Santos-Dumont flight "the most positive advance yet made in the science of aeronautics."

The Wrights spent 1907 building and testing a refined two-seat airplane. It was unveiled almost simultaneously in France by Wilbur and in Fort Myer, Virginia, by Orville in August 1908. The plane's maneuverability and endurance—with flights of up to an hour—amazed the press and the public. Not even Orville's crash of September 17, in which U.S. Army Lieutenant Thomas Selfridge was fatally injured, could detract much from their success. Wilbur continued flying and breaking records in France, carrying passengers, and teaching people to fly.

The Growth of Aviation Soars

After 1908, inventors who had been struggling for years started to make rapid progress, particularly in Europe. The Wrights, meanwhile, were locked in battles to enforce their patent rights. They continued to build and demonstrate airplanes and licensed their designs to others, but they never strayed far from their original design.

In Europe, by 1909, Louis Bleriot and Leon Levavasseur were flying monoplanes with single propellers in the front and control surfaces on a long tail, a layout that would become increasingly common. Levavasseur was one of the first to build a specialized

August 2, 1909
The Wrights deliver a Model A biplane to the U.S. Army.

August 22–28, 1909
The first large air meet is held in Rheims, France.

August 29, 1909
Glenn Curtiss wins the Gordon-Bennett Cup at Rheims with a then-blistering 46.5 miles per hour.

October 16, 1909
Count Ferdinand von Zeppelin forms Delag, the world's first commercial airline company.

1909–10
Igor Sikorsky builds two helicopters—neither can fly.

1910
▶ Count Ferdinand von Zeppelin launches the 20-passenger airship, *Deutschland*.

1910
Antonio Mattioni patents a ducted fan engine.

January 19, 1910
Army Lieutenant Paul Beck drops dummy bombs from an airplane piloted by Louis Paulhan.

July 24, 1910
August Euler patents a fixed forward-firing machine gun.

August 20, 1910
Army Lieutenant Jacob Fickel fires a rifle from a Curtiss biplane.

September 10, 1910
▶ Geoffrey de Havilland tests his first successful airplane.

September 23, 1910
Georges Chavez makes the first flight across the Alps but is killed on landing.

aircraft engine in quantity—a 25-horsepower V-8 named (like Levavasseur's plane) Antoinette. The Seguin brothers, Louis and Laurent, started to manufacture the Gnome rotary engine in 1909. It had seven cylinders in a star shape and was unusual because its crankshaft was bolted to the airplane and the entire engine and propeller rotated together. This helped to keep the cylinders cool. Its combination of high power and low weight made it very attractive.

Above: Louis Bleriot was a plucky man who ignored his injuries (he had been burned by the heat from his engine) to cross the English Channel in a craft powered by an engine notorious for its sudden failures.

Left: Louis Bleriot's mechanics and others watch ecstatically as he makes his historic flight.

October 11, 1910
Former President Theodore Roosevelt becomes the first U.S. president to fly in an airplane.

November 7, 1910
Famed pilot Philip Parmalee flies a Wright Model B with two packages of silk from Dayton to Columbus, Ohio, as an "aeroplane express" for Max Morehouse, the head of a dry-goods firm. Cost: $5,000.

November 14, 1910
Eugene Ely makes the first flight from a ship, the USS *Birmingham*.

1911
Harriet Quimby earns the first pilot's license issued to a woman in the United States.

1911
There are 81 licensed pilots in the United States, and 10 people are killed in aircraft accidents.

January 7, 1911
U.S. Army Lt. Myron S. Crissey drops a live bomb on a target in San Francisco Bay from a Wright biplane piloted by Philip Parmlee.

January 18, 1911
▶ Eugene Ely lands on the USS *Pennsylvania*.

January 26, 1911
Glenn Curtiss flies the first seaplane,

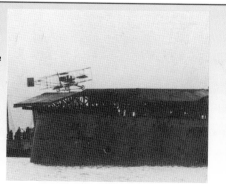

A beautiful contender to be the first to cross the Channel was Leon Levavasseur's *Antoinette*. The craft's name was for the daughter of Jules Gastambide, for whom Levavasseur had built the engine. Ironically, it was an Antoinette engine that powered Bleriot's aircraft on its successful flight.

USS *Birmingham;* two months later, he departed from San Francisco, landed on the USS *Pennsylvania,* took off again, and returned to the city. In September 1911, C. P. Rodgers set out from New York in a Wright biplane and arrived—after 82 flying hours and 15 crash landings—in Pasadena, California.

A large aviation meet in 1911 brought together a wide variety of airplane shapes. Voisin, Farman, and Curtiss airplanes resembled the Wright Flyer—biplanes with an elevator in front and a rudder behind the wing. Both Breguet and Bleriot favored front-engine biplanes. The fastest aircraft were monoplanes, but many designers and pilots distrusted them. Edouard Nieuport, whose monoplanes held the world records for speed (83 miles per hour) and range (449 miles) in 1911, was killed in September of that year when his airplane stalled in a tight turn.

The U.S. Army bought a Wright airplane in 1908. Other armies followed suit. Italy was the first country to use an airplane in warfare; in October 1911, Captain Carlo Piazza made the first operational reconnaissance flight by an airplane. Piazza flew a Bleriot plane out of Tripoli as part of Italy's campaign against Turkish forces. Although aviators were beginning to experiment with bombs and machine guns, the airplane's most important role was still reconnaissance and scouting.

For passenger transport, however, there was nothing to beat Count Zeppelin's airships. Zeppelin launched the *Deutschland* in 1910—the first of a series of Zeppelins with a 20-passenger enclosed cabin in the keel. By July 1914, these aircraft had carried more than 19,000 passengers.

But the technology of the airplane was advancing even more quickly. Curtiss had won the 1909 Gordon-Bennett race at an average speed of 47 miles per hour; three years later, designers were working on aircraft that were well over twice as fast. One of the best such designs was Louis Becherau's graceful Deperdussin

Aviation became a subject of national pride as well as a fashionable obsession. On July 25, 1909, Louis Bleriot made a 23.5-mile flight across the English Channel, winning a £1,000 prize from the London *Daily Mail.* New York *Herald* publisher James Gordon Bennett also sponsored an air race at one of the first great aviation meetings, a week-long festival held at Rheims, France, in August 1909. The race was won by America's Glenn Curtiss.

The more successful aviation pioneers started to build airplanes in quantity, selling some to wealthy enthusiasts and a few to the military. By 1911, Louis Breguet, Henry and Maurice Farman, and Gabriel Voisin were operating airplane factories in France, building no fewer than 1,350 planes in that year.

In the United States, Glenn Curtiss and the Wright brothers were the main aircraft manufacturers. In November 1910, pilot Eugene Ely succeeded in flying a Curtiss from the foredeck of the cruiser

---

with a water takeoff and landing in San Diego.

February 22, 1911
Airmail service starts between Allahabad and Naini Junction in India.

April 11, 1911
The College Park U.S. Army Flying School is formed in College Park, Maryland.

July 4, 1911
The first air cargo flight in the United

Kingdom is flown by Horatio Barber in a Valkyrie monoplane. The content: Osram lamps.

August 18, 1911
The Royal Aircraft Factory F.E.2 pusher flies for the first time.

September 1911
C. P. Rodgers begins the first U.S. transcontinental flight in the Wright biplane, *Vin Fiz.*

September 23, 1911
Earle Ovington carries the first U.S. airmail in a Bleriot monoplane.

October 23, 1911
Italy's Captain Carlo Piazza makes the first operational reconnaissance flight, spying on Turkish Forces in North Africa.

November 1, 1911
Italian pilot Giulio Gevotti drops

bombs on Turkish troops in Libya. It's the first wartime bombing.

November 5, 1911
Cal Rodgers completes the first U.S. transcontinental flight.

1912
Danish aviator J.H.C. Ellehammer develops a cyclic pitch control for motor blades for stabilized flight.

April 13, 1912
Britain forms the Royal Flying Corps.

April 16, 1912
▶ America's first woman pilot, Harriet Quimby, flies the English Channel in a Bleriot.

April 16, 1912
The first Schneider Trophy seaplane race is held.

A monoplane was easier to build than a biplane and had less drag. However, a properly rigged biplane was very strong structurally. No aircraft were designed with stress analysis in the early days, and many monoplanes, like this Deperdussin, broke up in flight, giving the type a bad reputation.

Many firms built monoplanes like this sleek-looking Nieuport. Monoplanes were easier to build and rig and had less drag than a biplane. However, because aeronautical engineering was just in its early stages, the monoplanes lacked inherent structural strength. This led many companies to turn to biplanes, which Nieuport did with great success.

racer. A monoplane, it had a streamlined, enclosed fuselage, formed around a solid mold from thin strips of tulipwood. A streamlined cowling covered the 160-horsepower Gnome engine. The most powerful aircraft engine in the world, it had two rows of radial cylinders mounted back-to-back. In September 1913, Maurice Prevost won the Gordon-Bennett race in a Deperdussin, at a speed of 126 miles per hour.

There would be no Gordon-Bennett race in 1914, however. On June 28, the Austrian Archduke Franz Ferdinand was shot by a Serbian activist in Sarajevo, and most of Europe was at war within little more than a month. The burgeoning field of military aviation was about to expand.

Eugene Ely made history when he flew a Curtiss Pusher from the deck of the *Birmingham* on November 14, 1910. It was a daring takeoff, and its implications were understood around the world: Aircraft could operate from ships.

May 1, 1912
Britain's A. V. Roe flies the first enclosed-cabin aircraft.

June 21, 1912
Tiny Broadwick is the first female to parachute from an airplane.

July 1, 1912
Harriet Quimby and passenger William Willard die in an accident at the Third Annual Boston Aviation Meet.

September 9, 1912
Jules Vedrines flies a Deperdussin at 108 miles per hour in Chicago.

November 12, 1912
Navy Lieutenant T. Ellyson is catapult-launched from a ship at anchor in the Navy Yard.

December 12, 1912
The ejection seat is tested near Paris.

1913
Lawrence Sperry demonstrates the gyroscopic automatic stabilizer in a Curtiss flying boat.

January 13, 1913
The first regularly scheduled freight service flies from Boston to New York in a Wright B. The cargo: baked beans.

April 16, 1913
The first Schneider Cup race is won by Maurice Prevost in a Deperdussin at 46 miles per hour.

May 13, 1913
Igor Sikorsky flies *Le Grand*, the world's first four-engine airplane and ancestor of the four-engine bomber.

CHAPTER TWO
Aviation Goes to War

AS THE WORLD GOES TO WAR,

THE YOUNG FIELD OF AVIATION FLIES INTO

A POSITION OF IMPORTANCE.

Captain Roy Brown of the Royal Flying Corps had just stared death right in the face. Pinned by three German fighter planes, Brown had evaded their fire by executing a half-loop with a roll into level flight at the top—a technical maneuver known to pilots on both sides of the war as an *Immelmann,* after the German ace who perfected it. Brown came out and immediately scanned the sky for Lieutenant Wilford May, who was flying his first combat mission. May was a boyhood friend from Canada. Brown saw his friend, but he also saw a red Fokker Dr.1 triplane fighter climbing out of the mist.

Right: Although built in relatively small quantities, the Fokker Dr.1 triplane captured the imagination of Allied pilots because of its rapid climb and maneuverability. It was the aircraft in which Baron Manfred von Richthofen was shot down. This is a reproduction; no genuine Dr.1s still exist.

Doused in smoke and castor oil from the hammering rotary engine in his Sopwith Camel, Brown clawed for altitude. Altitude was speed and surprise. As the German approached within gun range of his target, Brown dived. May and his pursuer had also traded height for speed and were skimming just above the ghastly battlefield of the Somme. Focused on his target, the German pilot did not see Brown's Camel.

Brown later recalled seeing the glint of the German's eyes when he turned to see his attacker. The pilot collapsed, and the triplane crashed. In the years since, there has been dispute about whether the man was hit by Brown's shot or by fire from the field below. Either way, the result was the same: Manfred Freiherr von Richthofen—known to his enemies and to history as the Red Baron—was dead at age 25. He had 80 kills to his credit.

War Takes to the Sky

The airplane was far from a decisive weapon in World War I. Although military airplanes were built in thousands, their combined firepower was small compared to artillery. In "Bloody April" of 1917, the Royal Flying Corps lost 330 aircrew; in contrast, more than 20,000 British ground troops were killed on the first *day* of the Battle of the Somme in April 1916. French Army Marshal Ferdinand Foch, as commander of the French College of War in 1911, described aircraft as "interesting toys, but of no military value."

But air warfare had a symbolic importance greater than its physical impact. For propagandists, the close-range battles between opposing fighter groups—quickly dubbed dogfights—were a distraction from the slaughter in the mud below them. For civilians, bombing raids were a threat that placed them on the front line. Young air commanders saw all this as just a start and envisioned air power as a way to make trench warfare unnecessary.

Foch's comments notwithstanding, the warring nations of 1914 were all experimenting with military aviation. Aircraft were used mostly for reconnaissance. A typical example was the British B.E.2c, designed by Geoffrey de Havilland for the Royal Aircraft Factory. Powered by a 90-horsepower, V-8 engine, the B.E.2c had a top speed of 75 miles per hour and could stay airborne for more than three hours. De Havilland had designed the airplane to be inherently stable: It tended to remain in straight and level flight unless the pilot moved the controls.

Alongside the two-seater reconnaissance planes flew faster single-seaters, usually called scouts. Dutch designer Anthony Fokker, working in Germany, produced one of the best-known scouts—the Fokker E.I ("E" standing for *eindecker*, or monoplane)—while T.O.M.

A GENIUS FOR GERMANY

Anthony Fokker was Dutch but was sent to Germany for his technical education and built his first airplane there in 1910 at the age of 20. At 25, he was one of the leading aircraft designers in Germany. When he was asked to copy the Garros propeller guard, Fokker thought it was crude and dangerous. Instead, he designed a mechanical linkage between the propeller and the gun, so that the rotating propeller fired the gun automatically when the blades were out of the way. Copied by other combatants, it was the essential invention that made the classic WWI fighter a reality.

Fokker's other great innovation of the war years was a cantilever wooden wing (that is, one without bracing struts or wires), which was introduced on the Fokker D.VIII and used on an entire series of later Fokker airplanes. Fokker died in New York in 1939, at 49 years of age.

Anthony Fokker

June 15, 1913
Alan and Malcom Loughead fly their first aircraft. They later form Lockheed Aircraft.

September 23, 1913
Roland Garros makes the first crossing of the Mediterranean.

November 13, 1913
Pilots from rival Mexican factions exchange revolver shots in the air over Naco, Mexico. No hits were registered in this first aerial combat.

November 18, 1913
Lincoln Beachey executes the first loop.

1914
The Chinese Army Air Arm is formed.

1914
▶ Curtiss introduces the JN, or Jenny.

1914
Elmer Sperry develops the first gyro-

scopic controls, the forerunner of the automatic pilot.

January 1, 1914
Tony Jannus flies a Benoist flying boat between Tampa and St. Petersburg, Florida, in the first regularly scheduled passenger airline.

April 25, 1914
Navy Lieutenant P.N.L. Bellinger makes the first U.S. combat flight off

Vera Cruz, Mexico. He is later hit by rifle fire, thus also suffering the first combat damage.

June 24, 1914
Igor Sikorsky sets a 1,590-mile distance record in an Ilia Mouromets four-engine aircraft.

July 1914
Rodman Wanamaker's Curtiss *America*, intended for transatlantic travel, makes its first flight.

July 18, 1914
The U.S. Army Aviation Section is created as part of the Signal Corps.

July 30, 1914
Tryggve Gran, a Norwegian pilot, makes the first flight across the North Sea in a Bleriot monoplane. His flying time is four hours and ten minutes.

August 1, 1914
Germany declares war on Russia. In subsequent days, it becomes a true world war, with Allies versus the Central Powers.

August 13–15, 1914
Four Royal Flying Corps (RFC) squadrons deploy to France.

August 22, 1914
The British RFC takes a reconnaissance of German lines.

August 25, 1914
Three RFC BE.2s force down a German airplane.

August 26, 1914
Russian Staff Captain P. N. Nesterov (the first man to loop-the-loop) destroys an Austrian airplane by ramming it, setting a precedent for Russian-style ramming in combat.

August 30, 1914
German Army Lieutenant Ferdinand von Hiddessen drops five bombs on Paris.

September 1914
The RFC uses aerial photography during the Battle of the Aisne.

October 5, 1914
Sergeant Joseph Frantz and Corporal Louis Quénault of the French Air Force shoot down a German Aviatik over Rheims. It's the first victory in aerial combat.

November 21, 1914
Four Avro 504s attack Zeppelin sheds in Friedrichshafen, Germany. It is the first true strategic bombing. One Zeppelin is destroyed.

December 11, 1914
The Royal Flying Corps (RFC) adopts a blue, white, and red roundel as its insignia.

December 21, 1914
The first German bombs fall on Great Britain. They are dropped by a Taube monoplane near Dover.

Right: The Fokker "Eindecker" (meaning one-winged, or a monoplane) was the first specialized fighter aircraft to enter combat. Equipped with a machine gun to fire straight ahead through the propeller, it revolutionized tactics and became known as "the Fokker Scourge."

Below: The de Havilland was designated the DH-4 in American service and mass-produced using American standards of measurement. It was powered by the American-designed and -built Liberty engine of about 400 horsepower.

Sopwith did the same in England. With 80-horsepower (or more) rotary engines, they could routinely exceed 100 miles per hour.

None of these airplanes was designed to carry a weapon. Reconnaissance crews occasionally carried bombs or grenades, and both pilots and observers carried rifles to engage enemy aircraft. A few aircraft were shot down in this way, but it was more common for both combatants to fire all their ammunition without hitting anything vital.

One of the first airplanes designed to shoot down other aircraft was in service by the end of 1914. The British Vickers FB.5 Gunbus had its engine mounted behind the wing. The pilot sat in front of the plane's engine, and the nose accommodated a cockpit for a gunner. With a clear field of fire, the gunner had a pretty good chance of shooting down anything that the Gunbus could

January 19, 1915
The first Zeppelin raids happen in Great Britain.

March 1915
The Battle of Neuve Chapelle takes place. It's the first time a battle is planned and fought entirely with maps created by photo-reconnaissance.

March 3, 1915
The United States forms the National Advisory Committee for Aeronautics

(NACA). (It will become the National Aeronautics and Space Administration [NASA] in 1958.)

April 1, 1915
Roland Garros uses a machine gun fired through a propeller to shoot down a German Albatros two-seater.

May 31, 1915
The first Zeppelin raid on London kills seven people.

June 1915
Ruth Law becomes the first female to do a loop.

June 6–7, 1915
Flight Sub-Lieutenant R.A.J. Warneford destroys a Zeppelin LZ 37 by dropping six 20-pound Hales bombs on it. He is killed 12 days later.

July 1915
Fokker E.1 monoplanes arrive at the front, the first to have a synchronized

gun firing through the propeller. The "Fokker Scourge" begins as they destroy the opposition.

August 12, 1915
Flying a Short 184 seaplane, Flight Commander C. H. Edmonds makes the first airdrop of a torpedo in combat against a Turkish supply ship in the Dardanelles campaign.

December 1915
The United States orders 49 aircraft,

with a value of $789,872. This brings the total military and commercial airplane deliveries since 1903 to 100.

December 12, 1915
Hugo Junkers' J1 *Blechesel*—or "Tin Donkey"—the first all-metal aircraft, makes its inaugural flight.

1916
The Caproni Ca 4 bomber makes its first flight.

One of the real geniuses behind Great Britain's aviation industry, T.O.M. Sopwith brought a whole line of successful fighters to the Royal Flying Corps and Royal Air Force, including the Pup, 1½-Strutter, Tripe, Camel, Dolphin, Snipe, and Salamander. The most famous of the Sopwith products was the tricky little Camel (pictured below), which probably killed more British pilots than any German airplane ever did. However, it also killed more Germans than any other British plane; in the hands of an experienced pilot, it was a deadly weapon.

Far Right: The environment in which World War I flyers flew became increasingly hostile as the war progressed. Flights took place at altitudes up to 20,000 feet, where temperatures were sometimes 60 degrees below zero. In an open cockpit, at even 100 miles per hour, the windchill factor required adequate protective clothing.

Far Right: The environment in which World War I flyers flew became increasingly hostile as the war progressed. Flights took place at altitudes up to 20,000 feet, where temperatures were sometimes 60 degrees below zero. In an open cockpit, at even 100 miles per hour, the windchill factor required adequate protective clothing.

catch—which was not much, since the nimbler scouts could avoid it with ease.

Early in 1915, some German pilots reported being attacked by a single-seater scout, armed with a machine gun that fired through its propeller. The mystery was solved in April when Roland Garros, a French pioneer pilot in pre-war France and now a hero with five combat victories, was forced to land behind German lines. Garros's Morane monoplane had been modified with a fixed machine gun. Wedge-shaped metal plates were fixed to the back of the propeller, protecting it from bullet strikes by deflecting the bullets to one side.

Anthony Fokker was instructed to reproduce the system, but went one better with a synchronized gun. Fokker monoplanes

Right: Most Fokker triplanes were painted more like this example than the usual all-red versions said to represent the "Red Baron's" aircraft. Slow, and thus unable to avoid combat, the triplane's maneuverability saved it. Early Dr.1s had quality-control problems that delayed their production, a common event with Fokker products.

January 12, 1916
German fighter aces Max Immelmann and Oswald Boelcke receive the "Blue Max" Pour le Merite medal.

April 1916
The French are the first to use air-to-air rockets, firing Le Prieur rockets from a fighter to down a Zeppelin L 77.

April 20, 1916
American pilots form Lafayette Escadrille to fight in France.

May 28, 1916
The Sopwith Triplane makes its first flight.

June 29, 1916
William E. Boeing test-flies his first airplane.

July 3, 1916
The Royal Flying Corps starts operations with the Sopwith 1 Strutter, its first fighter with a synchronized gun.

July 15, 1916
William Boeing organizes Pacific Aero Products.

September 1916
The SPAD VII fighter enters service.

September 2, 1916
Lieutenant Leefe Robinson shoots down the Schutte-Lanz SL 11 airship over Britain.

September 2, 1916
The first plane-to-plane radio contact takes place in North Island, California. The distance: two miles.

September 12, 1916
The Hewitt-Sperry radio-guide flying bomb is tested in the United States.

September 17, 1916
The Wright-Martin aircraft company is formed after the first of many mergers in the aviation industry.

1917
The Ansaldo A1, SVA 5, and Macchi M5 make their first flights.

February 1917
The Junkers J-1 armored ground assault plane enters service.

February 13, 1917
The Aircraft Manufacturers Association forms.

dominated the western front into early 1916, when British and French fighters with similar weapons entered service. For the rest of the war, the balance of air power over the front would swing rapidly from one side to the other; a fighter would rule the skies for a matter of months before a better aircraft appeared.

Most World War I fighters were biplanes. More powerful engines compensated for the fact that they had more drag than monoplanes, and pilots regarded rate of climb and turning ability as being at least as important as speed.

The classic British fighter of the era, the Sopwith Camel, was a compact machine in which the engine, the guns, and the pilot were grouped closely together, reducing the airplane's inertia in a turn. It was powered by a 130-horsepower Clerget rotary engine. The fighter pilot wore a heavy leather suit, boots, and

gauntlets. With the greater power, World War I fighters could climb to 20,000 feet, where temperatures are well below zero even in summer. Goggles protected the pilot's eyes from exhaust smoke and oil: Rotary engines, notoriously, were lubricated by a one-way system that used castor oil, which would not dilute the fuel. A silk scarf kept some of the oil out of the pilot's nose and mouth, without impeding his head movements.

Pilots either learned to keep their heads and eyes in constant motion or became part of the statistics: In 1917, the average RFC pilot on the western front lived for two months. Fighters had no armor protection, their fuel tanks were made of thin metal sheets, and pilots did not carry parachutes.

The airplane that von Richthofen made famous, the Fokker Dr.1 Triplane, was an oddity. It had an excellent rate of climb

The two-seat SPAD XVI was as unpopular with its pilots as the SPAD XIII was popular. It was, nonetheless, one of the aircraft used by Brigadier General Billy Mitchell, and in it, he carried the Prince of Wales on one flight over the lines.

March 1917
The Airco D.H.4, a fast, light bomber, enters service with the RFC.

April 1917
"Bloody April": The RFC loses 150 aircraft in action.

April 6, 1917
The United States enters World War I; the U.S. Army Aviation Section has 35 trained pilots and no combat aircraft.

April 10, 1917
NACA recommends the formation of Aircraft Production Board to supervise the wartime production of aircraft.

May 1917
▶ Gotha bombers attack the United Kingdom.

May 20, 1917
An American Curtiss *America* in service of the English is the first plane to destroy a submarine, a U-36.

May 25, 1917
Twenty-one Gothas raid England in the first mass bombing.

Summer 1917
The Junkers J.1, an all-metal biplane, enters service.

June 13, 1917
Eighteen Gotha bombers attack London.

Left: That's pretty good formation flying in four Curtiss JN-4s, probably not the most responsive aircraft in the business! The famous "Jenny" was—when coupled with the Liberty engine—America's most important contribution to the air war.

Right: The Germans, having found out to their distress that Zeppelins were an expensive and ineffective way to conduct a bombing campaign, turned to bombers. The Gotha series was one of the best, despite being difficult to fly when lightly loaded. The first bomber raids were conducted in broad daylight.

and was very maneuverable, due to its light weight and large wingspan. It was almost unbeatable when flown by the pilots of von Richthofen's famous "Circus." As Fokker said, the enemy pilots "never had a chance to realize how slow the Triplane was." Most German pilots would do better in Pfalz, Albatros, or Fokker biplanes, powered by inline Mercedes engines.

France's best fighter was the SPAD XIII biplane. The SPAD's outstanding feature was the light, powerful, and reliable Hispano-Suiza engine, a liquid-cooled V-8 that was eventually developed to produce 235 horsepower. The SPAD, Fokker said, "could dive away from any of the German planes like a streamlined brick."

The SPAD XIII was the favored fighter for the American Expeditionary Force fighter squadrons that came to France in 1917 and would have been placed into production in the United States if the war had continued.

The United States entered the war without one homegrown design that would have lasted more than a minute on the western front. The United States had fallen behind Europe techno-

logically. Although the planes of the immediate pre-war era were faster, more efficient, and more reliable than those of five years earlier, they were still mostly toys for the rich and daring—not fast enough to make much headway into a strong wind, slower than trains, and unable to carry much in the way of a useful load. These deficiencies were much more apparent in the United States, with its vast distances and well-developed rail network.

The U.S. Army showed more interest in aviation after 1915. In the previous year, Glenn Curtiss had merged the J and N series aircraft to create a small, 90-horsepower tractor biplane that could be used for reconnaissance or training. Curtiss called it the JN, but it was known affectionately as "the Jenny" to its pilots; it was practically the only U.S. aircraft type to be mass-produced during the war.

For a citizen of London, the fighter war on the western front was a secondary concern. The German Army and Navy had ordered airships before the war. They made their first raids on London in May 1915. It was not until September 1916 that the RFC managed to shoot down an airship, on a night in which 16 of the

July 1917
The Sopwith Camel enters service.

August 2, 1917
Squadron Commander E. H. Dunning lands a Sopwith Pup on HMS *Furious,* the first aircraft to land on a moving ship. Dunning is killed five days later.

September 1917
Zeppelin-Staaken R-planes take part in raids on the United Kingdom.

October 18, 1917
McCook Field in Dayton, Ohio, is established as an aeronautical experimental station by the Signal Corps.

October 19, 1917
The last German airships raid Britain.

December 17, 1917
The Glenn L. Martin Company is formed in Cleveland, Ohio.

March 4, 1918
The 94th Aero Squadron arrives on the warfront.

March 10, 1918
The Junkers D.1, a very advanced, all-metal, cantilever-wing monoplane, makes its first flight.

March 23–29, 1918
Air attacks by British aircraft cause the German advance to falter.

March 27, 1918
The Naval Aircraft Factory builds its first airplanes.

April 1918
Britain establishes the independent Royal Air Force.

April 21, 1918
Baron Manfred von Richthofen, known as "The Red Baron," is shot down and killed.

huge ships—some more than 600 feet long and able to carry four-and-a-half tons of bombs—raided England. The airships soon proved vulnerable. Filled with explosive hydrogen, most of the airships sent on bombing raids were eventually lost in action.

From May 1917, the airships were joined by long-range bomber airplanes. The first large bombers had been built in Russia. A young Russian engineer, Igor Sikorsky, had flown the first four-engine airplane in 1913—the *Russky Vitiaz (Russian Knight)*, also known as *Le Grand*. It was followed by more than 70 bombers of the IM (Ilia Mouroumets) class.

The first German bombers were built by the Gotha company and powered by 260-horsepower Mercedes engines. In a daylight attack on London in June 1917, Gotha bombs killed 162 people, and public unrest reached a dangerous level as it became apparent that the RFC had no effective defense against the bombers.

In September, the Gotha bombers switched to night raids and were joined by some of the most extraordinary aircraft of World War I: the Riesenflugzeuge (giant aircraft), or R-planes. The only R-plane design to be built in quantity was the Staaken R.VI. Powered by four 250-horsepower Mercedes engines, the R.VI had a 138-foot wingspan. The two pilots enjoyed the luxury of an enclosed cabin, and the crew wore electrically heated flying suits. Catwalks and ladders allowed the two mechanics to work on the engines in flight. Eighteen R.VIs were built.

But neither R-planes nor Fokker's legendary fighters could save Germany from defeat. The end of World War I left Europe shattered. It also left the aviation industry—which had barely existed eight years earlier—in utter disarray.

In the United States, the Army abruptly canceled contracts for thousands of aircraft. Thousands more aircraft were put up for sale. Some were Curtiss Jennies, and others were United States-built versions of the British de Havilland D.H.4, a fast, light bomber powered—in U.S. models—by a 400-horsepower Liberty engine.

In Britain, aviation enthusiasts had seized on the near-panic caused by the Gotha raids to bring about a revolution in air power: the formation of an Air Ministry and a Royal Air Force (independent of the Army) in April 1918. It would have little effect on the current war but a vast impact upon the next one.

The infant RAF was forced to shrink in the post-war years. The aircraft companies that had been building aircraft by the hundreds dismissed most of their workforces and kept going as best they could, building a few aircraft for export and repairing airplanes for the RAF.

After the Versailles Treaty was signed in 1919, the German aircraft industry was largely dismantled by the Allies. This, too,

The Germans fielded increasingly sophisticated aircraft, including the very large Riesenflugzeuge, which featured four engines, a 138-foot wingspan, and such modern innovations as oxygen and bomb sights.

April 29, 1918
◄ Captain Eddie Rickenbacker shoots down the first of 26 aircraft.

May 1918
At the instigation of NACA, General Electric installs an experimental turbosupercharger on a Liberty engine.

May 11, 1918
The first American-built de Havilland DH-4 arrives in France.

May 15, 1918
► The U.S. Post Office inaugurates its airmail service.

May 17, 1918
Stefan von Petroczy and Theodore von Karman make tethered flights up to 150 feet high in a gasoline-engine-powered helicopter.

May 19–20, 1918
Germans make their last WWI raid on Britain.

August 17, 1918
The Martin MB-1, the first American-designed heavy bomber, makes its first flight.

October 2, 1918
The Kettering Bug, an "uninhabited combat vehicle" and forerunner of guided missiles, makes its first flight.

November 11, 1918
The armistice ends World War I.

A STURDY WORKHORSE IS BORN

One of the most significant aircraft of the immediate post-war era was the **Junkers F 13** transport. Constructed entirely of metal, the F 13 included a Junkers trademark feature: To give the thin aluminum skins more strength (they tended to buckle easily), Hugo Junkers used corrugated aluminum panels for the wing and body. The airplane took the world's altitude record (22,150 feet) in 1919.

The F 13 remained in production until 1926, when it was replaced by the W 33, a modified aircraft for all-cargo operations. It was the *Bremen*, a W 33, that made the first east-to-west crossing of the Atlantic by a heavier-than-air airplane. The last example of the W 34—a version of the W 33 with a radial engine—was retired from active service in Canada in 1961.

had an unfortunate impact on aviation; German technology was years ahead of the rest of the world.

In building their giant airships, Germans had discovered the wonder of aluminum. Dr. Hugo Junkers designed the all-metal J 4 attack aircraft in 1918: 227 of these armored airplanes were built. By 1919, Junkers was testing the F 13, an all-metal, low-wing transport aircraft.

An even more remarkable aircraft was the Staaken E.4/20. Designed by Adolf Rohrbach late in the war, the E.4/20 was an 18-passenger, all-metal civil transport. It had a range of more than 700 miles and could attain 140 miles per hour (this at a time when the world's top airspeed record stood at only 163 miles per hour). A prototype of the E.4/20 was built, but the Allies—terrified of the plane's potential as a bomber—ordered the airplane scrapped after the war. Rohrbach's ideas were forgotten for most of a decade.

A Race for the Records

In the post-war era, aviation became the subject of national prestige. The war had interrupted the quest for speed and turned aviation in a different direction. Contests to make the first flights across the Atlantic, across the Pacific, and between other points on the globe picked up again—spurred, as they were before the war, by the lure of prizes and trophies.

The U.S. Navy made the first flight across the Atlantic in May 1919. Lieutenant-Commander A. C. Read and his crew flew in a Navy-Curtiss NC flying boat from Newfoundland to Lisbon, refueling in the Azores. Three of the four-engine NC boats, the largest U.S. airplanes built up to that time, attempted the crossing, but two of them landed in mid-ocean and were abandoned.

In June, RAF pilots John Alcock and Arthur Whitten-Brown saved national pride by making the first nonstop crossing of the

The Curtiss NC-1 was one of four gigantic flying boats built to cross the Atlantic Ocean. Only the NC-4 completed the journey in 1919, the first transatlantic crossing. It can be seen today in the Naval Air Museum in Pensacola, Florida.

1919
The first Lawson airliner is designed.

January 1919
Raymond Orteig offers a $25,000 prize for the first flight between New York and Paris.

February 5, 1919
The first sustained airline service starts with Deutsche Luft-Reederei between Berlin and Weimar, Germany.

February 7, 1919
The world air speed record of 171 miles per hour is set in a Nieuport 29.

March 22, 1919
The first regular international passenger service begins between Paris and Brussels by Lignes Aeriennes Farman.

May 16–27, 1919
▶ Lieutenant Commander A. C. Read and crew cross the Atlantic in a Curtiss NC-4 flying boat.

May 19, 1919
Movie director Cecil B. DeMille establishes a scheduled airline, Mercury Air Service, with Junkers airplanes.

May 26, 1919
Dr. Robert H. Goddard reports on "A Method of Reaching Extreme Altitudes," which is published by the Smithsonian Institution.

Atlantic, in a Vickers Vimy bomber. Their achievement was slightly tarnished by the fact that the field that they selected for their landing turned out to be a peat bog, which tipped the Vimy on its nose.

Just two weeks after Alcock and Whitten-Brown landed in Ireland, the British airship R.34—a copy of a 1916 Zeppelin—left its mooring mast in Scotland and flew westward to Long Island, New York. Days later, it made the eastward return flight. It was a dramatic demonstration of the range advantage of the airship. Both the 1919 airplane crossings had been eastbound. Cruising at about 80 miles per hour, contemporary airplanes were unable to battle headwinds coming westward across the Atlantic.

Navy and Army rivalry drove the record-setting in the United States. Army lieutenants John MacReady and Oakley Kelly flew nonstop from Mineola, New York, to San Diego, California, in May 1923. Their airplane was not American; it was a modified Fokker F.IV (designated T-2 in U.S. service) monoplane with a U.S.

engine. The following May, the Army launched four specially built biplanes on a flight around the world. The single-engine World Cruisers, which could be fitted with wheels or pontoons, were built in the United States; in fact, the four planes represented one of the first large contracts for a young company in Santa Monica, California. The company had been founded by a Scottish-American engineer named Donald Douglas. Only one of the four World Cruisers completed the epic 175-day flight.

In 1919, Raymond Orteig—the French-born owner of two New York hotels—offered a $25,000 prize for the first flight between New York and Paris, a distance of 3,400 miles. By 1926, several teams were preparing to make the flight.

French World War I ace Rene Fonck commissioned a specially built airplane from Sikorsky, who had escaped from the Bolsheviks to move to the United States. The Sikorsky crashed during take-off from Roosevelt Field on Long Island on September 21, 1926. Fonck and his navigator escaped, but his mechanic and radio

Left: The Douglas DWC was an important step for the Douglas company: Their fine product brought world fame. Powered by specially tuned and modified Liberty engines, the DWC crews were supported by an elaborate logistic system provided by the U.S. Army and Navy.

Right: The Levavasseur biplane *L'Oiseau Blanc* featured a jettison-able undercarriage and a water-tight fuselage compartment, but these did not save the famous French ace Charles Nungesser or his heroic companion, Francois Coli, who apparently perished in their attempt to cross the Atlantic. In recent years, there have been recurrent reports of parts of their airplane being found in Maine and the Canadian wilderness.

May 31, 1919
A Curtiss NC-4 completes the first transatlantic crossing.

June 14–15, 1919
John Alcock and Arthur Whitten-Brown make the first nonstop flight across the Atlantic. They go from Newfoundland to Ireland.

July 2–6, 1919
▶ A British Army R.34 airship crosses the Atlantic round-trip.

August 1919
Air Transport & Travel starts scheduled London–Paris flights.

September 18, 1919
Roland Rohlfs reaches 31,420 feet in a Curtiss L-3 triplane.

October 1919
KLM Royal Dutch Airlines is established.

November 1, 1919
Aeromarine, with three flying boats, opens an airline between Key West and Cuba.

December 10, 1919
The Smith brothers fly a Vimy from England to Australia.

December 27, 1919
Boeing's B-1 mailplane, the company's first commercial airplane, makes its first flight.

February 27, 1920
Major R. W. Schroeder reaches 33,113 feet in a turbosupercharged Packard-LePere, producing the first recorded contrail.

May 31, 1920
Italian pilots Arturo Ferrarin and Guido Masiero fly from Rome to Tokyo in SVA.9 biplanes.

June 4, 1920
The Army Reorganization Act officially establishes the U.S. Army Air Service.

November 25, 1920
A Verville Packard 600 wins the first Pulitzer Trophy race at 156.5 miles per hour.

December 14, 1920
The first fatal airline accident occurs in England.

1921
▶ Bessie Coleman studies in France to become the first licensed African American pilot.

1921
Curtiss CR-2 wins the Pulitzer Trophy race at an average speed of 197.8 miles per hour.

1921
George de Bothezat, a Russian-born engineer working for the U.S. Air

Service, builds a large, complex, moderately successful helicopter.

1921
The Soviets establish a laboratory for research on solid-propellant rockets.

February 22, 1921
American transcontinental airmail service starts between San Francisco and Mineola, New York, using DH-4s.

February 24, 1921
The Douglas Cloudster, the first of the Douglas line, flies.

April 14, 1921
KLM introduces the Fokker F.III five-passenger airliner. This begins a period of Fokker airline dominance.

June 8, 1921
The first pressure-cabin experiments at McCook Field occur with a de Havilland DH 9 aircraft.

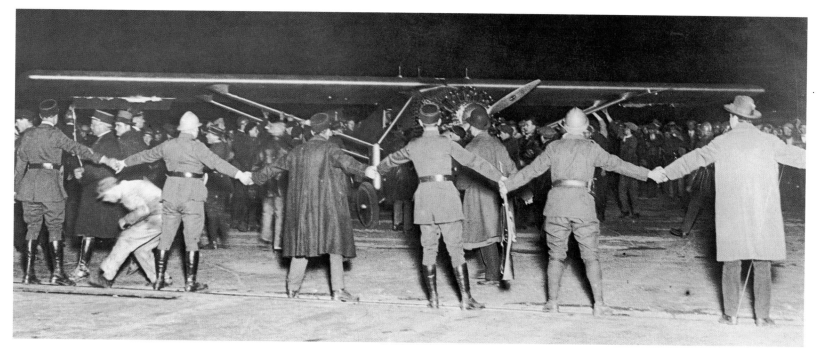

Opposite: In Charles Lindbergh, the world found the hero it was waiting for—a modest, intelligent, good-looking young man who was not only brave but smart. Lindbergh was the best prepared of all the contestants for the Orteig prize.

Left: Lindbergh was expecting to have difficulty finding a mechanic to help him hangar the *Spirit of St. Louis* after his arrival in Paris. Instead, he was met by a jubilant crowd of thousands who were determined to touch him if they could. The *Spirit* was badly damaged by souvenir hunters despite attempts by security to control the crowd.

operator died. The quest claimed two more lives a few months later. Noel Davis and Stanton Wooster, two U.S. military pilots, were killed on April 26, 1927, while preparing for a prize attempt in a modified Keystone bomber.

Charles Nungesser and Francois Coli departed from Le Bourget, north of Paris, on May 8, 1927. They were well prepared, with a Levavasseur biplane named *L'Oiseau Blanc (The White Bird)*. On May 9, Paris newspapers mistakenly reported that the airplane had landed in New York; in actuality, the airplane and its crew had vanished.

The prospects of a successful mission looked dim. With six lives lost, it wasn't surprising that the New York press played the story for its gallows-humor value—especially since one of the remaining pilots had set only one record in his life: Charles Lindbergh, a 26-year-old Minnesota congressman's son, had made a record four emergency parachute jumps. Lindbergh was to make his flight in an airplane half the size of *L'Oiseau Blanc*.

Lindbergh had persuaded friends in St. Louis, Missouri, to support an attempt on the Orteig prize. The *Spirit of St. Louis* was specially built by the Ryan company in San Diego. It weighed less than a ton empty but could take off at 5,135 pounds, including 450 gallons of fuel.

On May 20, 1927, Lindbergh took off from Roosevelt Field. Navigating by dead reckoning, using a clock, airspeed indicator, and compass, and occasionally descending to within sight of the sea to estimate the wind speed, he crossed the Irish coast three miles from his planned course. Lindbergh was sighted, and the news was wired to Paris: As he approached Paris in the late evening of May 21, a crowd of 200,000 people assembled at Le Bourget. Landing after 33½ hours in the air, Lindbergh found himself dragged from the airplane and later said that his feet had not touched the ground for half an hour. Finally, an American reporter put on Lindbergh's helmet to distract the crowd. While the crowd feted the decoy, two French pilots drove Lindbergh to the U.S. Embassy.

July 13–21, 1921
Brigadier General Billy Mitchell's Martin MB2 bombers sink the battleship *Ostfriesland* in a demonstration attack.

August 1, 1921
The RAF takes delivery of its first troop-carrying aircraft, the Vickers Vernon.

August 4, 1921
Lieutenant John MacReady gives the

first demonstration of crop dusting in a Curtiss JN-4D.

August 24, 1921
A British airship R.38 breaks up over the Humber River near Hull, England.

November 5, 1921
Bert Acosta wins the Pulitzer Trophy race in a Curtiss Racer at 176.7 miles per hour.

November 12, 1921
The first "in-flight refueling": Army

Lieutenant Wes May climbs from the wing of one DH-4 to another while carrying a five-gallon can of fuel.

November 28, 1921
Ludwig Prandtl's seminal NACA Report 116, "Application of Modern Hydrodynamics to Aeronautics," is published.

December 31, 1921
An estimated 1,200 commercial aircraft are in operation in the United

States; 146 airfields are available for 125 commercial companies in 34 states.

1922
France and Spain join forces to invade Morocco, using aviation in the effort.

1922
Emile Berliner begins a series of helicopter experiments. Etienne Oehmichen, a French automotive engineer, makes successful flights, in-

cluding a one-kilometer closed-course circuit. Raul Pateras Pescara flies his helicopter 736 meters; his aircraft features autorotation capability.

February 7, 1922
The Lawrance J-1 radial completes a 50-hour test; this will lead to a revolution in engines.

March 20, 1922
The U.S. Navy commissions its first aircraft carrier, the USS *Langley*.

A "FOOL" FLIES TO PARIS

The press who gave **Charles Lindbergh** the nickname "The Flying Fool" underestimated the man. Calculating and immune to panic—as well as a superb navigator—Lindbergh had carefully assessed what was needed to make a transatlantic flight.

No multi-engine airplane of the day could stay in the air long if an engine failed. Since an engine failure in the middle of the Atlantic meant ditching the plane anyway, Lindbergh reasoned, it made sense to use only one engine. The pilot also knew that aircraft size in itself meant nothing: what counted was the fraction of the total weight devoted to fuel, together with the efficiency of the airplane (which was related to wingspan), and the engine.

This Fairey Fox was an extremely radical aircraft when it debuted on January 25, 1925. Powered by an American Curtiss D-12 engine, it was faster than contemporary British fighters. The use of the D-12 engine inspired the Rolls-Royce Kestrel, which was installed in later versions of the Fox.

While Lindbergh became the first hero of the newsreel age, other fliers chipped away at the remaining "first across" records. Perhaps the most important of these flights took place 11 months later. The *Bremen*, a Junkers W 33, set out from Ireland on April 12, 1928, bound for New York in an attempt at the first east–west transatlantic flight. Four hundred miles from the coast, the airplane ran into a dense fog bank. With the compass almost useless in high latitudes, the crew became lost and headed northwest, crash-landing on Greenly Island in Labrador, Canada. The *Bremen* had crossed the Atlantic from east to west with World War I technology. The Junkers W 33 was a variant of the F 13, which had flown in 1919.

The race for distance in the air was matched in cost and intensity only by the quest for speed. In the 1920s, this too was driven by the rivalry between different service branches and between nations.

In the United States, the goal was to win the Pulitzer Trophy race. The Pulitzer races were held annually from 1920 to 1925 and were superseded by the National Air Races at Cleveland. Before the 1921 race, the U.S. Navy ordered two "prototype fighters"—pure racers, in fact—from Curtiss. Small, conventional biplanes, they broke no new ground except in their engine installations. The Curtiss D-12 was a liquid-cooled V-12 engine (developing more than 400 horsepower) and drove a propeller that was forged, machined, and twisted from a solid billet of aluminum. The D-12-powered CR-2 racer won the 1921 Pulitzer race at an average speed of 197.8 miles per hour. In the following year, the U.S. Army retaliated with its own Curtiss racers, setting the first lap speed above 200 miles per hour and going on to set a new air speed record of 224 miles per hour.

In Europe, all eyes were on the Schneider Trophy seaplane races. French arms manufacturer Jacques Schneider had stipulated that the winning nation would host the following year's race, and

March 23, 1922
NACA Report 159 on "Jet Propulsion for Airplanes" by Edgar Buckingham is published.

July 14, 1922
Aeromarine Airways, Great Lakes Division, operates 11-passenger Aeromarine Cruisers between Cleveland and Detroit.

August 15, 1922
An Aeromarine flying boat delivers a Ford car from Detroit to Cleveland.

August 18, 1922
Supermarine Sea Lion, flown by Henry Biard, wins the Schneider Trophy race at 145.7 miles per hour.

September 4, 1922
Lieutenant Jimmy Doolittle flies coast-to-coast in under 24 hours.

September 20, 1922
Sadi Lecointe sets the first world's air speed record over 200 miles per hour (205.23 mph) in a Nieuport.

September 27, 1922
Radar signatures are demonstrated at the Naval Aircraft Radio Lab.

October 18, 1922
Billy Mitchell sets the world's air speed record at 222.96 miles per hour in a Curtiss R-6.

December 27, 1922
Japan commissions the first aircraft carrier, *Hosho*.

1923
A Curtiss CR-3 wins the Schneider Trophy.

1923
The Department of Agriculture experiments with crop dusting.

1923
Air Union (a forerunner of Air France) is established.

1923
Hermann Oberth's classic *Die Rakete zu den Planetenraumen (The Rocket Into Planetary Space)* is published.

January 1, 1923
The Cox A-1 and Fokker A-2, intended to be airborne ambulances, debut.

The Curtiss Aeroplane and Engine Company was at the height of its powers with the development of the R series of racers. Here, flamboyant lady-killer Bert Acosta stands by the Curtiss CR racer and the Pulitzer Trophy. Note the huge Lamblin radiators—not exactly a low-drag installation.

January 9, 1923
Juan de la Cierva makes an officially observed flight in a C-4 autogiro.

February 23, 1923
The Collier Trophy is awarded to the U.S. Post Office Air Mail Service.

March 5, 1923
An auxiliary jettisonable belly is fixed to a Boeing MB3A at Selfridge Field in Michigan; it foreshadows the long-range fighters of World War II.

March 29, 1923
U.S. Air Service Lieutenant R. L. Maitland sets a world air speed record of 239.95 miles per hour in a Curtiss R-6.

April 20, 1923
The first aerial refueling with a hose occurs at Rockwell Field, California.

May 2–3, 1923
U.S. Army pilots Lieutenant John MacReady and Lieutenant Oakley

Kelly make the first nonstop trans-U.S. flight in a Fokker T-2 in 26 hours, 50 minutes.

June 26, 1923
Lieutenants L. H. Smith and J. P. Richter achieve the first complete mid-air pipeline refueling.

August 21, 1923
Navigation beacon lights between Chicago and Cheyenne are completed.

August 22, 1923
The giant Barling Bomber makes its first (unsuccessful) flight.

November 1, 1923
Dr. Robert H. Goddard successfully tests a liquid oxygen and gasoline rocket motor.

November 4, 1923
USN Lieutenant Alford Williams sets a speed record of 266.59 miles per hour in a Navy-Curtiss racer.

1924
Argentinian Paul Pescara builds a coaxial helicopter and flies 736 meters.

1924
Huff-Daland, manufacturers of military training planes, creates the first crop duster, revolutionizing agriculture.

1924
Travel Air Manufacturing Co. Inc. is organized in Wichita by Walter

that the nation that won the race three times in five years would win the trophy outright. As a recipe for international rivalry, it could not be bettered.

The first Schneider races were all-European. In 1923, the U.S. Navy's Pulitzer racers entered. The Curtiss CR-3 won easily, beating the fastest British airplane by 20 miles per hour. Richard Fairey, one of Britain's independent aircraft manufacturers, acquired rights to build the D-12 for a new bomber, the Fox, which could outrun any RAF fighter. The Air Ministry did not want to support a new aero-engine company and persuaded Rolls-Royce to build an engine patterned on the D-12. The resulting Kestrel was the first of a series of Rolls-Royce V-12 engines that would be vastly important in World War II.

A RACER TO REMEMBER

The first airplane to exceed 400 miles per hour was Reginald Mitchell's **Supermarine S.6B** racing seaplane. An all-metal airplane (apart from the fabric-covered control surfaces), the S.6B was virtually a flying radiator for the 2,350-horsepower Rolls-Royce R engine. Coolant was circulated through the double skins of the wings and the pontoon floats, and oil coolers were arranged along the body sides. At full bore, the most important instrument in the cockpit was the temperature gauge.

The Schneider Trophy contest became more intense. In 1924, in Baltimore, no team other than the U.S. Navy qualified, and the service sportingly declined to claim a flyover victory. The strongest competition in 1925 came from Britain's Supermarine S.4, but it crashed during practice in Baltimore, and the Navy once again won. A third victory in 1926 would end the contest and make the United States the outright winner of the Schneider Trophy.

A third victory wasn't entirely assured, however. Seaplane racing was not only expensive but dangerous. The racers were flying as fast as anyone had ever flown. Engines were tuned for power, not durability. They were flying at a low altitude, making tight turns to clear the buoys that marked the course. The U.S. Navy alone lost two seaplanes and their pilots in practice for the 1926 competition. Because of the costs and casualties, the U.S. government decreed in 1925 that the services should not build any new racers. In addition, the older Navy airplanes faced a new competitor in 1926.

Italian Fascists saw themselves as modernizers—the wave of the future. The movement was strongly influenced by the cultural and artistic tendency known as Futurism. Futurism was fascinated by machinery, particularly airplanes. Not surprisingly, then, Italian dictator Benito Mussolini decreed that Italy should win the Schneider Trophy.

In 1926, the Italian's Macchi M.39 monoplane did indeed win at Baltimore. The race also marked the last time the U.S. Navy would compete in it.

The Trophy contests of the next few years were a series of titanic duels fought between Italy and the United Kingdom. In general layout, the Italian and British Schneider racers were quite similar, and the races were more or less won and lost on engine power and reliability. In the 1927 contest, the British Supermarine

---

Beech, Clyde Cessna, and Walter Innes. This leads to two business aircraft dynasties.

March 4, 1924
To prevent a flood, two Martin MB-1s and two DH-4s bomb an ice jam on the Platte River in Nebraska.

March 31, 1924
Imperial Airways is formed.

May 19, 1924
Stanley Goble and Ivor McIntyre make the first round-Australia flight.

June 23, 1924
Russel Maughan flies a dawn-to-dusk transcontinental flight in a Curtiss PW-8.

July 1, 1924
The U.S. Post Office opens its first regular transcontinental airmail service, flying between San Francisco and New York.

September 28, 1924
▶ U.S. Army Douglas World Cruisers complete the first round-the-world flight in Seattle.

December 15, 1924
A Sperry Messenger hooks up to an Army Airship TC-3.

1925
S. C. Johnson & Son begins its tradition of operating business aircraft.

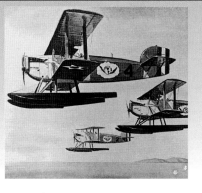

1925
Belgian airliner Ligne Aderienne Roi Albert begins its operation in Africa.

January 3, 1925
The Fairey Fox light bomber flies in England. It starts a chain of events that leads to the Rolls-Royce Merlin engine.

February 2, 1925
President Calvin Coolidge signs the

S.5 was powered by a Napier Lion engine delivering 900 horse-power. It won the race at an average speed of 281 miles per hour.

It was clear in 1929 (the race was now biennial) that the aging Lion had reached its limits. Sir Henry Royce detested racing, but following an appeal to his patriotism, he agreed that Rolls-Royce would build a new engine for a racing seaplane. The Rolls-Royce R engine was based on a bigger version of the Kestrel; the seaplane was the Supermarine S.6, designed by Reginald Mitchell.

In August 1929, a month before the race, the R reached a staggering 1,800 horsepower, twice as much as the Lion. The designers equipped the engine with an enormous supercharger that pumped air into the engine so that it could burn more fuel and produce more power. The S.6 won easily at 328 miles per hour.

Britain needed one more win in 1931 to close the contest. In Italy, Macchi and Fiat were designing the MC.72, with two engines mounted nose-to-nose and driving a two-stage propeller. But the British government, in the depths of the Depression, refused to fund the RAF's High Speed Flight for 1931. Financial rescue came at the last moment from Lady Houston, a wealthy patron; she provided £100,000 to support the British team.

Rolls-Royce coaxed another 450 horsepower out of the engine, but the race itself was anticlimactic. Two Italian pilots had died in MC.72s in the weeks before the race, which became a flyover victory for the British. Just after the race, the Supermarine S.6B racer set a world's air speed record of 407 miles per hour. But the world had not seen the last of Reginald Mitchell's works or heard the last snarl of a V-12 engine.

Racing and record-breaking were the stuff of headlines but were no way to make money, and despite Lindbergh's fame or the Schneider contest's glory, the airplane industry in the 1920s lived hand-to-mouth.

The Airline Industry Takes Wing

Military orders for planes were scant. General Guilio Douhet, who had commanded the first Italian air squadrons before the war, said in his 1921 book, *The Command of the Air*, that the airplane would be decisive in future wars. Other officers were influenced by Douhet, including Lord Hugh Trenchard, the first leader of the RAF, and the U.S. Army's combative Brigadier General Billy Mitchell, who proposed in 1921 to sink a battleship with bombs dropped from airplanes. "Good god!" commented Navy Secretary Josephus Daniels. "This man should be writing dime novels." In July, Mitchell's Martin MB-2 bombers attacked the captured German battleship *Ostfriesland* in a planned exercise and sent it to the bottom of the Atlantic.

Such pro-aircraft doctrines were considered threats to armies and navies. Mitchell himself made one intemperate statement too many and was court-martialed in 1925 (he resigned to avoid being discharged). Air forces were henceforth kept on a tight rein. Most military aircraft of 1930 looked like those of 1920.

Brigadier General Billy Mitchell spent his life and his career calling for the United States to build an adequate air force. He antagonized many, but his prediction that the Japanese would bomb Pearl Harbor early some Sunday morning was but one of many that came true.

Kelly bill, or Air Mail Act of 1925, authorizing private contract carriage of airmail.

February 18, 1925
NACA approves the "Standard Altimeter Calibration" system.

February 22, 1925
The de Havilland D.H.60 Moth, pioneering private aircraft, makes its first flight.

March 1, 1925
The first U.S. year-round airline opens. Ryan Airlines has two flights a day from LA to San Diego; ticket price is $22.50 (about $225 today).

April 13, 1925
Henry Ford inaugurates scheduled air freight service between Detroit and Chicago.

May 1, 1925
National Air Transport Inc. is organized to carry mail and passengers.

May 15, 1925
The Junkers G 23 airliner is introduced by AB Aerotransport. It will become one of the most important airliners of the period.

May 16, 1925
The Messerschmitt M-17, the first

plane manufactured by the company, makes its first flight and crashes with Willy Messerschmitt onboard, injuring him and the pilot.

July 1925
The radio beacon is developed for use in aircraft.

July 7, 1925
Boeing Model 40 makes its first flight. It's the first in a long series of Boeing airliners.

July 15, 1925
Dr. A. Hamilton Rice, in a Curtiss Sea-gull, explores the Amazon River by aircraft—the first exploration of its kind.

September 3, 1925
The Navy airship *Shenandoah* crashes.

September 4, 1925
The Fokker F.VII/3m "Tri-Motor" makes its first flight. It will become one of the most important airliners of the period.

Fighters were open-cockpit, two-gun biplanes with top speeds below 200 miles per hour; bombers were scarcely able to exceed 100 miles per hour.

The development of naval aviation was constrained by the 1922 Washington naval treaty, which limited the construction of aircraft carriers: The U.S. Navy was able to build only two carriers in the 1920s—the large and modern *Lexington* and *Saratoga*.

Commercial aviation was also a fledgling. Air Transport & Travel, formed by a struggling airplane builder, started scheduled passenger services between London and Paris in August 1919. Its first airplanes were war-surplus de Havilland single-engine bombers, modified to seat two to four passengers in an enclosed cabin.

Two months later, in Amsterdam, an airline company was formed under charter from the King. Known by its Dutch initials, KLM, it today can lay claim to being the oldest continuously operating

The USS *Saratoga* and the USS *Lexington* were built on the hulls of battle cruisers. At the time of their debut, they were probably the best aircraft carriers in the world. The *Lexington* was sunk, but the *Saratoga* survived World War II and was used in the Bikini atomic tests.

airline in the world. Many of KLM's starter aircraft were designed by Anthony Fokker. The crafts had wooden monoplane wings and steel-tube-and-fabric fuselages.

But business was generally poor, regardless of who owned the airline. Airplanes were little faster than trains. Their cabins were noisy and cold, and they flew at low altitudes, through the worst of the weather. Emergency landings were a regular event.

By the mid-1920s, most of the European airlines had been folded into larger companies, often supported or owned by national governments: Air Union in France was formed in 1923, Imperial Airways in the United Kingdom in 1924, and Deutsche Lufthansa in 1926. This stabilized the airline industry, which became a more reliable customer for the airplane builders.

Imperial Airways' name underlined the fact that the British and French saw national airlines as instruments of their colonial governments. The companies extended their routes from Europe into Asia and Africa. They wanted strong, reliable airplanes rather than those that were best in performance and economics, and to an increasing extent, they used flying boats for over-water flights.

Early commercial airplanes used liquid-cooled engines, but by the mid-1920s, they had been displaced by radial engines. These resembled the wartime rotary engines, but the cylinders and crankcase were firmly bolted to the firewall as logic dictates, eliminating the rotary engine's vile effects on handling. After engineers had overcome the mechanical challenges of radial engines, their merits became apparent. There was no coolant to leak, and most of the working parts were out in the open, where they could be easily inspected.

The most advanced transport aircraft of the 1920s were the monoplane Fokkers of KLM and Lufthansa's all-metal Junkers airplanes. A classic debuted in September 1925 when Fokker fit-

September 8–October 4, 1925
The First Commercial Reliability Tour is flown. It's designed to demonstrate the usefulness of aircraft to American consumers.

December 21, 1925
Florida Airways forms to operate between Tampa, Miami, Jackson, and Atlanta.

1926
Italy gains its first Schneider win at Baltimore.

1926
Ford acquires the Stout Metal Airplane Company.

1926
Airmail routes blossom all over the United States.

January 6, 1926
The German airline Lufthansa is formed.

February 6, 1926
Pratt & Whitney produce the first radial Wasp engine.

February 10, 1926
Ramon Franco and his crew land their Dornier Wal after the first east–west crossing of the South Atlantic.

March 16, 1926
Dr. Robert H. Goddard launches the first liquid-fueled rocket. It climbs 41 feet and lands 184 feet away.

April 6, 1926
Varney Speed Lines begins operations.

May 8, 1926
The Air Commerce Act is passed, authorizing the Weather Bureau to provide meteorological service to pilots.

May 9, 1926
Admiral Richard E. Byrd and Floyd Bennett allegedly reach the North Pole in a Fokker F.VII-3m. The success of the flight is disputed to this day.

May 20, 1926
President Calvin Coolidge signs the Air Commerce Act, the first Federal regulation of civil aeronautics.

June 11, 1926
The Ford Tri-Motor, a very important

ted the F.VII monoplane with three 200-horsepower Wright Whirlwinds. The F.VII/3m, the Fokker Tri-Motor, could carry ten passengers at around 100 miles per hour and was safe and reliable for its time.

Tri-Motors were built in Belgium, Poland, Czechoslovakia, Italy, and the United Kingdom. In the United States, General Motors was the part-owner of the Fokker Aircraft Corporation, which provided Tri-Motors to the emerging U.S. airline industry.

In the United States, some wartime pilots "barnstormed" across the country. After selecting a suitable field and town, the barnstormers then offered airplane rides and performed daredevil stunts such as wing-walking. Aside from that, the main business of aviation was flying the mail. Any qualified carrier could bid for U.S. Air Mail contracts; in the 1920s, the more successful companies gradually acquired their rivals and built up larger fleets of aircraft. The first United States-developed passenger-carrying aircraft were single-engine mailplanes like the Boeing 40A, operational from 1927, which could carry a pair of passengers as well as a load of mail.

But traffic soon picked up, and the demand for larger aircraft increased. Observing GM's move into aircraft manufacturing, Henry Ford acquired the Stout Metal Airplane Company in 1926. The company's founder, William Stout, was developing an airliner that was—to be frank—a copy of the Fokker Tri-Motor's shape, with corrugated-skin metal construction that owed a great deal to Hugo Junkers. But the combination of those influences with the trusted Ford name was a happy one. Ford's most successful product was the 5-AT, a 15-passenger airplane with three 420-horsepower Pratt & Whitney Hornet engines.

As the 1920s drew to a close, the U.S. airline industry was growing up. Western Air Express, one of the larger airmail companies, had acquired the Fokker Aircraft Corporation and was

moving toward forming a group of airlines that would offer service from coast to coast. Delta Air Transport was adding new air links in the South. William Stout, who once summed up his design approach in the precept "simplicate and add more lightness," also defined a commercial aircraft as "an airplane that can support itself aerodynamically and economically at the same time." With the world's expanding prosperity, it seemed definite that such a perfect aircraft would emerge soon. "Stocks have reached what looks like a permanently high plateau," remarked Yale economics professor Irving Fisher on October 17, 1929.

Black Thursday, the stock market crash that triggered the Great Depression, struck a week later; the aircraft industry that emerged from the economic cataclysm would be quite different from the one that entered it, with new leaders and new technology.

When World War I ended, there were thousands of aircraft and engines declared surplus. The Curtiss JN-4 was among the most popular of these among barnstormers, particularly when a Wright Hispano engine was installed. Most, however, used the original Curtiss OX-5 engine.

CHAPTER THREE

Flight
Comes of Age

WORLD WAR II TAKES THE FIELD OF AVIATION—FLYING

HIGH IN THE POST-DEPRESSION WORLD—INTO AN

EXPLOSIVE NEW ERA OF DEVELOPMENT.

In the fall of 1933, a gleaming silver twin-engine airplane stood at the end of the runway in Winslow, Arizona—a nothing-much-of-interest town located in the Painted Desert. At the airplane's controls was legendary test pilot Edmund "Eddie" Allen. The airplane was at its maximum takeoff weight and Winslow stands at 4,500 feet above sea level, so it was clear that the takeoff run would have to be long. Allen released the brakes, and the craft started moving. The wings began to lift, and the airplane rose a little as the shock struts in the landing gear extended. At that point, Allen's copilot, Tommy Tomlinson, cut the right engine as planned.

Right: One of the loveliest fighters ever built, the Supermarine Spitfire was designed by the famous Reginald Mitchell, who died just after the first flight of the prototype in 1936. He had no idea that more than 22,000 "Spits" would be produced.

Top right: The Boeing B-9 was the first modern bomber acquired by the U.S. Army Air Corps. With its cantilever monoplane wing and retractable landing gear, it was faster than contemporary fighters. Only 13 were procured before the more advanced Martin B-10 appeared.

Bottom right: A line of development, leading from the Boeing Monomail through the B-9 and the 247 (pictured here), leads directly to the famous Boeing B-17 of World War II. The Boeing 247 was the first modern airliner, making the contemporary Ford and Fokker three-engine transports obsolete overnight.

Opposite: Only one DC-1 was built, but that was enough to show that the Douglas line of transports was revolutionary.

Below: The Boeing Monomail featured a cantilever monoplane wing, all-metal construction, retractable landing gear, and a ring cowl. However, it retained the open cockpit placed toward the rear that was so favored by airmail pilots, who liked to have a lot of airplane between them and the crash site.

The airplane "shook and staggered, but it continued to climb," the third man in the cockpit, Frank Collbohm, recalled later. It ascended to 8,000 feet, clearing the peaks around Winslow, and flew another 280 miles to Albuquerque, New Mexico, without ever using the right engine. The new Douglas DC-1 had passed a critical test for its customer, Transcontinental & Western Air (TWA), and was now ready to make its mark on the aviation world. The impact is still felt today. While most of the DC-1's contemporaries have been museum pieces for 50 years or more, you can still find the DC-1's direct descendants hauling passengers and cargo.

Distance Marries Speed

The story of the DC-1 starts in 1926, when German Adolf Rohrbach—the designer of the before-its-time Zeppelin-Staaken E.4/20 airplane of 1919—gave a lecture in the United States. According to historian Charles Gibbs-Smith, the printed version of the lecture inspired a group of engineers at the Boeing company in Seattle.

Boeing was also an aircraft operator, with mail contracts between Chicago and San Francisco. With such long routes, it was not surprising that the company became interested in high-speed, long-range aircraft. In May 1930, Boeing flew the first example of a mailplane called the Monomail. With a single 575-horse-power Pratt & Whitney engine, the Monomail had a clean, 59-foot wing. The landing gear retracted into the wing. The main structure was made of aluminum alloy sheet, with sheet-metal stiffeners riveted to the inner surfaces.

The Monomail was a qualified success, but only because the day of the single-engine mailplane with a few passenger seats was almost over. Boeing obtained an Army contract for a high-speed twin-engine bomber, the B-9, and delivered the first aircraft in 1931: It cruised 60 miles per hour faster than the Army's in-service bombers and could outrun most fighters. In June 1932, as the economy recovered from the Great Depression, United Airlines—newly formed by the merger of Boeing Air Transport with National and Varney—ordered 60 Boeing Model 247s, an airliner with a similar wing to the B-9 and a descendant of the Monomail.

1927
L.M.C. Drilling and Production uses a Laird Swallow to fly to drilling sites; many oil companies followed, including Shell, Texaco, Phillips, Conoco, and Standard Oil.

January 28, 1927
Boeing receives a contract to fly airmail between Chicago and San Francisco with the specially built Model 40A mailplane.

March–April, 1927
A Portuguese Dornier Wal makes the first night crossing of the South Atlantic.

March 29, 1927
The first Aircraft Type Certificate is issued to the Buhl Airster CA-3.

May 8, 1927
Lieutenant Charles Nungesser and Captain Francois Coli disappear in an attempted Paris–New York flight.

May 21, 1927
▶ Charles Lindbergh lands in Paris after a nonstop solo flight from New York.

May 21, 1927
Standard Oil takes the delivery of a Ford Tri-Motor.

May 25, 1927
Lieutenant Jimmy Doolittle flies first outside loop.

June 28–29, 1927
In an Atlantic-Fokker C-2 named *Bird of Paradise*, Lieutenant Albert F. Hegenberger and Lieutenant Lester J. Maitland fly from Oakland, California, to Honolulu, Hawaii, the longest distance ever flown over the open sea.

July 1, 1927
Federal aids to air navigation on transcontinental airways is turned over to the U.S. Post Office.

A NEW GENERATION OF TEST PILOTS

The DC-1 test pilot **Edmund "Eddie" Allen** had also been a test pilot in World War I. He had been the first test pilot for the National Advisory Committee on Aeronautics (NACA) but had resigned to study aeronautical engineering at the University of Illinois and the Massachusetts Institute of Technology. Only after completing school did he return to flight testing.

Allen represented a bridge between the early designer-pilots and the dedicated flight-test teams of today. In 1942, Allen made the first flight of the XB-29 bomber. The early flights were disrupted by engine fires, but the airplane was badly needed for the war effort, so Allen continued the test program. In February 1943, he was killed with the rest of his crew after the second XB-29 caught fire in flight.

Edmund "Eddie" Allen

This was not good news for United's biggest rival, TWA. But when TWA approached Boeing to order 247s, it was told none would be available until United's order for airplanes was completed.

TWA's vice president for operations, a 30-year-old former Fokker salesman named Jack Frye, gathered a team of employees from engineering, operations, and sales and wrote a draft specification for an airliner that would surpass the 247. Frye mailed the specification to several companies, including Douglas Aircraft Company in Santa Monica.

Donald Douglas decided to bid on the TWA design request, but with a twin-engine aircraft rather than the tri-motor that TWA expected. The only element of the design that truly worried Douglas was a safety demand by TWA technical adviser Charles Lindbergh. He wanted the airplane to be able to take off from any field in TWA's system on one engine and be able to climb and clear the terrain around that airport. You did not say no to Lindbergh. The contract for a single DC-1 was signed in September 1932.

The DC-1 flew in July 1933. It wouldn't have passed Lindbergh's test had it not been for new technology: The plane used variable-pitch propeller blades that could be adjusted for best efficiency for takeoff, climb, and cruise. The blades also "feathered" (rotated in line with the airstream) to reduce the drag of a dead engine. TWA ordered the improved DC-2 into production. Entering service in 1934, it was an immense success. "Coast to coast in 18 hours," boasted TWA.

The next development was inspired by American Airlines, which wanted to take the lead in transcontinental service by offering passengers a sleeping berth. The result was the enlarged Douglas Sleeper Transport, or DST, first tested at the end of 1935.

The production version of the DC-1, the DC-2, carried 14 passengers and had split flaps, retractable landing gear, and a streamlined look that resulted in 193 sales.

July 4, 1927
The Lockheed Aircraft Company builds the first Vega. It becomes an important executive aircraft.

July 5, 1927
The Germans form a Society for Space Travel.

July 17, 1927
USMC DH-4s dive-bomb hostile forces in Nicaragua.

August 24, 1927
The de Havilland D.H. 71 Tiger Moth sets a light plane speed record of 186.47 miles per hour.

August 31, 1927
The U.S. Post Office turns over airmail routes to private contractors.

September 1, 1927
The American Railway Express Company starts a large-scale air express operation.

October 14–15, 1927
Dieudonné Costes and Joseph Le Brix cross the South Atlantic nonstop in a Breguet 19.

October 19, 1927
Pan American Airways begins international services with Cy Caldwell's Fairchild seaplane, *La Nina*.

October 28, 1927
Pan Am sets up its first base in Key West, Florida.

November 16, 1927
The U.S. Navy commissions its first combat-capable aircraft carrier, the USS *Saratoga*.

December 14, 1927
The USS *Lexington* (CV 2) is commissioned at Quincy, Massachusetts.

December 31, 1927
Art Goebel wins the Dole Race from California to Hawaii in a Travel Air Woolaroc.

1928
The NACA develops a cowling for radial engines.

January 7, 1928
The Polikarpov U-2 trainer makes its first flight. The general-purpose biplane will be built in greater numbers—40,000—than any other aircraft.

January 15, 1928
James Herman Banning becomes the

Child star Shirley Temple received the first eastbound ticket at Los Angeles Municipal Airport on September 18, 1936.

The DST could carry 14 passengers, including two in the Sky Room, a private compartment. It was an elegant way to travel, but Douglas was sure that the market was limited. Before the airplane entered service, the company was already selling a version of the aircraft as the 21-seat DC-3 "day plane."

Even before thousands of military DC-3s were built, the airplane transformed the aviation business. By the end of 1937, Douglas was building 36 of the airplanes per month, at $700,000 or more each; a mere seven years earlier, a respectable lifetime production for a large aircraft had been 36 total. American's founder, C. R. Smith, said that the DC-3 "was the first airplane that could make money just by hauling passengers."

By 1939, other important innovations had been widely adopted. Radio transmitters allowed a pilot to fix his or her airplane's position anywhere in the United States. The pilot reported the plane's position to controllers on the ground, who could warn of other airplanes in the area.

In 1929, a Pulitzer-race-winning pilot named James "Jimmy" Doolittle had made a safe blind landing at Mitchell Field on Long Island; he was guided only by a set of radio beams and receivers onboard the airplane. By 1939, a system based on the German Lorenz beam was in widespread use for landing guidance.

Other West Coast aircraft companies were following in Douglas's wake. By 1937, Boeing was building the four-engine Stratoliner, with a pressurized cabin that allowed flight at 25,000 feet,

The DC-2 was expanded into the DST, the Douglas Sleeper, which had Pullman-style sleeping bunks built in (inset). The DST was not as well received as its teammate, the Douglas DC-3, which became the most popular airliner in the world because it could earn a profit without a subsidy.

IT'S A LIVING

Flying became a good profession in the 1930s. **Commercial pilots** in the DC-3 era wore crisp, naval-style uniforms. In a contemporary account of an American Airlines transcontinental trip, published in *Fortune*, "Captain King" was a member of the Air Line Pilots' Association (ALPA): "a very de luxe union man with very de luxe wages." He made $8,500 a year (which would be about $108,000 today).

"Miss Jones," the stewardess on the *Flagship Arizona*, was a registered nurse making $125 a month (about $1,500 today). Medical training was important: The *Flagship Arizona* cruised only a few thousand feet above the ground, and the ride could be rough. Miss Jones could administer spirits of ammonia to the afflicted and, if these did not have the desired effect, could discreetly dispose of the now-soiled large cardboard carton handily stowed under each seat.

---

first African American to receive a federal pilot license.

February 1928
Bert Hinkler flies solo from England to Australia in an Avro Avian.

February 21, 1928
W. R. Grace and Pan American Airways form Pan-American-Grace Airways.

March 30, 1928
Major Mario di Bernardi sets a world speed record of 318 miles per hour in a Macchi M.52 floatplane.

April 12, 1928
A Junkers W.33 Bremen makes the first westbound Atlantic crossing by a heavier-than-air craft.

April 15–21, 1928
In a Lockheed Vega, Sir George Wilkins and pilot Carl Ben Eielson fly across the Arctic Sea from Alaska to Norway.

May 1, 1928
Pitcairn Aviation begins mail operations. It will become Eastern Air Lines in 1934.

May 15, 1928
The Australian Flying Doctor Service is inaugurated, setting the stage for business aviation in Australia.

May 16, 1928
TAT (which will become TWA in 1930) begins operations.

May 17, 1928
Sophie Pierce, the Lady Heath, lands an Avro Avian at Croydon after the first solo South Africa–Britain flight.

May 31–June 9, 1928
▶ Charles Kingsford-Smith (pictured) and Charles Ulm make the first transpacific flight from Oakland, California, to Brisbane, Australia, in a Fokker Trimotor.

Top: Unquestionably the most successful dirigible in history, the *Graf Zeppelin* seemed to herald a new age of air travel. Despite being filled with hydrogen, the carefully managed and flown *Graf* never had an accident and survived to be dismantled for its aluminum during World War II.

Middle: The British R100 was built by private funds. It proved to be a big success. Its fascinating story is told in engineer Nevile Shute's autobiography, *Slide Rule*. The R100's competition was the government-built R101, which crashed and burned on its first major flight. ·

Bottom: The United States used helium rather than hydrogen in its dirigibles, a vast improvement in safety, although somewhat costly in terms of efficiency. The *Akron* was built in the United States with the help of Zeppelin company engineers; it represented the peak of dirigible performance. Yet both it, and its sister ship, the *Macon*, crashed at sea.

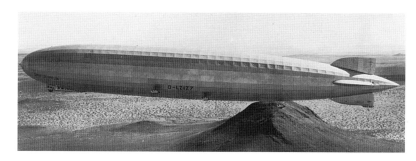

above most of the weather. Lockheed was producing a series of twin-engine transports, not quite as large as the DC-3 but somewhat faster.

Compared to the United States, in the rest of the world, aviation was a cottage industry. In Britain, in 1930, Handley Page flew the first HP.42 for Imperial Airways. It was a majestic four-engine biplane with a 130-foot wingspan. Within five years, though, the DC-2 had rendered it obsolete. Imperial Airways' privately owned rival British Airways, which was not compelled to buy British, bought Lockheeds and offered fierce competition.

Different crafts were needed for ocean flight. In the late '20s, the British and German governments launched the construction of airships three times as large in volume as the biggest World War I Zeppelins. The first, the *Graf Zeppelin*, flew in September 1928. With luxury accommodation for 20 passengers, the *Graf Zeppelin* made the first commercial air crossings of the North Atlantic and, in 1929, cruised around the world. The *Graf Zeppelin* made 144 Atlantic crossings before it was retired in 1937.

The British government ordered two airships: the R100 from Vickers and the R101 built by the Royal Airship Works. The

CALIFORNIA DREAMING

The airplane and movie industries both grew up in **Southern California.** With affordable land for airfields, reliable weather for test flying, and a business community to provide finance, it was a hospitable climate for the growing industry. California Institute of Technology (CalTech) in Pasadena was developing a strong aeronautical department, complete with wind tunnels and other test facilities.

The region also hosted visionary designers like Jack Northrop, whose ambition was to build flying-wing aircraft. CalTech's Theodore von Karman had worked with Germany's Hugo Junkers. Junkers shared Northrop's goal, and von Karman was able to help Northrop refine a new method of all-metal wing construction that was used on the DC-1, DC-2, and DC-3.

R101 crashed in northern France on its maiden voyage to India in October 1930. The accident killed the project's government leaders. The airship plan was abandoned, and the successful R100 was scrapped as a result.

In the United States, the Navy commissioned two giant airships for fleet reconnaissance. The *Akron* and *Macon* were filled with

---

June 11, 1928
A German sailplane, the *Ente,* or the Duck, flies with two Sander solid-propellant rockets for 60 seconds.

June 17, 1928
Amelia Earhart becomes the first woman to cross the Atlantic.

June 20, 1928
Braniff Airlines forms.

July 5, 1928
Arturo Ferrarin and Carlo de Prete land an S.64 on a beach after a 4,466-mile nonstop flight from Rome, Italy, to Natal, Brazil.

July 30, 1928
The first Aeronautics Branch Aircraft Accident Investigation Board is created.

August 1928
A British newspaper, the *Daily Mail,*

buys a de Havilland D.H. 61 to use as a flying newspaper office; it starts a trend among newspapers to own their own aircraft.

September 1928
The *Graf Zeppelin* makes its first flight.

September 1928
NACA begins coordination of university research programs on aeronautics and meteorology.

September 18, 1928
Juan de la Cierva, inventor of the gyroplane (autogiro), crosses the English Channel.

October 1928
NACA reports on Aircraft Accident Analysis.

October 31, 1928
There are 3,659 pilots with active licenses in the United States.

November 1928
Fred Weick reports on his low-drag, long-chord cowling for the new air-cooled radial engines, for which he will win the 1929 Collier Trophy.

December 19, 1928
Harold F. Pitcairn makes the first autogiro flight in the United States.

1929
Ed Link creates the first model of the

THE FALL OF A GIANT

The Zeppelin company had started work on the world's most modern airship in 1934, intended expressly for scheduled service on the North Atlantic. More than 800 feet long, the LZ 129 **Hindenburg** was designed to accommodate 72 passengers in cabins and would cruise at 70 miles per hour. To reduce the risk of fire, the new airship was powered by four 1,050-horsepower diesel engines (diesel fuel is safer than gasoline) and would have been filled with helium if the U.S. government had not banned its export. The vast ship first lifted off in March 1936, making more than 70 transatlantic flights in the following year, crossing the ocean in approximately two days.

helium, rather than inflammable hydrogen, and carried Curtiss fighters in an internal hangar. Both were lost in bad weather—the *Akron* in 1933 and *Macon* two years later.

On the afternoon of May 6, 1937, the new Zeppelin *Hindenburg* arrived over New York City, waiting for the weather to clear at Lakehust, New Jersey. Around 7:00 P.M., the airship was approaching the mooring mast when a flame appeared near the tail. Within seconds, the whole ship was ablaze. It was the end of the large airship as a passenger vehicle, with only 62 of the 96 people on board the airship surviving. Including the last Zeppelin

(the LZ 130, which was flown but never entered service), seven giant ships had been built and four of them had met violent ends.

From the late '20s, flying boats were favored for long-haul operations. Outside the United States and Europe, most of the world's richest cities were seaports. These cities had sheltered harbors where seaplanes could land and take off. Also important—designers could create seaplanes in a size that would strain the capacity of the runways at most airports.

In the United States, the long-range flying boat was associated with Juan Trippe's Pan American Airways. In 1931, Igor Sikorsky built the four-engine, 40-passenger S-40 for Pan American, and Trippe asked both Sikorsky and the Glenn L. Martin Company to design flying boats capable of crossing the Atlantic and Pacific oceans. In 1934 and 1935, Pan Am put the Sikorsky S.42 into service on its South American routes, and the Martin 130 launched scheduled service from San Francisco to Hong Kong.

If inanimate objects may be said to have hubris, surely that was the case with the *Hindenburg*. Perhaps not the most filmed dirigible in history (the *Graf Zeppelin* certainly was) but no dirigible has had its death agony repeated more often on television than the *Hindenburg*.

Link Trainer, the ancestor of all flight simulators.

1929
Transcontinental Air Transport shows the first in-flight movie.

1929
Fabrica Militar de Aviones in Cordoba, Argentina, begins manufacturing aircraft and engines.

January 1–7, 1929
▶ Major Carl Spaatz (pictured), Captain Ira Eaker, First Lieutenant Elwood Quesada, and Staff Sergeant Roy Hooe conduct an endurance flight in the Fokker C2-A *Question Mark*, setting a world record of 150 hours, 40 minutes.

January 9, 1929
Pan American opens a route between Miami and San Juan, Puerto Rico.

January 29, 1929
Weyman-Lepere Company acquires a license for Cierva autogiros in France. Cierva has developed a flapping hinge to prevent the rollover effect.

February 1, 1929
Boeing changes its name to United Aircraft and Transportation Corporation. Later broken up, it is the predecessor of United Airlines and United Technologies as well as today's Boeing.

February 14, 1929
The Pitcairn-Cierva Autogiro Company forms in United States.

March 30, 1929
Imperial Airways starts London–Karachi (Pakistan) passenger service, using a variety of aircraft over seven days.

June 17, 1929
Delta Air Service makes its first flight.

AN EARLY AIRLINE MOGUL

Aristocratic, energetic, and equally confident of his own judgment in business, politics, and technology, **Juan Trippe** formed Pan American Airways in 1927 at the age of 28. The airline served Havana and the other Caribbean playgrounds of Trippe's rich Yale and Wall Street friends.

Gradually, Pan American spread its network deeper into South and Central America, with Trippe exploiting his political connections to obtain exclusive U.S. mail contracts. The visionary Trippe also acquired a friend and close associate in Charles Lindbergh. Trippe's first Sikorsky S-40 was christened *American Clipper* by the First Lady, Mrs. Herbert Hoover, and Lindbergh captained the first flight.

Juan Trippe

Inspired by the U.S. designs, Great Britain's Imperial Airways ordered the Shorts C-Class flying boat in 1935. With four 900-horsepower engines and a clean, rather small elliptical wing, the C-Class was designed to replace all the landplanes used on the main Empire route, all the way to Australia.

In June 1936, Pan Am ordered six Boeing 314 flying boats. With a wingspan of 152 feet, a weight of 84,000 pounds fully loaded, and the power of four 1,600-horsepower Wright radial engines, the 314 was one of the largest airplanes ever built when it made its first flight in June 1938. Despite its size, cruising speed was a respectable 180 miles per hour.

The Boeing Clippers carried 40 sleeper passengers and a crew of ten, including relief pilots. Meals were prepared by selected hotel kitchens and served in a separate dining room, and there was a VIP compartment in the rear of the cabin. But the airplanes were still unpressurized and low-flying, and the trip, which took more than 20 hours, could be uncomfortable and exhausting. At Pan Am's landing in Foynes, Ireland, chef Joe Sheridan learned to revive the passengers with a mixture of strong coffee, cream, and whiskey, a recipe that American travelers took back home and called Irish coffee.

The Boeing 314 Clipper was the most advanced of all of Pan Am's Clipper fleet. It entered transatlantic service in 1939. It used the same wing and horizontal tail surface as the giant Boeing XB-15. Twelve were built, and they served around the globe during World War II.

Private Citizens Take to the Skies

The late '30s saw the appearance of some of the world's largest airplanes, while the skies also began to fill with smaller machines. One of the first airplanes designed for private ownership was Geoffrey de Havilland's D.H.60 Moth, flown in 1925. Sales of such aircraft picked up in the 1930s as the world economies started to recover. In Europe, governments fostered the development of flying clubs where people of average means could learn to fly.

A U.S. classic was born in 1933 when the J-2 Cub, powered by a horizontally opposed Continental engine, was put on the market by the Taylor Aircraft Corporation. After founder Gillbert Taylor left the company in 1936, owner William Piper gave it his own name. In 1937, Piper built 687 Cubs, all of them yellow with black trim. The following year's J-3 model sold for $1,300 (about $15,500 today).

Some small airplanes were less conventional. German enthusiasts led the way in developing the art of engineless flight, discovering that an efficient glider with slender, clean wings could stay airborne for hours, gaining height as it flew a tight circle in a column of rising air.

July 7, 1929
Transcontinental Air Transport sets up combined rail-air service, going coast to coast in 48 hours.

July 10, 1929
Nick Mamer and Art Walker fly nonstop round-trip from Spokane to New York in the *Spokane Sun-God*, which was refueled in flight.

July 17, 1929
Dr. Robert H. Goddard launches a rocket and recovers the instruments by parachute.

July 22, 1929
A Heinkel He 12 postal seaplane takes off of the ocean liner *Bremen* 250 miles from New York to speed mail service.

August 1929
The Germans test a rocket-assisted takeoff on a Junkers J-33, the world's first use of JATO/RATO.

August 8–29, 1929
The LZ 127 *Graf Zeppelin* makes its round-the-world flight. The only successful scheduled lighter-than-air ship transport takes 21 days, 7 hours, and 34 minutes.

September 1929
A Supermarine S.6 wins the Schneider race for Britain at Calshot, England.

September 24, 1929
At Mitchell Field, in thick fog, Lieutenant Jimmy Doolittle achieves the first instrument-only blind flight in a Consolidated NY-2 biplane.

September 30, 1929
Fritz von Opel flies a rocket-powered glider.

October 21, 1929
The largest aircraft of the time, the Dornier DO-X, a 12-engine giant flying boat, debuts and successfully flies for an hour with 169 people onboard.

November 1, 1929
A Soviet Tupelov ANT-4 flies from Moscow to New York, a 13,300-mile flight.

November 22, 1929
A Curtiss Tanager wins the Guggenheim Safe Airplane Contest.

November 28–29, 1929
Admiral Richard E. Byrd and Bernt Balchen fly over the South Pole.

and turn tightly at low speeds, like their old biplanes. Reginald Mitchell, designer of the winning Schneider Trophy racers, had created such a fighter to meet a 1930 specification, but it would have no chance of catching a bomber based on DC-2 technology. The RAF recognized this in 1934 when a stock DC-2 came in second in a much-publicized air race from London to Melbourne.

Far left: The Piper Cub came to symbolize the great American sports plane, thanks to the brilliant sales abilities of Bill Piper. In actual performance, the Cub was indistinguishable from a dozen other aircraft, including Aeronca and Taylorcraft. But Bill Piper sold the sizzle as well as the steak, and the Cub predominated.

Left: The Heinkel He 51 was one of the aircraft that formed the earliest squadrons of the German Luftwaffe. When it fought in Spain, the Germans were surprised to find that its performance was inferior to the Russian Polikarpov planes that opposed it. Even the Italian Fiat Cr-32 was a better fighter.

One significant private airplane came from Southern Germany. Flown in 1934, Professor Willy Messerschmitt's sleek, high-performance Bf 108 joined a number of German aircraft with rather puzzling features. Dornier Aircraft Company and the Heinkel company were flying prototypes of "fast transports" or "mailplanes," with passenger accommodation that was—to say the least—cramped. Some government-sponsored flying clubs in Germany were getting Heinkel He 51s—remarkable airplanes for trainee pilots; they packed a 750-horsepower BMW V-12 engine.

It was all part of Nazi Germany's secret re-armament program. In 1935, the wraps came off, and the Richthofen squadron—the first combat unit in the new Luftwaffe—was equipped with He 51s. Also, in 1935, Messerschmitt completed another new airplane. It closely resembled the Bf 108 in its layout, but it was larger, with a single seat and a Rolls-Royce Kestrel V engine. There was no disguising the Bf 109: It was a fighter.

Fighters Enter a New Era

Fighter plane technology was undergoing a change. The performance of the DC-2 was an important influence on fighter design. In the past, air forces had ordered monoplane fighters, such as the Boeing P-26, but insisted that they should be able to land slowly

Above: The Messerschmitt Bf 108 Taifun (Typhoon) was a stunning aircraft, with a performance that rivaled the post-war Beechcraft Bonanza. It was the direct ancestor of the famous Bf 109 fighter and was used in large numbers by the Luftwaffe. When you see a "Bf 109" in films today, it is most often a disguised Bf 108 acting the role.

1930
Keystone B-5A, the last of the biplane bombers, enters Air Corps service.

1930
Italian engineer Corridion D'Ascanio sets the helicopter altitude record (59 feet), distance record (1,180 yards), and endurance record (8 minutes, 45 seconds) in his design.

1930
U.S. airlines carry 374,935 passengers.

1930
NACA constructs a vertical wind tunnel to study spins.

January 25, 1930
American Airways (now American Airlines) forms.

January 26, 1930
▶ Frank Whittle gets a patent on a jet engine.

March 1930
The Pitcairn-Cierva PCA-2 autogiro flies, using a mechanical-drive rotor spin-up to assist takeoff.

April 2, 1930
The Grumman XFF-1 makes its first flight.

April 4, 1930
The American Interplanetary Society forms. It subsequently becomes part of IAS.

May 5–24, 1930
Amy Johnson becomes the first woman to fly solo between England and Australia.

May 6, 1930
The Boeing Monomail makes its first flight.

May 15, 1930
Ellen Church becomes the first airline stewardess for Boeing Air Transport, on a Boeing Model 80.

The Junkers Ju 87 made the term "Stuka" as famous as the term "blitzkrieg," with which it will always be associated. The angular dive-bomber was a perfect ground-assault weapon—but only when the Germans had air superiority. Once air superiority was lost, it was very vulnerable to attack.

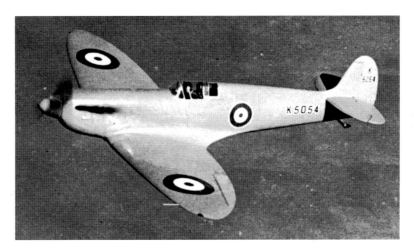

Mitchell started a completely new design, the Type 300, in late 1934. The Type 300 had a large, thin wing and the latest V-12 engine from Rolls-Royce. The wing housed eight machine guns based on the American Colt. The result was a clean, graceful aircraft capable of 360 miles per hour. It was named Spitfire, and its engine was known as the Merlin.

Messerschmitt's Bf 109 and Mitchell's Spitfire were the only fighters in production at the start of World War II that would still be in production at the end of it. They fought nose-to-nose over Britain, the Mediterranean, and northern Europe and set the pattern for a classic generation of airplanes.

As war approached and the world's air forces re-equipped, there were clear differences not only in airplane design but in the military doctrine that dictated what airplanes would be needed. The German Luftwaffe placed heavy emphasis on providing tactical support for a rapidly advancing army. The Condor Legion, the Luftwaffe detachment that supported Franco's Republicans in the Spanish Civil War, used dive-bombers as flying artillery. The specially designed Junkers Ju 87 dive-bomber was tested in Spain, and the results were so encouraging that the German Air Ministry decreed that all future bombers should be capable of dive attacks.

Above: Affectionately called the "Peashooter," the Boeing P-26 was a transitional fighter. The monoplane's all-metal makeup was new, but it retained the wire bracing, open cockpit, and fixed landing gear of the past.

Left: The Spitfire was a delightful aircraft to fly, and it proved amazingly adaptable to modification, as increasingly powerful engines were fitted to it. Designed as an interceptor for knocking down intruding enemy bombers, the Spitfire never had the range needed to be an escort fighter.

Opposite: The Hawker Hurricane was a private venture by the Hawker company. Designed by Sydney Camm, the Hurricane featured retractable landing gear, an enclosed cockpit, and no less than eight machine guns. It was really the star of the Battle of Britain, despite the glamour of the Spitfire.

The Royal Air Force was biased toward air defense and bombing. The most important aircraft in production as war approached were the Spitfire and the Hawker Hurricane. Also powered by the Merlin and armed with eight guns, the Hurricane was not as fast as the Spitfire but was easier to build and repair. At the same time, British companies were working on a new generation of fast, heavy bombers, carrying a large bomb load and armed for self-defense with machine guns in powered turrets.

July 16, 1930
TWA forms.

July–August, 1930
Wernher von Braun conducts his first "space-medicine" experiments, using mice and a centrifuge.

September 1, 1930
Dieudonné Costes and Maurice Bellonte, in a Breguet biplane, accomplish the first airplane flight from Paris to New York.

September 10, 1930
The Taylor E-2 Cub makes its first flight. It will later become the Piper Cub.

November 1, 1930
Wernher von Braun becomes an employee of the German Army under General Walter R. Dornberger.

October 5, 1930
A British R101 airship crashes near Beauvais in northern France.

December 30, 1930
Dr. Robert H. Goddard's rocket attains 2,000 feet and 500 miles per hour.

1931
The *Graf Zeppelin* starts the first scheduled South Atlantic air service.

1931
A NACA report shows that a boundary layer control could increase lift by as much as 96 percent.

1931
Alexander Lippisch flies the first delta-wing aircraft.

January 1931
Italian aviation minister Italo Balbo leads the first formation flight across the South Atlantic.

January 7, 1931
Guy Menzies lands his Avro Avian in Wellington, New Zealand, after a record flight from Sydney, Australia.

February 1931
The first official rocket-mail is established in Austria.

February 28, 1931
Imperial Airways starts its London–Central Africa service.

April 1931
The Junkers Ju 52/3m makes it first flight.

By contrast, though, U.S. fighters were slow. A U.S. contemporary of the Spitfire, the Curtiss Model 75B, was no less than 65 miles per hour slower than the British fighter, but it was bought in large numbers because it was the best U.S. design available.

Above: The Mitsubishi A6M came as a complete surprise to the United States, despite the warnings about it that had been sent from Major General Claire Chennault and others. It proved to be the dominant aircraft in the Pacific in the early months of the war.

Above right: The Bristol Blenheim was developed from a private venture, and it was Britain's most modern bomber when war began on September 3, 1939. Although it was underpowered and poorly armed and armored, the Blenheim was used extensively, primarily because it was all that was available.

Japan, meanwhile, was investing heavily in carrier-based aircraft. The first example of the Imperial Japanese Navy's most important airplane, the Mitsubishi A6M, flew in April 1939. Unlike most contemporary carrier-based aircraft, the Type 0, or Zero, could hold its own in speed, carried a heavy armament (including a 20-millimeter cannon), and possessed an extraordinary range of more than 1,000 miles.

The U.S. Army Air Corps fielded a mixed bag of aircraft, a result of conflicting doctrine and budget cuts. The most spectacular military airplane in service in 1939 was the Boeing B-17B Flying Fortress four-engine bomber. With turbo-supercharged engines, the B-17 could reach altitudes of 25,000 feet. Speed, altitude, and guns would protect the airplane from defenses, the Air Corps argued; the gyro-stabilized, computer-controlled Norden bombsight, a closely guarded secret, would put its weapons precisely on target.

WWII's War in the Sky

The first German air campaigns of World War II went according to plan for the Luftwaffe. A few obsolete Polish aircraft were no match for Bf 109s, and the Ju 87s were able to operate with impunity. When the German army rolled into France in April 1940, the Bf 109 again proved superior to French fighters. The most severe losses were among the RAF's day bombers, Fairey Battles and Bristol Blenheims. When they were designed, they were faster than contemporary biplane fighters, but they could easily be overtaken by the Bf 109. Some sorties by Fairey Battles against heavily defended bridges were almost literally suicidal.

Airplanes played another new role in the invasion of France. The Belgian fortress of Eben Emael was seized by elite German troops who flew over its perimeter defenses in wooden gliders towed behind transport planes. In May 1941, troops dropped by parachutes and gliders were critical to the German invasion of Crete.

April 8, 1931
Amelia Earhart establishes the autogiro altitude record of 18,415 feet in her Pitcairn autogiro.

May 27, 1931
NACA opens the first full-scale wind tunnel in Langley, Virginia.

May 27, 1931
August Piccard, with Paul Kipfer, makes the first balloon flight into the stratosphere (51,777 feet).

May 31, 1931
The first drone plane is flown by radio control from another plane.

June 23–July 1, 1931
Wiley Post and Harold Gatty fly around the world in 8 days, 15 hours, and 51 minutes in a Lockheed Vega *Winnie Mae.*

July 29–August 26, 1931
Charles and Anne Lindbergh make their survey flight to Japan.

September 29, 1931
The Supermarine S.6B sets a 407 miles per hour world air speed record. It's the first one at more than 400 miles per hour.

October 1931
The giant U.S. Navy airship *Akron* is commissioned.

October 3–5, 1931
Clyde Pangborn and Hugh Herndon make the first nonstop transpacific

flight, in a Bellanca Pacemaker. It takes 41 hours and 13 minutes.

1932
Aeroflot is formed. It will become the world's largest airline.

March 20, 1932
The Boeing P-26 makes its first flight. It is the first all-metal monoplane fighter of the Air Corps.

May 9, 1932
Captain Albert Hegenberger flies a

Consolidated NY-2 solo from takeoff to landing entirely on instruments.

May 20–21, 1932
► In a Lockheed Vega, Amelia Earhart becomes the first woman to fly solo across the Atlantic.

June 1932
United Air Lines orders 60 Boeing 247s.

July–August 1932
Germany begins formal rocket

In the summer of 1940, Adolf Hitler's commanders contemplated an invasion of Britain. As Hitler's directive of July 16 made clear, this task could not be performed until the RAF's fighter force had been eliminated. This was the overriding goal of the Luftwaffe in the Battle of Britain.

Before the war, the British fighter force was being expanded to the size that was believed necessary to defeat a Luftwaffe attack launched from Germany—not from bases as little as 30 miles from England. It had never reached that necessary size and had been further weakened by losses in Norway and France. At the beginning of July, the RAF had fewer than 600 fighters available against 2,600 German aircraft in northern France.

The most important engagements in the Battle of Britain took place between early August and mid-September 1940. In mid-August, the Luftwaffe concentrated its attacks on British fighter airfields. Losses were heavy on both sides, but the RAF could afford them less. By the beginning of September, 27 out of 97 flight commanders present at the beginning of July had been killed and 12 more had been seriously wounded.

On September 7, the Luftwaffe switched its attacks to London, believing the last few RAF fighters would be drawn into a final, decisive battle. But London was a distant target, and the fuel-thirsty Bf 109s had to turn for home after a few minutes' combat, leaving the bombers unescorted. The RAF could focus its forces on one stream of enemy aircraft rather than defending all its bases.

It was another eight days before the Luftwaffe could aim another major raid at London—eight days free of airfield attacks. Both sides had exaggerated their victories in the previous weeks, but the German crews were shocked on September 15: The two main waves of German bombers were attacked by more than 300 Spitfires and Hurricanes. The invasion was abandoned, and the military airplane had both won and lost its first decisive battle.

Aircraft versus aircraft, the Spitfire and Bf 109 were evenly matched. But one of the most critical factors in the Battle of Britain was not an airplane but a chain of primitive radar stations on the British coast. The British were not unique in developing radar, but the RAF had developed a simple system for using radar to track targets and to control fighters.

In November 1940, the British city of Coventry was attacked by 500 German bombers at night. The bombers were led by a special force of "pathfinders"—elite squadrons with specially trained crews using radio beams to navigate to the target. The accuracy and destruction were unprecedented for a night raid.

THE *BISMARCK* SINKS INTO HISTORY

In May 1941, the sinking of the **Bismarck** set the scene for the use of airplanes in sea warfare. On May 18, the German battleship *Bismarck* and the battle-cruiser *Prinz Eugen* sailed to attack convoys in the North Atlantic. Six days later, the British battle-cruiser, *Hood*, caught *Bismarck* off Iceland and was blown up in minutes with the loss of all but three of the 1,500-man crew. The Royal Navy was desperate to catch *Bismarck*, but it was an RAF Consolidated Catalina flying boat—a craft known to the U.S. Navy as the PBY—that found the ship on May 26.

Fifteen Fairey Swordfish biplanes, from the carrier *Ark Royal*, found the *Bismarck* and attacked with torpedoes, wrecking her rudder. The British capital ships sank the *Bismarck* the next morning. The world's most modern battleship had been crippled by obsolete biplanes (the Swordfish was about as big and fast as a modern crop duster), but the U.S. Navy was still unworried. "It is significant that despite the claims of air enthusiasts, no battleship has yet been sunk by bombs," read a photo caption in the program for the 1941 Army-Navy football game. The game was played on November 29, and the caption referred to a photo of the USS *Arizona*—sunk eight days later at Pearl Harbor.

development under Walter Dornberger.

July 2, 1932
Franklin D. Roosevelt becomes the first U.S. presidential candidate to fly.

September 1932
TWA orders its first DC-1.

September 3, 1932
Jimmy Doolittle wins the Thompson Trophy in a Gee Bee R-1.

November 4, 1932
Wichita's Beech Aircraft Company makes the first flight of the Model 17 Staggerwing biplane, which will become a successful executive aircraft.

1933
Hamilton Standard develops a controllable-pitch propeller.

1933
NACA helps to develop retractable landing gears, props, airfoils, and flaps.

1933
Austrian Ernst Sanger publishes *Rocket Flight Engineering*. It is the first academic book on rocketry.

February 6, 1933
A Fairey Long-Range Monoplane sets a long-distance record of 5,410 miles.

February 8, 1933
The Boeing 247 debuts. It is the first "modern" airliner.

March 1, 1933
A radio system for blind-landing aircraft is demonstrated at Newark, New Jersey.

March 30, 1933
The Sikorsky S-42 flying boat makes its first flight.

March 30, 1933
The first Boeing 247 is delivered to United Airlines.

Above: Designed by Isaac "Mac" Laddon, the Consolidated PBY was an immediate success and was subsequently built in greater numbers than any other flying boat in history. The PBY-5 was an amphibian, which greatly increased its utility. The Catalina was used as a torpedo bomber, patrol plane, air-sea rescue craft, and anti-submarine warfare plane.

Above: The North American B-25 made history when then-Lieutenant Colonel Jimmy Doolittle led a flight of 16 Mitchells in his famous April 18, 1942, raid on Tokyo. The B-25 was fast and rugged and served with distinction in every theater of war.

Lower right: When Consolidated Aircraft Corporation president Reuben Fleet was asked to build Boeing B-17 bombers under license, his engineers told him that they could create a better bomber of their own design. Many believe that they did with the B-24 Liberator, which was built in greater numbers than any other American warplane: More than 18,000 were built.

It was the start of a long game of cat and mouse between bombers and defenders. The defenders would use fake transmissions and powerful "jamming" signals to throw the enemy's bombers off track; the attackers would invent new bombing aids and switch radio frequencies to avoid jamming. Both sides modified light bombers (like the Bristol Blenheim) and twin-engine fighters (the Messerschmitt Bf 110) to carry airborne radar to hunt down bombers at night.

The air war soon spread to the ocean. Most navies entered World War II believing that the airplane's primary role was to act as a scout for their mighty battleships. Even the sinking of the *Bismarck* in May 1941 didn't kill this conviction. Japan, however, regarded the aircraft carrier as a strategic weapon—a fact that was clearly demonstrated in the December 7 attack on Pearl Harbor.

Six Japanese aircraft carriers had crossed the Pacific Ocean and launched 353 aircraft 200 miles from their targets. Surprise was total. The Japanese force lost only 29 airplanes. Eight U.S. battleships were sunk or damaged, and although all but three—the *Arizona*, *Oklahoma*, and *Utah*—were later repaired, none could play a part in a major action for some time. On December 10, Japanese land-based bombers sank the British battleship *Prince of Wales* and the battle-cruiser *Repulse* off the coast of Malaya.

Crucially, though, the attack on Pearl Harbor missed the carriers *Lexington*, *Saratoga*, and *Enterprise*, which were all away from port on different missions. In the Battle of the Coral Sea in May, opposing carriers clashed directly: The U.S. carrier *Lexington* was sunk, and the *Yorktown* was damaged; the Japanese *Shoho* was also sunk.

April 4, 1933
Rear Admiral William Adger Moffett and 72 others die in the crash of the *Akron* airship.

July 1, 1933
The Douglas DC-1 makes its first flight.

July 1–15, 1933
Italian General Italo Balbo leads the flight of 24 Savoia Marchetti S.55 flying boats from Italy to Chicago.

July 9–December 19, 1933
The Lindberghs make a 29,000-mile survey flight of Atlantic air routes.

July 15–22, 1933
▶ Wiley Post flies solo around the world in the *Winnie Mae*.

July 28, 1933
Clifford Anderson and Albert Forsythe become the first African Americans to fly a transcontinental round-trip.

August 1933
Frank Caldwell demonstrates the first practical variable-pitch propeller.

August 5–7, 1933
French Air Force pilots Maurice Rossi and Paul Codos establish the world's distance record of 5,657 miles, in a Bleriot Zapata.

August 17, 1933
Soviets launch the first hybrid (solid/liquid propellent) rocket.

August 30, 1933
Air France is established.

September 30, 1933
The Soviet balloon *USSR* flies to 60,695 feet.

December 20, 1933
The Martin M-130 *China Clipper* makes its first flight.

December 31, 1933
The Polikarpov I-16 debuts. It will become the first cantilever monoplane

The Japanese Naval Air Force was an elite organization, built up before the war with rigorous training from which all but the best were washed out. The Zero, maneuverable and heavily armed but lightly armored, was ideal for such pilots.

But in wartime, the JNAF could not afford to be as selective about its pilots and could not spend as much time on their training. Japan's ship-building capability was far smaller than that of the United States. The U.S. loss of the *Lexington* was a massive setback; for Japan, losing a carrier was a disaster.

On April 18, 1942, Lieutenant Colonel James Doolittle—who had performed the pioneering blind-landing test in 1929—led a small group of North American B-25 Mitchell bombers in a reprisal raid on Tokyo, launching the land-based Air Corps bombers from the carrier *Hornet*. The raid caused little damage but persuaded Japanese commanders to bring forward the date of a planned operation to establish a base on Midway Island in the Pacific.

The Japanese strike force heading for Midway was centered on four large carriers—*Kaga*, *Akagi*, *Hiryu*, and *Soryu*. The battle started early on June 4 with attacks on Midway. The U.S. commanders launched land-based torpedo bombers to intercept the Japanese forces; the bombers were annihilated, as was the next wave of torpedo-armed attackers from *Enterprise*, *Hornet*, and *Yorktown*. But as the Zero fighters attacked the low-flying bombers, U.S. Navy dive-bombers appeared above the Japanese fleet, leaving three of the carriers wrecked and sinking. The fourth, *Hiryu*, was sunk later in the day.

The U.S. aircraft industry, by mid-1942, was building much better combat aircraft. Production capacity had been expanding since 1940, as the United States built up its own forces and supplied aircraft to the United Kingdom under the Lend-Lease program—including the PBY Catalina that had found the *Bismarck*.

Lessons from air battles in Europe had been studied. More heavily armed and armored versions of the B-17 and the Consolidated B-24 Liberator were being developed.

Left: The Republic P-47 was the biggest and heaviest fighter in the world at the time of its appearance, and for many pilots, these were not desirable qualities. Yet the P-47 proved itself in combat, both as a medium-range escort fighter and as a superb close-air-support weapon.

Below: The Chance Vought F4U was a tremendous departure from previous Vought crafts, but designer Rex Beisel created one of the best fighters of World War II in the Corsair. It, like the Republic P-47, used the Pratt & Whitney R-2800 of 2,000 horsepower.

---

with retractable gear in squadron service in the world.

December 31, 1933
About 150 autogiros have been built worldwide.

January 10–11, 1934
Six Consolidated P2Y-1 flying boats fly from San Francisco to Hawaii.

January 18, 1934
Qantas Empire Airways is established.

February 9, 1934
Postmaster General Jim Farley cancels all airmail contracts and recommends the army fly airmail.

February 18–19, 1934
On the eve of cancellation of airmail contracts, Captain Eddie Rickenbacker and Jack Frye set a transport transcontinental record of 13 hours and 2 minutes in a DC-1.

February 19, 1934
The U.S. Army begins its responsibility for airmail. The results are disastrous.

May 11, 1934
The Douglas DC-2 makes its first flight.

June 12, 1934
Franklin Roosevelt signs the Air Mail Act of 1934.

July 1934
Britain announces a major expansion of the RAF.

July 1, 1934
The U.S. Aeronautics Branch becomes the Bureau of Air Commerce.

July 10–August 20, 1934
Lieutenant Colonel Hap Arnold leads a flight of Martin B-10s to Alaska.

July 11, 1934
The Federal Aviation Commission is appointed.

July 28, 1934
Major W. E. Kepner and Captains

A. W. Stevens and O. A. Anderson fly to 60,613 feet in a pressurized balloon capsule.

October 20, 1934
The MacRobertson England–Australia air race begins. The modern American transport planes, the DC-2 and Boeing 247, come out on top.

December 1934
The first rotary-wing aircraft—a Rota Autogiro—is accepted by the RAF.

U.S. fighter designers were producing large, powerful, and heavily armed fighters. Beside the Bf 109 or the Spitfire, the huge Republic P-47 Thunderbolt looked like a water buffalo that some joker had entered for the Kentucky Derby, but its Pratt & Whitney R-2800 radial engine—fitted with a huge General Electric turbosupercharger and a 12-foot propeller—could provide 2,000 horsepower at 27,500 feet altitude. At such heights, the "Jug" could walk away from its smaller rivals. An R-2800 and a big propeller also motivated the Chance Vought F4U Corsair, the best carrier-based fighter of the war years, and the Grumman F6F Hellcat.

The Lockheed P-38 Lightning had two turbocharged engines packed together with their cooling systems in twin slender booms that carried its tail surfaces. The P-38 was complicated and expensive to build, but it was very fast and had an excellent range. P-38s were used in April 1943 to intercept and shoot down the airplane carrying Admiral Isoruku Yamamoto, architect of the Pacific campaign.

These fighters carried six or eight .50-caliber machine guns and were fitted with armor around the cockpit. The fuel tanks were lined with a rubber material that expanded when wet, sealing any bullet holes in the tanks. These features were particularly important for rookie pilots; the armor and self-sealing tanks gave many new pilots a second chance after being hit.

In 1941 and early 1942, the fighter war in Europe and North Africa was different from the Battle of Britain. The German daylight bomber offensive had ended; Germany had delayed any plans to invade Britain and instead attacked Russia in June 1941. The German army advanced rapidly with tactical support from bombers and fighters, as it had done in France the previous year.

The Soviet Union's air power was in poor shape. Russian designers were not untalented; in fact, the Polikarpov I-16, used in the

Spanish Civil War, had been one of the world's first fighters with retractable landing gear, and it proved effective against the He 51. But Joseph Stalin's tyranny had taken a heavy toll. Designers who failed to deliver what they had promised—or who simply fell out of favor—were arrested and forced to continue their work in labor camps. Stalin's purge of his officer corps in the late 1930s had eliminated many good tactical minds.

After the invasion, political considerations were subordinated to survival. Complete aircraft factories, located in the path of the Ger-

Above: The Soviet Union sent designer Boris Lisunov to the Douglas factory in Santa Monica to study the DC-3, for which a manufacturing license was obtained. The result was the production of more than 2,900 Lisunov Li-2 duplicates of the great Douglas transport.

Left: The Polikarpov I-16 was an extremely advanced aircraft that allowed the Soviet Union to be the first to equip its all-metal monoplane fighters with retractable landing gear. It fought well in the Spanish Civil War but was obsolete by the time World War II came, and many were lost in combat.

Opposite: Lockheed's Hall Hibbard and Kelly Johnson knew that they needed 2,000 horsepower to get the performance required for their new fighter. With only 1,000-horsepower engines available, they created the radical twin-engine, twin-boom Lockheed Lightning. The central nacelle was the perfect spot for a heavy armament package.

December 31, 1934
Helen Richey becomes the first female airline pilot in the United States.

January 22, 1935
A Federal Aviation Commission report on U.S. aviation recommends strengthening civil and military aeronautics.

February 12, 1935
The USS *Macon*, a Navy airship, crashes, ending U.S. interest in rigid lighter-than-air crafts.

March 9, 1935
Hermann Goering discloses the existence of the Luftwaffe.

March 28, 1935
◀ The Consolidated PBY prototype debuts.

May 18, 1935
The world's largest aircraft, the *Maxim Gorki*, crashes near Moscow.

May 28, 1935
The Messerschmitt Bf 109 prototype makes its first flight.

July 11, 1935
Laura Ingalls becomes the first woman to fly nonstop from the east to west coast of the United States.

July 23, 1935
The British receive a key report on radar.

Opposite: The Boeing B-17 prototype, the Model 299, first flew on July 28, 1935. Hailed by the Seattle press as a "Flying Fortress," the B-17 became one of the most important Allied bombers of World War II. It was continuously modified, and the B-17G shown here had a 13-gun armament.

Inset: The German Luftwaffe learned that the weak point of early Boeing B-17s could be found in a head-on frontal attack. Boeing countered this with the installation of the twin-gun "chin" turret shown here.

man advance, were dismantled, and their machinery was shipped east to new sites behind the Ural Mountains, safe from both invasion and bombing. In the winter of 1941, new fighters were being built in the open air there in sub-freezing temperatures.

A new generation of designers came to the fore, including Alexander Yakovlev and Artem Mikoyan. Russian fighters such as the Yak-3 and MiG-3 did not match the absolute performance of airplanes like the Bf 109 or the new German Focke-Wulf Fw190, but they were rugged and performed well at low altitudes, where most of the combat over the eastern front took place. They were also easy to build. The Yak-3 had a wooden wing and a steel-tube fuselage structure, placing fewer demands on Soviet aluminum production.

On the eastern front and in north Africa, the airplane took on a new role—that of an anti-tank weapon. Before the war, Russian designer Sergei Ilyushin had designed a robust, heavyweight ground attack airplane with a 20-millimeter high-velocity cannon in its wings and up to half an inch of armor around its cockpit. Designated Il-2, it became known as the Shturmovik, or "attacker." Stalin would say that it was necessary to the Red Army "like air, like bread." Il-2s were built and shot down in tens of thousands. More than 44,000 of the Il-2 and its descendants were built; 14,000 of them were lost in 1943 and '44 alone.

Perhaps in imitation of the Il-2, the Luftwaffe ordered a new version of the Junkers Ju 87 dive-bomber with a pair of 37-millimeter guns under the wings. The RAF produced a similar version of the Hawker Hurricane fighter and used it extensively in northern Africa. Later, both the RAF and the U.S. Army Air Corps (now called the U.S. Army Air Force) abandoned the heavy-gun fighter in favor of unguided rockets. Increasingly, the fighter was seen not as a pure interceptor for air defense but as a multipurpose weapon.

In 1942, the USAAF and Royal Air Force started preparing for the largest, most costly, and most controversial air campaign of the war: the bombing of Germany. Commanders such as Sir Arthur Harris, the leader of RAF Bomber Command, and his U.S. counterparts like General Carl Spaatz, commander of the USAAF in Europe, believed that a massive bombing campaign against Germany could end the war with fewer casualties than a land invasion.

The most famous USAAF bomber of World War II is the Boeing B-17, the star of movies such as *Memphis Belle* and *Twelve O'Clock High*. The first B-17s to be used in Europe were used by the RAF, as Fortress Is, and were flown on a few high-altitude bombing missions. The USAAF took the more heavily armed B-17E into action in Europe in August 1942. (They were not the first U.S. heavy bombers to attack Europe, though; in June, oil refineries at Ploesti in Yugoslavia had been hit by Consolidated B-24 Liberators. Actually, more Liberators

THE MOSQUITO BUZZES INTO ACTION

One of the unique airplanes of World War II was the **de Havilland Mosquito.** In the early 1930s, as most of the aircraft industry switched to metal construction, the de Havilland company developed a new way of building in wood. The wing and body skins were a sandwich comprised of two thin layers of strong spruce plywood glued to a thick core of light balsa wood.

The structure could be assembled quickly around molds, using newly rediscovered, very strong casein glues. In 1940, de Havilland used this technique to build a light bomber with two Merlin engines. The Mosquito was used as a bomber, a fighter-bomber with cannon and rockets, a night-fighter with radar, and a long-range reconnaissance airplane. As a bomber, it could carry a load almost as heavy as the far bigger B-17.

Another legacy of the Mosquito arose from the fact that the casein glues broke down in hot climates. Searching for a replacement, chemists invented the first practical epoxy-resin glues. This family of adhesives is the basis for most modern composite materials, from fiberglass to carbon fiber.

July 28, 1935
The Boeing Model 299 bomber, the prototype of the B-17, makes its first flight.

August 15, 1935
Wiley Post and Will Rogers are killed in a crash in Alaska.

September 13, 1935
Howard Hughes sets a landplane speed record of 352 miles per hour in a Hughes Racer.

November 6, 1935
◄ The Hawker Hurricane makes its first flight.

November 11, 1935
Albert Stevens and Orvil Anderson reach 72,395 feet and set an altitude record in their balloon, *Explorer II.*

November 22, 1935
Pan Am starts the first transpacific mail service. It goes from San Francisco to Manila in a Martin *China Clipper.*

December 17, 1935
The Douglas DC-3 makes it first flight.

December 22, 1935
Louis Breguet and Rene Dorand fly their "gyroplane."

January 3, 1936
The Air Transport Association is formed.

March 5, 1936
A Supermarine Spitfire prototype flies.

March 17, 1936
A passenger is fined for smoking in the restroom of an Imperial Airways plane.

March 26, 1936
A Pitcairn AC-35 Roadable autogiro is flown.

April 12, 1936
The Bristol Type 142 makes its first flight. It is designed as an executive aircraft for Lord Rothermere and called

Britain First; it will become the prototype for the Bristol Blenheim bomber.

June 7, 1936
Major Ira Eaker flies blind from New York to Los Angeles.

June 15, 1936
The Vickers Wellington makes its first flight.

June 21, 1936
Pan Am orders six Boeing 314 Clipper flying boats.

June 26, 1936
Henrich Focke develops the Focke-Achgelis Fa 61 helicopter. It is the first helicopter capable of sustained, repeatable flights.

July 6, 1936
The federal government takes over air traffic control.

July 20, 1936
General Francisco Franco uses German Ju 52s to ferry his Moorish

troops from Spanish north Africa to Spain to begin the Spanish Civil War.

September 28, 1936
The Bristol 138A research aircraft establishes an altitude record at 49,444 feet.

October 21, 1936
Pan Am's Martin 130 flying boat leaves San Francisco for the first commercial transpacific flight.

December 21, 1936
The Junkers Ju 88, the most versatile of German bombers, makes its first flight.

March 1937
The Heinkel He 112 is flown with a 650-pound-thrust rocket engine. Erich Warstiz is the pilot.

April 1937
Wernher von Braun and his group move to Peenemunde, Germany, for research on rocket weapons.

THE MAKING OF A CLASSIC

The **North American P-51 Mustang,** probably the best all-round fighter of the war, was an airplane of Anglo-United States extraction, the result of an unplanned convergence of three separate developments in 1940. In March, the British Air Ministry asked Rolls-Royce to design a high-altitude engine: Rolls-Royce responded with the Merlin 60, an engine with a two-stage supercharger. In September, Britain reached an agreement with Packard under which the U.S. automaker would build large numbers of Merlins.

In October, North American Aviation, a young West Coast company formed by a former Douglas executive, flew the first prototype of the NA-73X. North American had designed and flown the NA-73X prototype after the British asked them to build the indifferent Curtiss P-40. It entered production as the P-51A—Mustang I to the British, who liked the reliable airframe but hated its Allison engine. In 1942, the P-51 airframe was mated to the Packard-built Merlin 60, creating the classic P-51B.

Opposite: Painted in the colors of the famous ace, Colonel Clarence "Bud" Anderson, the North American P-51 "Old Crow" struts its stuff. Anderson, besides being an ace and a gentleman, also wrote one of the best (if not *the* best), personal memoirs of World War II in *To Fly and Fight.*

than B-17s were built—18,000 versus 12,000. The Liberators always outnumbered the B-17s in Europe, carried a heavier bombload, and flew farther and faster than the Boeing. It is one of the mysteries of history that the B-24 is so much less well-known than the B-17, although it was certainly less loved by its crews.)

To support the bombing campaign, the United States massively expanded its aircraft industry. Martin, Lockheed, and Douglas were enlisted to build the Fortress and Liberator. (Disney artists painted a fake housing tract on the roof of Lockheed's factories in Burbank to disguise them in the event of air attacks.) Finally, the government constructed enormous airplane factories in places such as Omaha, Wichita, Tulsa, and Fort Worth, tapping an untouched labor pool. At its peak, the system produced a Liberator every 55 minutes.

The RAF, meanwhile, was building up its own heavy bomber force. Before the war, the Avro company had started development of the Manchester, a craft powered by two Rolls-Royce Vulture engines. The engine was horribly unreliable. With a massive supply of Merlin engines available from Packard, the Air Ministry approved a modified aircraft with four Merlins. The Lancaster (as it was called) became Britain's most successful bomber.

The RAF and USAAF shared a belief in decisive bombing but disagreed radically on how it should be done. U.S. commanders planned to attack in daylight, using the Norden bombsight to destroy the factories that were deemed vital to the German war effort. Flying in tight formation and armed with multiple machine guns, the USAAF believed the bombers would be able to beat off any fighter attack.

The RAF was convinced bombers could only survive at night. Lower accuracy was inevitable, but RAF Bomber Command leader Arthur Harris targeted not the factories, but the housing, morale, and lives of the workforce. With fewer, smaller guns and less ammunition, the Lancaster could carry 12,000 pounds of bombs—more than either U.S. type.

In early 1943, President Franklin Roosevelt and Prime Minister Winston Churchill merged the approaches into a round-the-clock bombing campaign. Both forces built up their strength during the first half of the year and were launching raids of hundreds of aircraft against German targets by the summer.

But the German defenses were resolute, well equipped, and innovative. Bomber losses were heavy. Raiding the ball-bearing factories at Schweinfurt in Bavaria on August 17, deep within Germany, the U.S. 8th Air Force had 36 airplanes shot down and 27 more damaged beyond repair. On an October return mission, dubbed "Black Thursday," 60 out of 291 bombers were

April 9, 1937
A Mitsubishi type 97 Kamikaze flies from Japan to England.

April 12, 1937
The Whittle jet engine passes its bench test.

April 22, 1937
Captain Eddie Rickenbacker buys Eastern Airlines for $3.5 million.

May 6, 1937
▶ The *Hindenburg* crashes upon landing in Lakehurst, New Jersey.

June 18, 1937
A Tupolev ANT-25 makes a nonstop flight from Moscow to Pearson Field in Washington state, close to Portland.

July 2, 1937
Amelia Earhart disappears in her round-the-world flight attempt.

July 4, 1937
Hanna Reitsch makes the first controlled flight of a Focke-Achgelis Fa61 helicopter.

July 12–14, 1937
Soviet pilots in an ANT-25 establish a new distance record of 6,306 miles, flying from Moscow to Columbia.

July 30, 1937
George Herrick demonstrates the "Convertiplane."

August 5, 1937
The Lockheed XC-35, the first pressurized-cabin airplane, debuts.

August 23, 1937
The first wholly automatic landing is made at Wright Field in Ohio.

December 1937
The Hawker Hurricane enters service with the RAF.

1938
The U.S. Army buys nine Kellet Autogiros to be used for liaison work.

April 28, 1938
NACA performs full-size tests of the Brewster F2A fighter in the Langley Tunnel. It results in a 31-mile-per-hour speed increase after alterations are made to the design.

May 31, 1938
The Boeing 314 makes its first flight.

June 1938
The Supermarine Spitfire enters service with the RAF.

June 23, 1938
The U.S. Civil Air Authority is created by the Civil Aeronautics Act.

July 10–14, 1938
Howard Hughes and his crew set a round-the-world speed record in a

Lockheed 14, covering 14,791 miles in 3 days and 19 hours.

July 18, 1938
▶ Douglas "Wrong-Way" Corrigan files a flight plan for California from Brooklyn but "accidentally" flies to Ireland instead.

July 30, 1938
The Pan American *Hawaiian Clipper* disappears.

August 22, 1938
The Civil Aeronautics Authority becomes effective.

August 24, 1938
The Heinkel He 178 makes its first test flight with a jet engine.

October 19, 1938
The Curtiss XP-40 prototype makes its first flight.

November 5, 1938
Two Vickers Wellesley bombers set a

Right: The first ballistic missile weapon to be used in combat, the V-2 was impossible to intercept. However, it was not accurate, and it proved to be extremely expensive (in terms of natural resources) to produce. The Germans would have been better off if they had concentrated on the V-1 flying bomb.

Below: The Boeing B-29 was the most important bomber of World War II, and the *Enola Gay* was the most important B-29. By dropping the atomic bomb on Hiroshima (and with the attack on Nagasaki three days later), the Japanese were forced to surrender.

shot down. Missions into Germany were abandoned until the long-range Merlin-powered Mustangs were available in large numbers.

In the RAF, too, the odds of a crew surviving a tour of 25 operational missions were not good. The Luftwaffe combined radar-equipped night fighters with anti-aircraft guns. Early-warning radars detected the incoming bomber forces, and more accurate tracking radars were used to vector night fighters into position. The RAF installed radars on its bombers to detect fighters; the Luftwaffe fitted night fighters with a homing device tuned to the radar. Devices and tactics such as these helped the German fighters to shoot down 94 out of 795 bombers attacking Nuremberg in March 1944.

A Deadly New Era of Military Aviation

After the Nuremberg raids, both bomber forces began preparing the ground for the invasion of Europe, planned for the long days of summer. They were also heavily engaged in defending against Germany's advanced weaponry that emerged in 1943–44.

Among the first such weapons were the Fritz-X and Hs293, a pair of radio-guided anti-ship gliding missiles. The first Fritz-X missiles to be used in action, in September 1943, sank the Italian battleship *Roma* off Salerno in the Mediterranean. In June 1944, just after the invasion started, the Luftwaffe launched the first V-1 "flying bomb," or cruise missile, at the United Kingdom.

The V-1 was a simple, cheap weapon, powered by a pulse-jet engine that gave it a characteristic motorbike-like noise. More than 9,500 of the weapons were launched against the United Kingdom, and attacks ceased only when the launch sites were overrun by Allied ground troops.

More dangerous, much more sophisticated, and far more expensive was the A-4 missile, or V-2. In a stupendous leap of tech-

new long-range record, flying 7,162 miles from Ismailia, Egypt, to Darwin, Australia.

December 10, 1938
James Wyld develops a regeneratively cooled liquid rocket motor that becomes the basis for JATO systems.

December 31, 1938
The Boeing 307 Stratoliner, the first pressurized commercial airplane, makes its first flight.

1939
NACA continues development of laminar flow airfoil.

January 27, 1939
The Lockheed Lightning makes its first flight.

February 1939
NACA begins re-evaluating jet propulsion for aircraft.

April 1939
◀ The prototype for the Mitsubishi A6M Type 0 "Zero" fighter debuts.

April 20, 1939
The first free-flight tunnel is placed into operation at Langley Field.

April 26, 1939
Fritz Wendel, in a Messerschmitt Me209V1, sets the world's air speed record of 469.22 miles per hour.

Luftwaffe had a few Messerschmitt Me 262 fighters in service, along with a handful of other types of jets such as the Arado Ar234 bomber and reconnaissance aircraft. Britain's Gloster Meteor jet had mainly been used to intercept V-1s.

As the war in Europe entered its last winter, scientists in a secret laboratory in Los Alamos, New Mexico, were working on a weapon that would truly change the course of history: the atomic bomb. The USAAF had decided in 1943 what airplane would carry it. Boeing had proposed the Model 345 to the USAAF in May 1940. Weighing half again as much as the huge Model 314 flying boat, it would have a pressurized cabin and four 2,200-horsepower engines and would cruise at 30,000 feet. It would carry 20,000 pounds of bombs, and its defensive guns would be aimed by computerized sights.

The first XB-29 flew from Seattle in September 1942. In February 1943, the second prototype crashed, killing all aboard. During 1943, the USAAF and Boeing investigated the accident and worked to fix the craft's problems. As aircraft rolled off the production lines, they were parked in long lines until modification crews could incorporate the changes resulting from the development program. As if these challenges were not enough, the USAAF planned to launch its first operational missions against Japan from China, which could only be supplied from the air.

The first missions were flown in the summer of 1944; in November, the B-29 force moved in its entirety to air bases in the newly recaptured Mariana Islands, which could be resupplied more easily. By the following summer, more than 800 of the bombers could be assembled for raids on Japan. The country had suffered enormous casualties from low-altitude firebomb raids even before August 6, 1945. On that day, a B-29 named *Enola Gay* dropped the first nuclear bomb on Hiroshima; three days later, *Bock's Car* attacked Nagasaki. The war was over, but what would replace it was unlike any peace that the world had ever known.

Left: Colonel Paul Tibbets (right) is seen in conversation in front of the aircraft he named after his mother, Enola Gay Tibbets. The **Enola Gay** dropped the first atomic weapon ever used in warfare on Hiroshima, Japan.

nology, a team of German Army engineers led by Wernher von Braun succeeded in developing a 225-mile-range ballistic rocket with a 1,650-pound warhead. It was powered by a liquid-fueled rocket engine, and its silence offered no warning of an attack; it hit the target at more than three times the speed of sound. The only defense against an A-4 was to destroy its launching sites. Some 2,700 A-4s were fired in 1944 and '45, mostly against London or Antwerp.

Entering service toward the end of the war, the V-1 and V-2 were too late to affect the outcome of the conflict or its timing. The same was true of the first jet combat aircraft. By the end of the war, the

---

May 9, 1939
Dale White and Chauncey Spencer begin a program to include African Americans in air-training programs.

May 27, 1939
The Petlyakov Pe-2 bomber debuts. Some 11,247 are made, but it is largely unknown in the United States.

June 20, 1939
The Heinkel He 176, the first aircraft to use a liquid-propellant rocket, makes its first flight.

June 28, 1939
Pan Am inaugurates its first transatlantic airplane passenger service.

August 27, 1939
The Heinkel He 178, the world's first jet aircraft, debuts.

September 1939
▶ Igor Sikorsky flies the first successful helicopter.

September 1, 1939
Germany invades Poland; World War II begins.

September 3, 1939
Britain declares war on Germany. Bristol Blenheim carries out the first operational sortie of the war.

September 4, 1939
RAF Wellington bombers attack German warships in the Elbe estuary. Five are shot down.

December 18, 1939
Directed by radar, Luftwaffe fighters shoot down 12 out of 24 RAF bombers attacking Wilhelmshaven, Germany.

December 29, 1939
The Consolidated B-24 Liberator, the most widely produced U.S. heavy bomber, makes its first flight.

CHAPTER FOUR

Aviation Jets Into the Future

THE COLD WAR LEADS AVIATION TECHNOLOGY TO NEW HEIGHTS AS THE COMMUNIST BLOC AND THE WEST STRIVE FOR SUPERIORITY IN THE SKIES.

The cockpit of a Spitfire PR.XI was quite cramped, but it was a relatively safe haven in World War II. Nothing could fly higher than the Spitfire's reconnaissance version, so imagine the shock when a shadow fell across the cockpit. The bigger surprise was the source of the shadow: an obsolescent Wellington bomber. The view offered an even stranger sight: Its propellers were stopped and feathered. Such sightings became increasingly common as the war continued. In great secrecy—using specially built airplanes and modified test beds like the Wellington—engineers were developing a new machine that would change history. The age of the jet was dawning.

Right: When the first Boeing YB-52 took off on April 14, 1952, no one at Boeing or anyone else would have believed that it would still be in first-line service 50 years later. Fitted with precision guided munitions, it became the weapon of choice in the conflict in Afghanistan.

By the end of World War II, aviation had changed beyond recognition. The industry had built large airplanes in the thousands. Hundreds of aircraft had crossed the world's oceans. Long-distance air travel had become routine. Troops and supplies regularly arrived by air. New airfields had been built worldwide, with mile-long concrete runways.

But the end of the war saw the advent of an innovation that was so important it divides the history of aviation into two distinct eras: the invention of the jet engine.

The jet is a gas-turbine engine. Air is drawn into a spinning compressor, and the compressed air is then mixed with fuel and burned. The expanding gases pass through a turbine. Part of the energy from the turbine is used to turn the compressor, and the rest is available for power. As airplane speeds approached

One of the great engineers at Lockheed was Nathan Price, who not only designed the XJ-37 jet engine in 1938, but also an extremely advanced fighter to go with it. Unfortunately for Price and Lockheed, the U.S. Air Force declined to pursue the project.

THE JET LEAVES ITS INVENTOR BEHIND

Briton **Frank Whittle** produced his first designs for jet engines in the early 1930s, receiving his first patent at the age of 25. With no official encouragement, Whittle obtained private finance for a company called Power Jets and ran his first engine in March 1937. The engine raced out of control, and the only speed records, Whittle would later recall, were set by the fleeing observers.

Frank Whittle

Whittle was awarded a contract for a flight-worthy engine in 1939. As the jet engine's potential military importance became apparent, the Air Ministry selected the Rover car company to build the engines in quantity. When this arrangement proved unworkable, the government transferred the contract to Rolls-Royce. Power Jets was prevented from building any production engines at all. Whittle spent most of the rest of his life as a consultant in the United States.

400 miles per hour, a few people realized that the gas turbine could eliminate the problem of declining propeller efficiency at high speeds. Instead of using the turbine to drive a propeller, the exhaust could be allowed to accelerate out of the back of the airplane, driving it by reaction.

An RAF officer, Frank Whittle, obtained a patent in 1932 for a simple jet engine. The Air Ministry thought Whittle's assumptions were overly optimistic and did not think them worth keeping secret. In the following year, Hans von Ohain, at the University of Gottingen in Germany, also designed a jet. Whittle formed a company called Power Jets to develop his engine; von Ohain joined forces with aircraft manufacturer Ernst Heinkel in

December 30, 1939
The Ilyushin Il-2 prototype flies. It will be the Soviet's most important ground-assault plane.

March 10, 1940
Pan Am takes delivery of the first pressurized Boeing 307 Stratoliner.

March 26, 1940
U.S. commercial airlines complete a full year without a fatal accident or serious injury.

May 10, 1940
The Luftwaffe flies more than 1,000 sorties in support of the invasion of France.

May 14, 1940
The RAF loses 39 out of 71 Fairey Battles and Bristol Blenheims in raids on bridges near Sedan, France.

May 29, 1940
▶ The Vought XF4U makes its first flight.

June 30, 1940
The CAA reorganizes into the Civil Aeronautics Board.

July 8, 1940
The Boeing Stratoliner enters service with Pan Am.

July 10, 1940
The Battle of Britain begins with attacks on shipping, ports, and radar stations.

August 1940
The DFS 194, the prototype of the Me 163 rocket fighter, debuts.

August–September, 1940
The Battle of Britain rages.

August 13, 1940
The Luftwaffe launches attacks on RAF airfields.

August 28, 1940
The Italian Caproni-Campini N.1, a

1936. Both teams succeeded in running engines in 1937. The Heinkel group flew the world's first jet aircraft, the purely experimental He 178, in August 1939—less than a week before Germany's invasion of Poland.

Neither Britain nor Germany launched a massive effort to develop jet engines. Britain had more urgent needs, and Germany's leaders were confident that the war would be over before the jet engine would be operational. Whittle, von Ohain, and two other German teams—BMW and Junkers—continued to work on the problems of efficiency, stability, and control. In March 1941, Heinkel flew the He 280, a prototype jet fighter; the Gloster E.28/39, the first British jet, flew in May.

Only one jet aircraft was built in large numbers in World War II. The compact, rugged Messerschmitt Me 262 had a heavy cannon armament grouped in the nose. The first one was completed in April 1941 but made its inaugural flight with a piston engine because the jets were not ready. The craft's first attempted jet flight (with two BMW engines) ended with a double flame-out.

A reliable Junkers engine was available in July 1942, but the landing gear had to be redesigned, and it was November 1943 before a modified design flew. Finally, some 1,400 Me 262s were built—too late to affect the outcome of the war. Britain produced a relatively small number of twin-jet Gloster Meteor fighters, but none of them is known to have engaged in combat against any other airplanes, although they did shoot down some V-1 missiles.

The British and U.S. industries were testing more powerful jet engines. The jet could be scaled up easily to produce more than 4,000 pounds of thrust; piston engines of equivalent power were heavy and complex. Rolls-Royce had been enlisted to build the Whittle engines and was working on the 3,000-pound-thrust Nene. The de Havilland company had started the design of a

The Messerschmitt Me 262 was the world's first operational jet fighter. Powered by Junkers Jumo 004 engines, it was at least 120 miles per hour faster than the North American P-51 Mustang. Fortunately for the Allies, it entered the war too late to have significant impact.

The first product of what became known as Lockheed's "Skunk Works," the XP-80 was the first operational jet fighter used by the United States. It did yeoman work during the Korean War and led to other designs, including the T-33 trainer and the F-94 night-fighter series.

piston-engine-powered jet aircraft, makes its first flight.

September 7, 1940
Luftwaffe switches strategy and attacks London.

September 15, 1940
The last major attack of the Battle of Britain occurs.

October 7, 1940
The RAF forms the first electronic warfare unit.

October 26, 1940
The North American P-51 Mustang makes its first flight.

November 14–15, 1940
The Luftwaffe makes its first major use of radio navigation aids in a raid on Coventry.

November 15, 1940
The de Havilland Mosquito flies for the first time.

January 9, 1941
▶ The Avro Lancaster, the most successful British heavy bomber, makes its first flight.

February 10, 1941
The RAF makes its first operational paratroop drop in Italy.

February 25, 1941
The RAF starts night bombing raids on Germany.

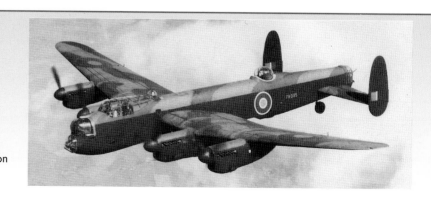

The Cold War Heats Up Aviation Development

The end of World War II ushered in an era of unparalleled progress in aviation—and in the related technologies of missiles and space vehicles. In 1945, a few experimental airplanes had exceeded 600 miles per hour. Fifteen years later, passenger airplanes would reach that speed routinely, military aircraft would be flying at 1,500 miles per hour, and 2,000-mile-per-hour airplanes were being designed.

The force behind this progress was, of course, the Cold War. Because the superpowers threatened each other at arm's length, the long-range weapons of aerospace took priority over ships and tanks. The rivalry between the West and the Soviet Union was completely unlike a shooting war: An investment in technology was not held back by the need to replace destroyed airplanes or produce ammunition.

After 1945, the Western and Russian air forces shrank in size, as they had after World War I. This time, though, they also began to modernize, replacing piston-engine airplanes with jets.

At first, strategic bombers were an exception to the scaling back. In 1945, nobody knew how to make a jet bomber that could reach the Soviet Union from the United States or vice versa. In 1941, the USAAF had considered the possibility that the United States might end up at war with a power an ocean away. The service issued a requirement for a bomber with a range of 10,000 miles—more than the world's airplane distance record of the time—carrying a 10,000-pound bomb load (military leaders later cut the range to 4,000 miles with a 10,000-pound bomb load).

Two extraordinary airplanes designed to meet that requirement were flown in 1946. Convair's B-36 was a monster with six 28-cylinder, 70-liter engines buried in the 230-foot wing. The airplane packed no fewer than sixteen 20-millimeter cannons for self-defense. The rival Northrop XB-35 had no body or tail: The

Above: The Convair B-36 came about because U.S. planners feared that England might be invaded and that the United States would have to bomb Europe from American bases. Work was delayed during the war, and the first B-36 did not fly until August 8, 1946.

Opposite top: The Tupolev Tu-95 Bear has been one of the most successful, longest-lived bomber types in history. This photo was taken in 1983 over the Mediterranean Sea. The basic design has been produced in many variants, including tanker and transport.

Opposite bottom: Jack Northrop was always a proponent of the flying wing. The XB-35 carried out his designs to perfection, but arrived just when the jet engine was becoming dominant. Unfortunately, the jet version of the XB-35, the YB-49, proved to be unsuitable as a bomber. It lacked stability.

2,700-pound-thrust engine, the Goblin, in 1941. Lockheed designed the XP-80, the first high-performance U.S. jet, specifically for use with the Goblin.

Drawing on its experience with superchargers and steam turbines, General Electric formed two jet-engine teams. Both were to work on developing 4,000-pound-thrust engines. One was based on the design favored by Whittle and de Havilland, with a wide centrifugal compressor; the other was an axial jet with multiple rows of blades. The former engine, the I-40, powered the Lockheed P-80A, a scaled-up version of the XP-80, on its inaugural flight in June 1944.

The impact of the jet revolution can be gauged by one fact: Not a single large airplane piston engine designed after 1940 actually went into production. Where the piston engine was not replaced by the pure jet, it was ousted by the turboprop, a gas turbine geared to a propeller.

engines, bombs, fuel, and cockpit were all housed inside the wing. The Air Force built more than 350 B-36s, most of them with two jet booster engines under each wing; the XB-35 remained a prototype, as did a jet-powered development, the YB-49.

The Soviet Union faced a challenge in developing a strategic bomber, having never produced a homegrown aircraft that equaled the performance of the B-24 or the British Lancaster. However, the Soviets did possess three intact Boeing B-29s that had made emergency landings in the city of Vladivostok. The Tupolev design bureau dismantled the airplanes and copied them piece by piece. More than 1,000 of the resulting Tu-4s were built.

The first Tu-4 flew in the summer of 1946, but it was not until three of the aircraft flew over Moscow in August 1947 that the type's existence was confirmed. Thus began a battle of one-upmanship that would last decades.

The Soviet side was cloaked in secrecy. In its closed society, travel by foreigners was tightly restricted, and entire cities were off-limits to most Soviet citizens as well as foreigners. The Soviet leaders used this secrecy to exaggerate their military strength; the West responded with real increases in its forces. With such a formula, the arms race could only accelerate.

New technology frequently made weapons obsolete in a few years. In 1944–45, the United States and Britain ordered new jet fighters and bombers designed for speeds around 500 miles per hour. A typical example was the North American B-45 Tornado bomber, powered by four of the new GE axial-flow J35 jet engines and fitted with a thin, unswept wing. Another was the Republic F-84 Thunderjet, with a single J35, flown in 1946.

A New Design Idea Takes Wing

As these airplanes were being designed, Allied engineers and intelligence specialists swarmed across Germany. What they

February 14, 1942
The Douglas DC-4 (C-54) makes its first flight.

March 16, 1942
Charles Morris gets the first commercial helicopter pilot's license from the CAA.

March 19, 1942
GALCIT Rocket Research Project becomes the Aerojet Corporation.

April 18, 1942
▶ Lieutenant Colonel Jimmy Doolittle leads the first U.S. raid on Tokyo.

May 7–8, 1942
The Battle of Coral Sea: The first sea battle in history in which no ship saw another. The combat (between Japanese and U.S. and Australian forces) was done entirely by the air forces. The battle sets the stage for the rest of the war.

May 26, 1942
The Northrop XP-61 Black Widow makes its first flight.

May 30–31, 1942
The first RAF "thousand-bomber" raid occurs in Cologne.

June 4, 1942
U.S. Navy dive bombers sink four Japanese carriers at Midway.

July 1, 1942
The first battle of El Alamein takes place. RAF aircraft fly almost 5,500 close-support sorties in seven days.

July 18, 1942
The Me 262 jet fighter debuts.

August 17, 1942
USAAF bombers make the first raid on Europe, attacking railway yards in Rouen, France.

radically revised their designs to incorporate swept wings. The North American XP-86 Sabre first flew in October 1947; the B-47 flew in December.

Russian designers were not far behind. In 1946, Britain's Labour government had agreed to sell twenty 4,000-pound-thrust Rolls-Royce Nene jets to the Soviet Union. In late 1947, the Klimov VK-1, a reverse-engineered Nene, powered the first example of Mikoyan's swept-wing MiG-15 on its first flight.

In November 1950, the MiG-15 appeared over Korea, clearly outclassing the Lockheed F-80s and the British-built, Australian-flown Meteors and threatening the slower B-29s and other World War II-era bombers. Sabres were rushed into the theater.

Swept-wing, 600-mile-per-hour fighters became standard among the world's air forces in the 1950s. Outside the United States and Russia, the first such airplane to enter service was Sweden's Saab J29, nicknamed the Barrel because of its rotund body. The UK's Hawker Hunter took longer to develop, but it was a tough and versatile fighter that enjoyed a long career, and France's Dassault also was the start of a successful line of jet fighters.

The most widely built version of the Sabre was different from those used in Korea, but it set an important pattern for the future. The F-86D had a more powerful engine with an afterburner—an extra fuel burner in the jetpipe that boosted the thrust at the expense of high fuel consumption. It had a radar and an onboard computer. What it did not have was a gun. Instead, it was armed with 24 unguided rockets. More than 2,000 F-86Ds were built and were issued to Air Defense Command (ADC) squadrons throughout the United States.

The USAF was formed in 1947, winning its independence from the Army, and now included four major operational commands: ADC; Tactical Air Command, armed with fighter-bombers; Air

The North American B-45 was the USAF's first operational jet bomber. It was also used as a reconnaissance plane, sometimes flying covert missions over the Soviet Union.

found amazed them. There was a Messerschmitt prototype, the P.1101, with a wing that was swept 40 degrees backward. Junkers chief designer Brunolf Baade was designing a bomber with a sharply swept wing and jet engines in slim pods that were hung from the wings on slender pylons. Alexander Lippisch, who had been responsible for the Me 163 Komet rocket-powered fighter, was preparing to test a glider with no horizontal tail and a triangular wing.

When this intelligence reached the United States, North American Aviation was developing a straight-wing fighter for the USAF, the XP-86, and Boeing was working on its first jet bomber. Boeing aerodynamicist George Schairer, who was in Germany with one of the research teams, sent a telegram advising the company to stop work on the original design. Boeing and North American

---

September 21, 1942
The Boeing XB-29 makes its first flight.

October 1, 1942
The Bell XP-59A, the first U.S. jet, makes its inaugural flight.

October 3, 1942
The Germans launch a V-2 rocket.

December 1942
Arthur Young's Bell Model 30 experimental helicopter design is rolled out.

1943
The German Doblhoff becomes the first helicopter powered by rotor-blade tip-jets.

January 1, 1943
The Casablanca Directive authorizes the joint U.S.-British bomber offensive.

January 9, 1943
The Lockheed Model 49 Constellation makes its first flight.

January 11, 1943
Franklin Roosevelt becomes the first U.S. President to fly while in office.

March 5, 1943
The Gloster Meteor, the first operatonal British fighter, makes its inaugural flight.

April 11, 1943
Frank Piasecki flies the single-main-rotor PV-2 helicopter.

May 16–17, 1943
RAF Lancasters breach the Mohne and Eder dams in Germany with specially designed mines.

July 24–25, 1943
The RAF raid on Hamburg sees the first use of "chaff," fine pieces of metal foil dropped by aircraft to confuse enemy radar.

August 1, 1943
Women in combat: Soviet fighter pilot Lieutenant Lidiya "Lilya" Litvak (known as "The White Rose of Stalingrad") is killed in action after 12 victories.

August 17, 1943
The first USAAF raid on Schweinfurt, Germany, occurs. Ten percent of the airplanes are lost.

The North American F-86 Sabre gained immortal fame in the famous dogfights with the MiG-15 during the Korean War. The MiG was slightly faster and had a greater altitude capability, but the F-86 was a far better gun platform and won most of the dogfights in "MiG Alley."

Transport Command; and Strategic Air Command (SAC), responsible for nuclear-armed bombers.

In 1948–49, the Soviet blockade of Berlin showed that the Soviet Union had no intention of withdrawing from its Eastern European conquests of the mid '40s. The city survived through the efforts of the USAF, RAF, and civilian pilots, who poured supplies into Berlin through appalling weather. In the shadow of an unknown Soviet nuclear threat, and led by the hard-driving General Curtis LeMay, SAC grew to dominate the U.S. military budget.

LeMay's first aim was to replace the B-29 and the improved B-50 with B-47s. By 1957, more than 2,000 B-47s had been built; the last was retired in 1967. The craft never dropped a bomb in anger, following the motto of LeMay's SAC, "Peace Is Our Profession." Actor Jimmy Stewart, a real-life bomber pilot in World War II, starred in the movie *Strategic Air Command*, which took the audience from the days of the B-36 to the advent of the jet.

The B-47's swept wings were not the only way to build a jet bomber, although that solution would come to dominate the world of aviation. Britain's Avro Vulcan was a delta-shape aircraft, almost a flying wing with only a small cockpit section ahead of its leading edge. The Vulcan's outstanding features were its service ceiling—it could fly at 60,000 feet—and its maneuverability at high altitude, which was often a nasty surprise to hotshot fighter pilots who took bar bets from wily Vulcan crews.

A DYNAMIC DUO

The **North American F-86 Sabre** and the **Mikoyan-Gurevich MiG-15** were evenly matched, each better and worse than the other in different respects. The bigger and more powerful Sabre had refinements that made a great difference to its effectiveness. Among these was a radar gunsight that measured the speed and range of a target and showed the pilot how far ahead of the target he should aim his guns in order to hit it. The USAF also developed new tactics to cope with jet speeds, launching fighters in small groups—"finger-four" formations—to patrol over targets.

Mikoyan-Gurevich MiG-15

North American F-86 Sabre

Also, under an operation called Project Moolah, a large sum of money was offered to any pilot who would defect to South Korea and bring his MiG-15 with him. The project was successful; an airplane was obtained and tested extensively. Tactics were changed accordingly, and the Sabre was modified to exploit its advantages over the MiG.

Designers Speed Toward Development

In the United States, some equally radical designs were being tested in California, under a series of projects that could be traced back to the war years.

Later fighters, such as the P-38, P-47, and higher-powered Spitfires, could dive at speeds of almost 500 miles per hour, around seven-tenths the speed of sound. At near-supersonic speeds, air flowing around an object became compressible and shock waves started to form. In the case of the P-38, shock waves rendered the tail ineffective and caused a number of crashes.

In the United Kingdom, the government's Royal Aircraft Establishment modified a Spitfire for high-speed dive tests. They reached Mach 0.92—92 percent the speed of sound, or more than 600 miles per hour—before the propeller fell off, indicating that the maximum safe speed had been attained. In 1943, RAE scientists designed a small plane for research at higher speeds. The body of the Miles M.52 was shaped like a high-velocity bullet, the only shape that was known to work at supersonic speeds. It had a very thin, straight wing and an all-moving tail.

In December 1943, the National Advisory Committee on Aeronautics held a meeting on high-speed research. Several participants had recently returned from the United Kingdom—and it was at this meeting that engineers from NACA and the Bell company recommended that NACA should build a specialized high-speed research airplane. Late in 1944, the Bell company received a contract for an airplane with a bullet-shaped body, a thin, straight wing, and an all-moving tail. (It's only fair to state at this point that many respected historians regard the resemblance between the M.52 and the Bell design as pure coincidence.)

The crucial difference was that the Bell XS-1 was powered by a rocket rather than a jet. Bell and the USAAF had hoped that the airplane could take off from a runway, but it could not carry

Above: The United States was surprised when the MiG-15 appeared in the skies over Korea in November 1950. It should not have been: The airplane had been demonstrated at the Tushino Airshow years before. The MiG-15 was an excellent airplane, with performance equivalent to the North American F-86.

Right: The Vought F8U Crusader was one of the most popular fighters of its time and proved itself as a "MiG-Killer" during the Vietnam War.

Far right: The swept-wing Saab J29 astounded observers when it first flew in September 1948. Some 661 J29s were built, and they established Sweden as a powerhouse in the fighter business.

September 8, 1944
The V-2 is used in battle for the first time.

September 10, 1944
The Fairchild C-82 cargo plane makes its first flight.

September 14, 1944
Colonel Floyd B. Wood, in a Douglas A-20, intentionally flies into a hurricane to gather weather data.

October 25, 1944
Japanese aircraft carry out the first Kamikaze suicide attacks. The escort carrier *St. Lo* is sunk.

November 1–December 7, 1944
The International Civil Aviation Conference is held in Chicago. It lays the basis for ICAO.

November 7, 1944
Theodore von Karman organizes the AAF Scientific Advisory Group.

January 20, 1945
Robert T. Jones of NACA formulates swept-back wings to overcome shock-wave effects at critical Mach speed.

February 1945
The Bachem Natter vertical-launch rocket interceptor is tested.

February 1945
The USAAF issues a contract for development of the Bell XS-1 supersonic aircraft.

March 14, 1945
The RAF drops a Grand Slam bomb on a key viaduct in Germany.

May 1945
Boeing begins development of gapa (ground-to-air pilotless aircraft) anti-aircraft missiles for the USAAF.

May 2, 1945
▶ Wernher Von Braun (pictured), Walter Dornberger, and others flee to the West.

enough fuel; instead, it was launched in flight from a B-29. The RAE/Miles team could never produce a jet engine powerful enough to take the M.52 supersonic, though, and the project was eventually abandoned in 1946.

The XS-1 had been tested at Muroc Air Force Base in California. In the early wartime years, the USAAF had set up a secret flight-test center on the edge of Muroc Dry Lake, in the high desert north of Los Angeles. The first U.S. jet airplane, the mediocre Bell P-59, was shipped there in disguise, with a fake wooden propeller on its nose.

Close to Muroc was a fly-in restaurant, horse ranch, and guest house owned by Florence "Pancho" Barnes, one-time holder of the women's air speed record. When the pilots were not flying, they relaxed at Pancho's, where pulling rank was forbidden, and the steaks were legendary.

Captain Chuck Yeager performed the first supersonic airplane flight in the XS-1 on October 14, 1947, using a length of broom-handle to close the cockpit door, because he had cracked two ribs while riding at Pancho's. The normal door-closing effort was temporarily outside his range of motion.

It was the start of a wild and dangerous era at Muroc. North American's George Welch dove a Sabre at supersonic speed soon after Yeager's flight. In June 1948, Northrop's jet-powered YB-49 flying-wing bomber broke up over the high desert, killing Captain Glen Edwards and his crew. The base was renamed in Edwards' honor.

Experimental airplanes designed for flight at two or three times the speed of sound were already being designed in the late 1940s, while North American started designing a scaled-up Sabre with a thinner wing and greater power. This craft, the F-100 Super Sabre, flew in 1953 and became the USAF's first operational

THE MAN BEHIND THE WWII AVIATION STRATEGIES

The most influential military leader of the Jet Age was USAF **General Curtis E. LeMay.** Rising quickly through the USAAF command in World War II, LeMay took over the B-29 force in the Marianas Islands in early 1945. He ordered the bombers stripped of their complex defensive guns and switched to high-speed, low-level night attacks on Japanese cities. Losses were minimal, and the devastation was immense.

In October 1948, LeMay took over the USAF's Strategic Air Command and transformed it into an organization on a proper war footing. In LeMay's experience, almost every unit failed on its first mission. For SAC, however, there was only one mission. As one officer summed it up: "In SAC, we work very hard to find the best way to do something—then, we all do it that way all the time."

General Curtis LeMay

May 8, 1945
VE Day: Germany surrenders.

August 6, 1945
A B-29 bomber drops the first atomic bomb on Hiroshima.

September 20, 1945
The first turboprop aircraft, a modified Gloster Meteor with Rolls-Royce Trent engine, flies.

September 26, 1945
The Army Wac Corporal is fired. It is the first U.S. rocket with liquid propellent.

October 23, 1945
The last of 10,174 military DC-3/C-47 aircraft is handed over.

November 6, 1945
Ensign Jake West, in a Ryan FR-1 Fireball, makes the first jet landing on a carrier.

November 7, 1945
An RAF Gloster Meteor IV sets the first official world's air speed record (606 miles per hour) in a jet aircraft.

December 3, 1945
The 412th Fighter Group receives their first U.S. jet fighters: Lockheed P-80As.

December 8, 1945
▶ The Bell Model 47, which becomes the first CAA-certified helicopter and

the first commercial helicopter in America, flies.

1946
The Department of Agriculture uses the Sikorsky HSN-1 for mosquito control.

1946
The Soviet Union takes over the V-2 missile production in Germany.

The beautiful Hawker Hunter was probably the most successful of all British jet aircraft. It was used for a long time by a number of air forces. In recent years, some "vintage" Hunters have been brought back to flying status.

The J57 powered the F-100; the first carrier-based supersonic fighter, the F8U Crusader; and a generation of long-range airplanes, including the B-52 bomber, flown in 1952.

If the United States could build intercontinental jet bombers, then it could be surmised that the Soviet Union could, too. Air Defense Command took second place only to SAC among the USAF's priorities, and the F-100 became the first of the "Century series" of supersonic fighters. One of the boldest such projects was the Convair F-102, featuring a thin-section delta wing.

The F-102 was intended to perform an automated attack using unguided rockets and AIM-4 Falcon radar-guided air-to-air missiles. Packing all this equipment and a large fuel load into the fighter resulted in a stout fuselage, and it became clear before the YF-102 made its first flight in late 1953 that it would not be supersonic. Using new data from NACA, the airplane was redesigned with a longer body and other changes. The F-102A Delta Dagger and its more powerful follow-on, the 1,400-mile-per-hour F-106A, remained in service for many years.

supersonic airplane. At around the same time, Mikoyan developed the supersonic MiG-19, with a sharply swept wing and two jet engines.

The F-100 was one of the first airplanes to use a very important engine, the Pratt & Whitney J57. P&W had been slow in developing jets and found itself eclipsed by General Electric. While the company built Rolls-Royce jet engines under license, it also developed a new second-generation engine, more efficient and more powerful than its rivals.

Another remarkable fighter of the 1950s emerged from the fertile minds of Lockheed's Skunk Works. Fighter pilots returning from Korea told Lockheed that they did not want a bomber-destroyer like the F-102; they wanted an aircraft that was fast, simple, high-flying, and fast—and did they mention fast? Kelly Johnson's team chose to reduce supersonic drag by using a very thin, unswept wing. The Lockheed fighter would use the new Sidewinder guided missile.

The F-104 Starfighter was tricky to fly, and some years later, when the airplane was in service with the re-established German Luftwaffe, it was said that the definition of an optimist was a Starfighter pilot who quit smoking. The airplane was much more complex than originally planned, but the Starfighter was true to its original concept in one respect: It was amazingly fast, the first

AMERICA'S JET BOMBER

The **Boeing B-47** was one of the fastest and heaviest airplanes in the world when it was built, and its slender swept wings, out-rigged engines on pylons, and bicycle landing gear had never been seen before except on Baade's drawing board in Germany.

The first B-47 did not have enough range to attack targets in Russia. Boeing added fuel tanks under the wings, installed rockets in the rear fuselage to get the overloaded bomber off the ground, and devised a new in-flight refueling system that used a telescoping boom under the tail of a tanker airplane.

January 1946
Leon Plympton becomes the first private helicopter owner. He creates the New England Helicopter Service with a surplus Sikorsky R-6.

January 1, 1946
The British Ministry of Aviation takes possession of an unused bomber airfield at Heath Row, near London. Today, Heathrow is the oldest continuously operated major airport.

January 10, 1946
A Sikorsky R-5 helicopter sets an altitude record at 21,000 feet.

February 4, 1946
Pan Am launches its transatlantic service using the Lockheed Constellation.

February 15, 1946
The XC-116, a military-funded prototype of the DC-6, makes its first flight.

March 12, 1946
The U.S. Civil Aeronautics Administration issues the first commercial certificate to a helicopter, the Bell 47.

April–September, 1946
The United States tests 64 V-2 missiles at White Sands, New Mexico.

April 19, 1946
The USAAF and Consolidated-Vultee launch Project MX-774, which will later lead to the Atlas missile.

production fighter capable of Mach 2, and in 2002, it still held the world record for speed at low altitude.

Tactical Air Command did not buy many F-104s. With the development of small nuclear bombs in the early 1950s, TAC took on the nuclear strike role. Its priority program was the Republic F-105, a big, heavy fighter that had a complex weapon-delivery system.

Another outstanding U.S. fighter of the era was the aforementioned Chance Vought F8U Crusader, flown in 1957. This carrier-based fighter's wing hinged around its rear spar, assuming a higher angle for more lift on landing and takeoff while the fighter's fuselage remained in a flat attitude. The U.S. Navy also disagreed with the Air Force's view that any fighter-size jet had to be supersonic; one of the best Navy airplanes of the 1950s was the Douglas A4D (later, A-4) Skyhawk. The Skyhawk was so small that it did not need folding wings, but it was efficient and had a remarkably long range.

Small size was also the goal of Russia's first Mach 2 fighter, tested in 1956. The Mikoyan MiG-21 had a single 11,000-pound-thrust engine, and like the F-104, it carried a single cannon and two missiles—K-13s, which bore a more-than-suspicious resemblance to Sidewinder missiles. High-supersonic fighters were also developed in Western Europe. Sweden's unique Saab J 35 Draken, with a double-delta wing that was almost as deep as the airplane's body, was flown in 1955; Dassault created its delta-wing Mirage; and the United Kingdom produced the twin-jet English Electric Lightning.

Missiles Take Aim at Airplanes

Military airplane developments in the late 1950s, however, were clouded by a developing controversy: Would they be replaced by missiles?

In Russia, in the mid-1950s, the Tupolev and Myasishchev design teams were creating long-range bombers. Myasischchev's 3M bomber had four jet engines; Tupolev's Tu-95 combined a swept

Left: The distinctive Avro Vulcan became one of the most popular aircraft in the Royal Air Force because of its great capability while retaining excellent flying qualities. It was used with success in the Falklands War.

Right: The Bell XS-1 (later called the X-1) in which Captain Charles "Chuck" Yeager exceeded the speed of sound on October 14, 1947, was at once a simple and a sophisticated aircraft. Its fuselage was patterned after a .45 caliber bullet, and its wings were straight and thin.

wing with four 12,000-horsepower turboprop engines, combining long range with near-jet speeds over the target. Nikita Khrushchev, who had consolidated his power over the Communist Party following the death (by natural causes) of Joseph Stalin and the deaths (by other causes) of Stalin's loyalists, doubted whether the bombers were necessary.

At a secret base near Sverdlovsk, an engineer who had once been sent by Stalin to his almost certain death in the goldmines of Kolyma was busy developing an intercontinental ballistic missile (ICBM). Sergei Korolev had been placed in charge of the R-7 ICBM project in 1953, after working for eight years on developments of the German A-4 missile. The huge R-7 missile, capable of launching a 12,000-pound warhead over 5,500 miles, was in full development by 1956.

The same debate was raging in the Pentagon, where LeMay wanted a massive supersonic bomber to replace the still-brand-new B-52. General Dynamics in Fort Worth was building the first supersonic bomber—the delta-wing, medium-range B-58 Hustler—but this was seen as a stepping stone to a larger intercontinental aircraft.

Above: The North American F-100 Supersabre was the first U.S. operational fighter with a supersonic capability. The "Hun," as it was called, was a demanding aircraft, and pilots flew it with respect, but it did an excellent job in reconnaissance and close air support in Vietnam.

Right: The famous "coke-bottle" shape of the Convair F-102A's fuselage is plainly visible here. The prototype F-102 did not have its fuselage pinched in this manner and was a subsonic aircraft. The use of the area-rule formula developed by NASA's Dr. Richard Whitcomb turned the F-102 into a supersonic fighter.

Far right: This Northrop B-62 Snark being launched at Patrick Air Force Base in Florida was a subsonic missile with a range of 1,500 to 5,000 miles. The designation B-62 was given to convey that the craft was still, essentially, a bomber.

March 6, 1947
The first operational U.S. jet bomber, the XB-45 Tornado, makes its first flight.

March 21, 1947
The last DC-3 is rolled out and becomes part of Sabena's fleet. It crashes one year later in thick fog.

March 28, 1947
The first DC-6s are delivered to American and United.

April 4, 1947
The International Civil Aviation Organization is founded.

April 15, 1947
The Douglas D-558-1 research aircraft makes its first flight.

April 24, 1947
The Kellet XR-10 makes its first flight, becoming the first all-metal, twin-engine helicopter in the world.

June 12, 1947
Anne Shaw Carter becomes the first licensed female helicopter pilot.

June 19, 1947
Colonel Al Boyd, in a Lockheed P-80R, sets the speed record of 623.8 miles per hour.

July 2, 1947
The MiG-15 prototype makes its first flight.

July 8, 1947
The Boeing 377 Stratocruiser makes its first flight. It's the world's most luxurious aircraft, but it won't be a money-maker.

July 17, 1947
President Harry Truman signs the National Security Act, which activates the Armed Forces Unification Act and establishes an independent U.S. Air Force.

July 18, 1947
President Harry Truman forms the Finletter Commission to study how to give the United States the "greatest possible benefits from aviation."

August 11, 1947
The last DC-4 of the 1,242 ever built is delivered to South African Airways.

August 20, 1947
The McDonnell XH-20 Little Henry is

91900

UNITED STATES AIR FORCE

GRACE UNDER PRESSURE

One of the great true legends of aviation history was the creation of the **Boeing B-52** bomber. In October 1948, several senior Boeing engineers were meeting Air Force customers at Wright-Patterson Air Force Base in Dayton, Ohio. The Friday meeting went badly.

The Boeing engineers were told that the XB-52, a turboprop-powered replacement for the B-36, was going to be axed. Two other Boeing engineers working on a bomber with the new J57 jet engine and a more efficient wing had also gone to Dayton. Over the weekend, the team prepared a preliminary design for a bomber with eight J57s. Aero-

dynamicist George Schairer bought balsa wood at a hobby shop, and the Boeing team had a presentation of the new design, complete with a display model, ready by Monday.

The Air Force reprieved the XB-52. The airplane flew in 1952—and the last B-52s were, at the time of this writing 50 years later, still flying combat missions.

Northrop had started developing an intercontinental nuclear missile in 1945. The toughest challenge was guidance: Northrop invented an inertial guidance system linked to an automatic, electronic star tracker. Named Snark, after an imaginary beast in a Lewis Carroll poem, the extraordinary weapon actually entered service in 1957.

Even more ambitious was the North American Navaho. Launched by a rocket booster, the ramjet-powered Navaho was designed to cruise at 2,000 miles per hour. The program was canceled in 1957, but the Rocketdyne booster engine powered the first U.S. ICBM, the Convair Atlas.

Despite the promise of the ICBM—which appeared impossible to intercept—and the potentially huge costs of the supersonic bomber, SAC persisted with the bomber project, aiming at speeds of Mach 3 or 2,000 miles per hour. But by 1956, only one airplane

The most important multi-jet aircraft in history, the Boeing B-47 is the direct ancestor not only of the KC-135 and the B-52 but also of the Boeing series of transports, from the 707 to the 777. The B-47 gave the Strategic Air Command a military dominance never before possible.

---

the first ram-jet-powered helicopter in the world.

October 1, 1947
The North American XP-86 Sabre makes its first flight.

October 1, 1947
Los Angeles begins the first scheduled helicopter mail service.

October 14, 1947
▶ Captain Chuck Yeager, flying in a

Bell XS-1, makes the world's first supersonic flight.

November 2, 1947
▶ The Hughes HK-1 *Spruce Goose* flying boat makes its first and only flight. It has the greatest wingspan (320 feet) of any airplane ever built.

December 17, 1947
The Boeing XB-47 makes its first flight. It is the most important multi-engine jet in history.

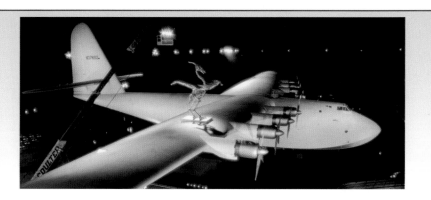

Right: The world's first supersonic bomber, the Convair B-58 Hustler proved too costly to operate, especially when its high loss rate was taken into consideration. A handsome aircraft, it was perhaps "too much, too soon."

Opposite top: The Republic F-105 Thunderchief was the workhorse of the Vietnam War. The Mach 2.1 fighter was originally intended to deliver nuclear weapons. It was modified to carry conventional weapons in the attack role, and then became a Wild Weasel that worked to suppress enemy defenses, the toughest mission of the war.

Opposite bottom: The Douglas A4D Skyhawk was one of the great Ed Heinemann's best achievements. Tasked to build a heavy Navy attack fighter, Heinemann countered with the tiny, lightweight, fast, and efficient Skyhawk.

Right: After World War II, the French aircraft industry found itself in a terrible state and years behind the major powers. Marcel Dassault undertook to change that, and he did so with a magnificent series of fighters, of which the Ouragan was one of the earliest successes.

had reached Mach 3—and it was not an encouraging story. The first Bell X-2 blew up under its B-50 mother-ship on a captive test flight; the second crashed in September 1956 after reaching Mach 3. The pilot was killed. Nevertheless, North American was awarded a contract in 1957 to develop the Mach 3 XB-70 bomber, with engines burning special high-energy boron fuel.

But boron fuel was by no means the most radical idea studied in the 1950s. In 1954, the Central Intelligence Agency asked Kelly Johnson's Skunk Works to build a small, single-seat reconnaissance aircraft that could fly unscathed over the Soviet Union at altitudes above 70,000 feet. The airplane was to be operated in secret, and the development team located a small airstrip beside Groom Dry Lake in Nevada for flight tests. It was on the edge of the Atomic Energy Commission's nuclear test site, which was divided into numbered areas for the purpose of tracking fallout from nuclear tests. The Lockheed/CIA base was in Area 51.

Named U-2, the sailplane-like jet made its first flight in 1955 and performed its first operational mission in July 1956. For almost four years, U-2s roamed over the Soviet Union, gathering vital intelligence. But the CIA did not believe that the U-2 could be immune from attack for more than a few years and asked Lockheed to design a supersonic follow-on airplane. The result was the CL-400, which resembled a giant F-104 but was fueled by liquid hydrogen. The engines had been tested before the project was canceled in 1957.

Even more incredible was the USAF's plan to build a nuclear-powered airplane. In July 1955, the USAF flew a working nuclear reactor aboard a modified B-36. It was followed at all times by an airplane carrying airborne troops who would parachute in to seal off the area if the B-36 crashed.

Far more practical was another Skunk Works design. Since World War II, air forces had been looking for a transport that could

December 30, 1947
The Soviet Union accepts the design of the MiG-15.

1948
The New York Police Department acquires a Bell Model 47 helicopter.

January 30, 1948
▶ Orville Wright dies.

April 28, 1948
The Constellation makes the first

nonstop New York–Paris passenger flight. It takes 16 hours and 1 minute.

May 3, 1948
Howard Lilly is the first NACA test pilot to be killed in the line of duty; he was flying a Douglas D-558-1.

June 1948
The SE 3101 is the first helicopter flown in France after the war.

June 26, 1948
▶ The Berlin Airlift begins.

July 16, 1948
The Vickers Viscount, the world's first turboprop airliner, makes its first flight.

September 1948
Mikhail L. Mil's Mil Mi-1 becomes the first Soviet mass-produced helicopter, starting off the Mil dynasty of helicopters.

76

land in a short airfield, like a glider, but then take off again. The turboprop made it possible. In August 1954, Lockheed flew the first prototype of the C-130 Hercules, a high-wing transport with four Allison turboprops and a rear ramp and low cargo floor for rapid loading.

The jet age made another decisive contribution to military mobility. The helicopter and its ancestor, the gyroplane, had been under development by enthusiasts, inventors, and dedicated engineering teams since the 1920s. The first helicopter that flew under control was in 1937. It was the German Focke-Achgelis Fa61, which had two side-by-side rotors.

It was the Russian émigré Igor Sikorsky, working in the United States, who developed the helicopter as we know it today, with a single main rotor and a smaller tail rotor. After several years of

September 1, 1948
The Saab J-29 jet fighter makes its first flight.

October 14, 1948
The Hiller 360 is certified, making it the third commercial helicopter in the United States.

1949
The Kaman K-225 helicopter is used for crop dusting.

1949
The Hiller Model 360 makes the first U.S. helicopter transcontinental flight.

1949
Petroleum helicopters are launched to tend to oil rigs in Louisiana; the practice becomes an industry standard.

February 8, 1949
The Boeing B-47 sets a transcontinen-

tal speed record with an average speed of 607.8 miles per hour.

February 24, 1949
A two-stage V-2/WAC Corporal missile is launched from White Sands, New Mexico, reaching a 244-mile altitude.

February 26–March 2, 1949
The USAF Boeing B-50 *Lucky Lady II* completes the first nonstop round-the-

world flight in 94 hours, with four in-flight refuelings.

March 7–8, 1949
Bill Odom flies the Beech Bonanza from Hawaii to Teterboro, New Jersey.

April 26, 1949
Dick Reidel and Harold Harris set the world endurance flight record at 1,008 hours and 1 minute.

May 13, 1949
The English Electric Canberra makes its first flight.

July 27, 1949
The de Havilland Comet makes its first flight.

August 9, 1949
The first emergency use of an ejection seat is carried out by J. L. Fruin after he loses control of a U.S. Navy Banshee aircraft.

A MAGNIFICENT MISSILE

One of the most ingenious weapons of the Cold War era was the **Sidewinder** air-to-air missile (AAM), developed by U.S. Navy scientists at China Lake, California. It was based on a standard five-inch rocket. The nose section incorporated control fins and an infrared seeker that was designed to home in on the heat from a target's jet engine.

The rear-mounted wings were fitted with "rollerons"— moving control surfaces that were adjusted by slipstream-driven gyroscopes. Later designated AIM-9, it was the world's dominant short-range AAM until the 1990s.

investigation, Sikorsky flew the experimental VS-300 in 1939, and a few production helicopters entered service with the U.S. Army in 1944.

Performance, however, was an issue. Pilots who had been recruited for "a secret program" were puzzled when they arrived

August 25, 1949
The Bristol Type 171 Sycamore becomes the first British commercial helicopter.

September 1949
The Sikorsky S-52 becomes the first helicopter to loop. It has all-metal rotor blades, the first ever fitted to a helicopter.

September 4, 1949
The Avro 707 delta-wing research plane flies; it is the forerunner of the future Vulcan bomber.

September 23, 1949
President Harry Truman announces that the Soviet Union has exploded a nuclear device.

November 7, 1949
The Sikorsky S-55 makes its first flight.

December 31, 1949
About 26.5 million people flew commercially in 1949.

January 1, 1950
British European Airways uses Sikorsky S-51s to launch the first commercial scheduled passenger helicopter service.

May 9, 1950
The CAA begins the purchase of the Distance Measuring System.

June 25, 1950
The Korean War begins; helicopters are used extensively for medical evacuation, rescue, resupply, etc.

July 29, 1950
Vickers Viscount, the first turbine-engine airliner, enters the service.

September 4, 1950
A downed F-80 pilot stuck behind enemy lines is picked up in a helicopter rescue.

September 22, 1950
Colonel David Schilling leads the flights of two F-84E aircraft for the first nonstop transatlantic jet crossing.

October 15–21, 1950
The first omnirange (VOR) frequency airways are placed in operation.

November 7, 1950
The last British Overseas Airways Corporation flying-boat service is conducted.

SKUNKING THE COMPETITION

One of the young engineers who traveled West to look for work in the early 1930s was **Clarence L. "Kelly" Johnson.** Joining the struggling Lockheed company in 1933, Johnson told his bosses that their new Model 10 transport would be unstable. Johnson devised a twin-tail layout that set the pattern for an entire family of successful aircraft.

Ten years later, asked to design a new jet fighter, Johnson picked a small team of engineers. Working in secrecy in a corner of the Burbank, California, factory, Johnson's team built the XP-80 in 143 days. Workers nicknamed Johnson's operation the Skunk Works, after the moonshiners' secret lair in the *Li'l Abner* comic strip.

The Skunk Works went on to become the most renowned special-projects operation in history, with a tradition of achieving apparently impossible results in very short periods of time under conditions of complete secrecy. Johnson himself could be a tyrant—his successor, Ben Rich, described him as "W.C. Fields without the humor"—but in turn he made sure that his people worked without interference from bosses or micro-managing customers.

at their training base: To save weight, they and their fellow recruits were all below-average size.

The helicopter was more widely used in the Korean War. Its role in medical evacuation was later embedded in the public consciousness through the *M*A*S*H* TV series, which featured Bell's simple and reliable Model 47 or H-13.

In any helicopter, the engine was a huge fraction of the empty weight. Turbine engines offered a tremendous weight savings. The first turbine helicopter flew in 1951, and in 1955, the U.S. Army ordered the first example of a Bell helicopter that was designed from the ground up for turbine power. The first XH-40 flew in October 1956—but it is better known today as the UH-1 or Huey.

Between them, the C-130 and the Huey made ground forces airmobile as never before. Remarkably, the latest versions of both aircraft were still in production in 2002, at the time of writing—while the amazing supersonic bombers and fighters of the 1950s are long retired. Apparently, the race is not always to the swift.

Above left: Igor Sikorsky began his career investigating helicopters but then switched to large aircraft. In the late 1930s, he returned to his first love and produced the VS-300, the first of a long line of Sikorsky helicopters.

Above right: The jet engine improved performance in helicopters. The Bell XH-40 made its first flight in 1956. When it was adopted by the Army, its name changed to the UH-1 Iroquois but was quickly nicknamed "Huey."

Opposite top: Called "The Missile With a Man in It," the Lockheed F-104 was designed by Kelly Johnson at the famous Lockheed Skunk Works. The USAF found the F-104 too small and too short-ranged, but it became extremely popular in Europe.

Opposite bottom: The Saab J 35 Draken ("Dragon") proved that the J 29 had been no fluke. With its unusual "double-delta" configuration, Draken was ideal for Sweden's often quite limited airfields.

November 8, 1950
A USAF F-80C shoots down a MiG-15 over Korea in the first jet-versus-jet dogfight.

1951
The Sud-Est SE 3120 helicopter, Alouette 1, is flown.

1951
For the first time in history, airline passenger miles (10.6 million) exceed rail passenger miles (10.2 million).

January 16, 1951
The USAF establishes Project Atlas, the first ICBM.

February 18, 1951
Auster light aircraft are used in Antarctic exploration.

February 21, 1951
The English Electric Canberra, the first British jet bomber, becomes the first jet to cross the Atlantic unrefueled.

February 23, 1951
The Dassault MD.452 Mystere makes its first flight, beginning the "Dassault dynasty."

March 29, 1951
Flight Safety Inc. begins operations at the Marine Air Terminal in LaGuardia with one Link Simulator. It will eventually grow into a huge business.

June 11, 1951
A Douglas Skyrocket attains the speed of 1,200 miles per hour over Edwards Air Force Base.

June 20, 1951
The Bell X-5 variable-sweep aircraft makes its first flight.

August 1951
The Viking sounding rocket reaches a speed of 4,100 miles per hour and an

altitude of 135 miles, a record for a single-stage rocket.

August 15, 1951
The Douglas Skyrocket reaches 79,494 feet, the highest altitude ever attained by a human being to date.

December 1951
The Civil Reserve Air Fleet (CRAF) is proclaimed, which allows the military to use commercial airliners during emergencies.

CHAPTER FIVE

Commercial Aviation Spreads Its Wings

AS AVIATION TECHNOLOGY POWERHOUSES ITS WAY INTO A NEW ERA, THE MAGIC OF JET FLIGHT BECOMES AVAILABLE TO THE RICH AND FAMOUS.

In August 1955, a group of top airline and industry bosses met in Seattle, where Boeing chair Bill Allen hosted them aboard yachts to watch the Gold Cup hydroplane races on Lake Washington. As the gathering watched the activities, a large plane in Boeing's trademark chocolate and yellow appeared over the lake. Allen had asked his chief test pilot, Tex Johnston, to show the company's new Model 367-80 jet transport prototype.  Johnston arrived at 300 feet, pitched the huge jet up into a climb, and performed an immaculate 360-degree barrell roll. He then rolled it again at the other end of the lake.

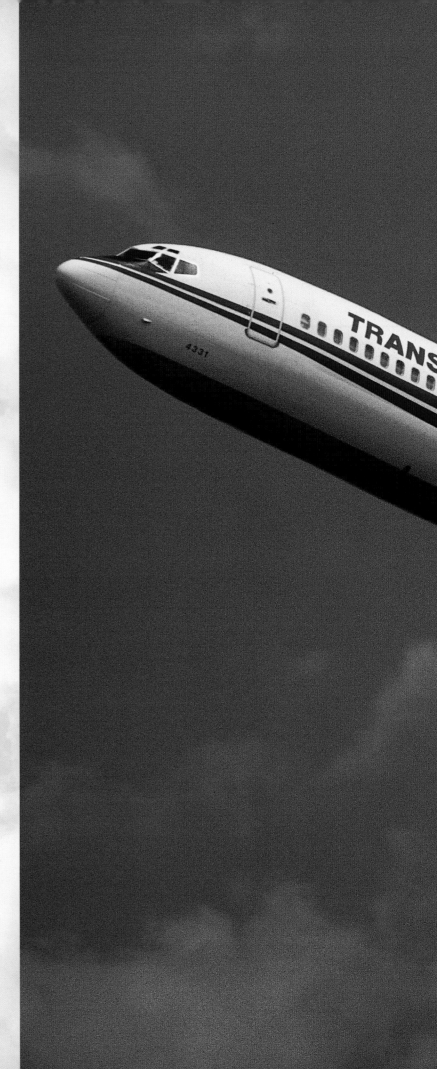

Right: The 727 solved its takeoff requirements with a very clever wing that was loaded with high-lift devices on its leading and trailing edges. Three rear-mounted engines provided ample power, but the T-tail required pilots to learn a new landing technique.

Opposite: The Douglas DC-4 was introduced to the service as the military C-54, and in that role, it did heroic work during the Berlin Airlift. It was faster than the DC-3 and much more comfortable, but it was not pressurized.

A shocked Allen watched with horror and then reportedly asked to borrow the heart pills of another passenger, saying, "I need it worse than you do." In 1977, Allen remarked, "It has taken me 22 years to reach the point where I can discuss the event with a modicum of humor."

The prototype that Johnston had demonstrated in such dramatic fashion would set the pattern for a whole new generation of aircraft and put Boeing on the top of a whole new industry.

The Airline Industry Takes Off

The Douglas DC-4 and Lockheed Model 49 Constellation had been the world's only modern airliners in 1945. They dominated air transport for a decade. In 1940, American, Eastern, and United ordered DC-4s for the prestigious transcontinental routes. The USAAF took over the DC-4 production line, building several hundred to be used as military transports called C-54s. TWA, owned by the demanding and technology-fascinated Howard Hughes, commissioned Lockheed to build the faster and more elegant Constellation airliner. Development of the Constellation continued, but it had the same engine as the desperately needed B-29, and only 15 Constellations were delivered in wartime.

TWA and Pan Am Constellations became the first landplanes to fly scheduled trips over the North Atlantic in 1946. TWA put the "Connie" into service on transcontinental routes, clocking in a time that beat American Airlines' DC-4s by three hours. Douglas had expected this and persuaded the USAAF to order the first prototype of the more powerful DC-6 before the war. Like the Constellation, it had a pressurized cabin, which allowed it to cruise above the roughest weather.

In the early 1950s, Douglas and Lockheed "stretched" the airplanes again, increasing capacity, speed, and range in the Super Constellation and DC-7. They could fly from New York to Europe nonstop—a stop in Gander, Newfoundland, was required on the upwind Europe–New York return leg. The pinnacles of both series were 1956's DC-7C Seven Seas and the Lockheed Starliner, both of which offered two-way, nonstop transatlantic range.

BOAC, KLM, Lufthansa, Air France, Alitalia, and other European airlines re-equipped with U.S. aircraft. Newly independent countries such as India and Pakistan formed their own airlines. Officially, the United States did not have a single "flag-carrier" airline—but it was hard to tell that from looking at Juan Trippe's Pan Am, which dominated U.S. international services.

In 1944, the Allies had formed the International Civil Aviation Organization (ICAO) to set standards for airplane operations. ICAO allocated a three-letter code to every major airport, set standards for radio frequencies, and defined a single phonetic alphabet: ABC was *Alfa Bravo Charlie*, irrespective of where in the world you were.

The International Air Transport Association (IATA) was given wide latitude to set fares. Through IATA, airlines agreed on fare codes and a ticket format; they used the dollar as their medium of exchange and devised a system of "interline" accounting. An airline passenger could take a long, complex trip with one fare and one multipage ticket. Airlines were also early adopters of credit cards.

A COMPANY BY ANY OTHER NAME

Airlines were among the first global companies to have names that were **acronyms** or were blends of two common words. The roots of the names were not all that memorable—so airline personnel made up their own colorful versions. The British Overseas Airways Corporation (BOAC) was "Better On A Camel." TWA became "Try Walking Across." Belgium's flag carrier, Sabena was "Such A Bloody Experience, Never Again."

December 10, 1951
A Navy Kaman K-225 helicopter, modified to be the world's first shaft-powered turbine helicopter, makes its first flight.

December 12, 1951
The de Havilland (Canada) DHC-3 Otter makes its first flight. The plane will become an important business aircraft.

1952
Kamov helicopters demonstrate a counter-rotating coaxial rotor arrangement, which will become the basis of many Soviet helicopters.

January 1952
The new twin-engine airliners appear.

April 15, 1952
The Boeing YB-52 heavy bomber makes its first flight.

May 1952
The USAF announces that four animals (two monkeys, two mice) have been launched 36 miles into the air in a missile and recovered alive and unharmed.

May 2, 1952
The British Overseas Airways Corporation offers the first jet passenger service. A BOAC de Havilland Comet jets between London and Rome.

May 20, 1952
Boeing starts work on the Model 367-80 jet transport prototype.

June 18, 1952
NACA's H. Julian Allen conceives the "blunt nose principle," a key for designing vehicles capable of re-entering the atmosphere.

July 29, 1952
The North American RB-45 makes the first nonstop transpacific flight by jet.

November 1952
The first Westland-built version of an S-55 helicopter flies.

November 1, 1952
The United States explodes the first hydrogen bomb.

November 19, 1952
SAS flies a commercial airline flight over the North Pole to establish Scandinavia–United States routes.

December 16, 1952
The first USAF helicopter squadron begins operations.

1953
Jean Ross Howard learns to fly helicopters and launches the "Whirly-Girls."

January 3, 1953
The Cessna 310 makes its first flight.

January 6, 1953
Luftag is formed; it will become Lufthansa in 1954.

January 12, 1953
The first flight tests of an angled deck carrier are conducted in the USN.

February 1, 1953
The 12,571st Chance Vought F4U, the last of the World War II propeller fighters, is delivered.

April 3, 1953
BOAC starts a London–Tokyo jet service with the Comet.

April 18, 1953
▶ Vickers Viscount, the first turbo-prop airliner, enters service.

May 18, 1953
The Douglas DC-7, a longer-range version of the DC-6, makes its first flight.

THE GREAT SILVER FLEET

"nonskeds." When they started to compete with Pan Am's Caribbean flights, Trippe retaliated with the first tourist-class flights, which featured cheaper airfares and slightly smaller seats.

The success of the new class led to the introduction of separate tourist-class flights across the Atlantic in 1952. Tourist-class passengers could be fed only sandwiches—sparking the "sandwich war" when Scandinavian Airlines System offered the region's traditional open-faced sandwiches, which were more hearty than typical American fare. Competitor TWA cried foul, and SAS was forced to pay a $25,000 fine to the IATA.

Within a couple of years, the tourist and first-class traffic was mixed on the same airplane. Coach-class service started in the United States, cutting fares and expanding traffic. In 1955, airlines carried more domestic passengers than the railroads.

Apart from Douglas and Lockheed airplanes, the only long-range airliner to sell in more than boutique numbers at the time was the Boeing Stratocruiser. Flown by Pan Am, BOAC, and Northwest

Pre-war airplanes were luxury transports. After the war, a few small airlines in the United States started operations with ex-military airplanes crammed with smaller seats and charged $99 for a transcontinental flight. Because they flew only when they could fill their airplanes, they were called "non-scheduled airlines" or

Opposite: Many people consider the Lockheed Constellation to be the most beautiful of all airline transports. The "S" shape of the fuselage and the three vertical surfaces were all there for good engineering reasons, but they also looked just right.

Left: The interior of piston-engine transports provided far more room than is found in today's jets. A flight was an occasion, and people dressed for it: men in suits and ladies in their suitable finery. And the stewardesses—not yet flight attendants—were young, pretty, and attentive.

Below: To compete with the pressurized Lockheed Constellation, Douglas created the DC-6, which became one of the most beloved of the piston-engine transports because of its superb flying qualities.

January 10, 1954
A BOAC Comet breaks up over the Mediterranean.

February 28, 1954
The Lockheed XF-104, the first Mach 2 aircraft to enter operational service, makes its first flight.

March 1954
The Kaman Huskie HTK-1 becomes the first twin-turbine engine helicopter.

April 8, 1954
A second Comet breaks up. The aircraft is grounded and will not return to service until 1958.

May 1, 1954
Early warning aircraft units, RC-121s, are formed.

July 15, 1954
The Boeing 367-80, a 707 prototype, makes its first flight. It will have a profound influence on military jet designs.

July 31, 1954
◄ Britain's first successful jet fighter, the Hawker Hunter, enters the service.

September 1, 1954
The USAF orders the first KC-135 tankers, based on the 367-80.

October 17, 1954
The Sikorsky XH-39 sets the helicopter altitude record at 24,500 feet. It is piloted by Army Warrant Officer Billy Wester.

Right: The visibility was marvelous from the Stratocruiser cockpit. Some pilots actually experienced difficulty orienting themselves because there was nothing ahead by which to judge the aircraft's attitude, or relative position.

Opposite: The Boeing Stratocruiser was developed from the Boeing B-29 and was widely regarded as the most luxurious air transport of its time. It was also the most expensive to operate and consequently found few buyers.

Below: The final expression of the lovely Lockheed Constellation airliners, the Model 1649 Starliner represented the peak of piston-powered transport performance. Passengers and pilots loved the Constellation, but the planes never made any money for Lockheed until they were converted to military use, as with the EC-121. This is the prototype Starliner.

Orient, it is best remembered for the spiral staircase that led to a cocktail bar in the lower half of the fuselage. Boeing built only 55 Stratocruisers but was consoled by selling 900-plus KC-97 military versions to the U.S. Air Force.

Convair, meanwhile, developed the CV-240, CV-340, and CV-440 Convairliners to complement the DC-6s and Constellations on shorter routes, appealing to passengers who had become used to pressurization and speed. All over the world, though, it was DC-3s that opened up most new air routes.

The British government knew the end of the war would bring about a resurgence of commercial aviation. At the end of 1942, a government committee concluded that British industry should develop a range of advanced airliners—some powered by turbine engines—and leapfrog over the expected U.S. competition.

In July 1950, the four-turboprop Vickers Viscount became the first turbine-powered airliner in service; eventually a respectable 445 Viscounts were built. The boldest new design to emerge from

the committee, though, was kept secret until 1949. The world's first jet airliner, the 44-seat, four-engine de Havilland Comet debuted in May 1952. The Comet cruised at 500 miles per hour and 40,000 feet, almost twice as fast as the Constellation and 10,000 feet higher.

The Comet 1 was designed for European services and multistop flights to Johannesburg and Singapore, but the transatlantic Comet 3 was on the drawing board. The first U.S. order, from Pan Am, was taken in late 1953.

In January and April 1954, though, two Comets broke up in flight over the Mediterranean. The Royal Navy salvaged the wreckage of one of the planes and found the pressurized cabin had failed due to metal fatigue. By the time a redesigned Comet entered service in 1958, it faced new competition.

Boeing had been studying commercial jet transports since 1947. Boeing's leaders believed that a jet transport could put the company back into the airliner business and that it would also make

February 26, 1955
George Welsh, in a North American F-100, makes the first-known supersonic ejection.

March 25, 1955
▶ Chance Vought XF8U-1 carrier-based fighter exceeds Mach 1 on its first flight.

April 7, 1955
Lockheed's YC-130 Hercules debuts.

May 17, 1955
The first of 60 Viscounts is delivered to Capital Airlines. It's the first non-U.S. aircraft bought by a U.S. airline since the 1920s.

May 27, 1955
Sud-Est Aviation SE 210 Caravelle, the first rear-engine twin-jet airliner, makes its first flight.

June 15, 1955
The Tupelov Tu-104 passenger jetliner makes it first flight.

July 20, 1955
An NB-36H makes the first flight carrying an atomic reactor.

August 2, 1955
Colonel Horace Hanes sets the first supersonic speed record (822 miles per hour) in a North American F-100 Super Sabre.

October 8, 1955
The first U.S. Navy supercarrier, the *Saratoga,* is launched.

October 13, 1955
Pan Am orders twenty 707s and twenty-five Douglas DC-8s.

November 24, 1955
The Fokker F.27 Friendship makes its first flight.

December 1955
An aircraft spraying water puts out a forest fire for the first time.

December 20, 1955
The Douglas DC-7C makes its first flight.

1956
Vertol (formerly Piasecki) flight-tests a new helicopter.

1956
The last GE 47 turbojet engine is produced.

1956
Cessna introduces the Model 172.

February 1, 1956
The U.S. Army activates the Army Ballistic Missile Agency at Redstone Arsenal, in Huntsville, Alabama, to develop the Redstone and the Jupiter intermediate-range ballistic missile.

March 10, 1956
Britain's Fairey Delta 2 research airplane sets the air-speed record at 1,132 miles per hour.

April 1956
Dr. John von Neumann is given the Enrico Fermi Award for his work on computers and nuclear development.

April 26, 1956
The Naval Aircraft Factory is decommissioned.

May 21, 1956
The first H-bomb is dropped from a B-52 in the Bikini Islands.

May 24, 1956
The Piper Comanche makes its first flight.

June 21, 1956
Convair launches the Model 880 jetliner with orders from American.

June 22, 1956
The USSR explodes an H-bomb at a 22-mile altitude via missile.

Top: The Boeing C-97 used B-29 technology to develop a cargo plane that was subsequently adapted to air-refueling duties (a variant called the KC-97). It was also employed by airlines in a civilian version, the Stratocruiser.

Bottom: Both Convair and Martin tried to replace the DC-3 with modern twin-engine transports. Convair produced the CV-240, CV-340, and CV-440 (shown here), while Martin built the similar 202 and 404. Neither company made any money on these projects because it was cheaper to buy surplus C-47s and refurbish them.

Opposite page top: The Vickers Viscount was unquestionably the most successful British transport in the post-war period, with more than 400 built. It was a delightful aircraft for passengers, particularly on Continental Airlines, where champagne was served from takeoff to landing.

Opposite page bottom: One of the most important aircraft in history, the Boeing 367-80 was the prototype for the famous 707 series of airliners. First flown on July 15, 1954, the 367-80 went on to become a versatile test aircraft for Boeing. It was recently restored for a flight to the Seattle Museum of Flight.

July 4, 1956
▶ The Lockheed U-2 makes its first spy flight over the Soviet Union.

July 7, 1956
The de Havilland Comet 2 enters service with the RAF Transport Command.

August 31, 1956
The KC-135 tanker makes its first flight.

September 20, 1956
The three-stage Jupiter C makes its first successful flight.

September 27, 1956
Captain Milburn Apt achieves the first Mach 3 flight in a Bell X-2 before crashing and dying.

October 11, 1956
The ultimate piston-engine airliner, the Lockheed Starliner, makes its first flight.

November 11, 1956
The Convair XB-58 Hustler, the world's first supersonic bomber, makes its first flight.

November 15, 1956
A Scandinavian Airlines System DC-7C flies 6,505 miles nonstop from Los Angeles to Stockholm, a record for a commercial aircraft.

November 26, 1956
Secretary of Defense Charles E.

A RADICAL COMBINATION OF OLD FEATURES

One of the most important aircraft designs in history, the **Boeing 367-80,** set the pattern for most of the jet airliners that followed. The main characteristics of its shape were a low-mounted, upward-angled swept wing, engines in separate pylon-mounted pods, a short landing gear, and complex lift-increasing flaps on the wings. A few of these features had appeared on earlier airplanes, but the combination of all of them was radically new.

The wings were mounted low on the body because the airlines hated the idea of high-wing airplanes like the B-47. This meant that the wings had to be angled upward, to keep the wingtips clear of the ground when the plane was pitched nose-up for takeoff. The "bicycle" landing gear of the B-52 would not work. Because the B-52 is in flying attitude on the ground, the wings generate lift, and the brakes do not work very well. The 367-80, therefore, had short-legged landing gear attached to the wing and folding into the body. The 367-80 had four JT3 engines in individual pods: Twin pods were ruled out because one disintegrating engine might wreck its neighbor. New, more effective wing flaps slowed the airplane down on approach.

Right: The Boeing 707 revolutionized air transport, bringing prices down and providing a level of comfort and speed never before possible.

Below: The de Havilland Comet gave the British aerospace industry an unimaginable lead when it was first flown on July 27, 1949. Unfortunately, three crashes caused it to be grounded, the victim of metal fatigue in the pressurized cabin.

an excellent tanker for the Strategic Air Command's B-47 and the new B-52. By 1952, Boeing was flush with cash from the bomber business and decided to build a jet transport on its own money—gambling the then-enormous sum of $16 million (which would be almost $105 million today).

The Airlines Jet Ahead

The 367-80 was rolled out in Seattle in 1954, but it was not the best of times. Two examples of the world's only other jet trans-

port lay at the bottom of the Mediterranean, and the rest of the fleet was grounded indefinitely. Neither the USAF nor the airline industry had yet placed orders for the new jet. As the new Boeing jet made its ground runs before the first flight, half the landing gear popped through the top of the wing. Things did not look good.

Renamed 707, the airplane made its first flight in July. Tests went well, and by September, the USAF had ordered the first military-version KC-135 tankers. The airlines still had not committed, however, and Douglas was starting to talk about a new jet, the DC-8. In October 1955, Pan Am ordered both Boeing's 707 and Douglas's DC-8.

Between 1955 and 1962, Douglas and Boeing competed for the market as Douglas and Lockheed had done in the previous ten years, each matching the other's improvements. The first versions had one-stop transatlantic range, but bigger versions that could go directly from the United States to Europe were flying by 1960. Later, both companies introduced cargo versions of their airplanes.

There was little room for other competitors. General Dynamics and General Electric teamed on the Convair 880 and 990 but

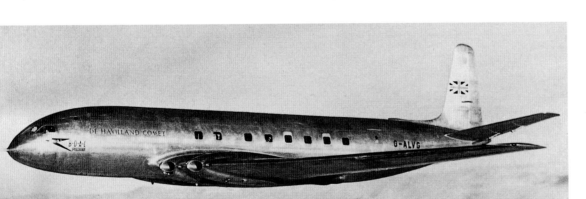

Wilson gives the USAF jurisdiction over ICBMs.

1957
France's Sud-Aviation converts the Alouette I to turbine power to become the Alouette II.

1957
The Mil Mi-6, the first Soviet turbine-powered helicopter, is built in great numbers.

January 18, 1957
Three USAF Boeing B-52s fly around the world nonstop in 45 hours and 19 minutes.

March 4–15, 1957
The Navy nonrigid airship ZPB-2 completes a nonstop transatlantic crossing and sets a new world endurance record for unrefueled flight: 264 hours and 14 minutes.

April 4, 1957
The British government declares that crewed military aircraft will be replaced by missiles.

May 31, 1957
An intermediate-range ballistic missile, the Jupiter, makes its first successful flight.

June 2, 1957
Joe Kittinger makes the first solo balloon flight in the stratosphere.

June 11, 1957
The Atlas ICBM makes its first test flight.

July 16, 1957
John Glenn flies a Vought F8U-1 from Los Angeles to New York at 760 miles per hour.

July 31, 1957
The North American DEW line is completed.

August 1957
The R.7, the first Soviet intercontinental ballistic missile, is launched. The flight takes place at what will become Baikonour Cosmodrome in Kazakhstan.

August 5, 1957
The CAB starts requiring flight data recorders (the "black boxes").

August 18, 1957
Paul Bikle establishes a world glider speed record of 55.02 miles per hour.

Top: Convair attempted to crash the airline market with the 880 and then the 990. These were slightly smaller aircraft than the 707 or DC-8, but they were also faster. Unfortunately, they didn't find a market, and Convair suffered huge losses from the jet transport program.

were forced out of the market by 1962. GD's $200 million loss on the program was the biggest in history. Britain's graceful rear-engine Vickers VC10 sold only 54 copies. The Soviet Union produced the world's largest airliner, the Tu-114, by putting a passenger fuselage on the wings of the Tu-95 bomber, but for the Soviet Union, international air service was a matter of prestige rather than economics.

Middle: Shortly before its maiden flight on June 29, 1962, the very capable and beautiful VC10 poses for its photograph. Only about 53 were built, and some were converted to become tankers in the Royal Air Force.

Bottom: Like Douglas, Lockheed had thought the turboprop was the way to go and so produced the handsome Electra II. The aircraft had unexpected structural problems, and crashes soon dried up the market. Lockheed turned the Electra into a military plane, the P-3 Orion, and proceeded to make a lot of money.

A Battle for the Shorter Airline Routes

For a time, it was less certain that jets would dominate the shorter air routes. The jet's main rival was the turboprop airplane. Lockheed designed a compact, fast turboprop airliner around the same Allison engines as the C-130. But two of the Lockheed Electras broke up in flight, and the airplane was grounded until the cause—a violent oscillation of the propellers—was found and fixed. Sales never recovered.

Sud-Est Aviation in France developed the elegant Caravelle, with engines mounted on the tail. The first jets ordered for U.S. short-haul flights were 20 Caravelles, bought by United in 1959.

August 26, 1957
The USSR announces a successful ICBM test.

October 4, 1957
Soviet Union launches *Sputnik*, the first artificial satellite.

October 28, 1957
▶ The first production of the Boeing 707 rolls out.

November 1957
Sputnik 2 is launched with the dog Laika inside. Laika is the first living creature in space.

November 3, 1957
The Tupolev Tu-114, the world's largest airliner at the time, makes its first flight.

November 21, 1957
NACA establishes its committee on space technology, headed by H. Guyford Stever.

December 1957
NACA's Max Faget proposes the ballistic shape of the Mercury spacecraft.

December 6, 1957
The Vanguard three-stage rocket fails on launch, enraging the humiliated U.S. government and pleasing the Soviet Union.

December 17, 1957
The Atlas ICBM is fired successfully. It will be the first U.S. space launcher.

Right: Douglas was actually concentrating on turboprops as the next step in airliners when they were surprised by Boeing's 707. It was almost a year before they announced they would build the DC-8, which was externally almost identical to the 707.

Opposite: Affectionately called "Fat Albert" when it was introduced, the wide-bodied Boeing 737 has become the best-selling jet airliner in history.

This was a shock to the U.S. industry. Boeing and Douglas were heavily committed to the 707 and DC-8 and had yet to make any money on them. But Boeing's leaders felt they had no choice and decided in 1960 that they would go ahead with a new short-range jet if they could secure orders from United and Eastern, then the two largest U.S. airlines. The resulting 727 was a bold design, with three engines in the tail and a complex wing design. The first orders were placed at the end of November 1960, and the airplane carried its first passengers in early 1964. Douglas used a pair of the same engines—Pratt & Whitney JT8Ds, scaled-down versions of the engines on the latest 707s—on a smaller jet, the DC-9, which went into service in 1965. Boeing responded later with its own twin-jet 737, flown in 1966.

Once again, Boeing and Douglas swamped the competition: The British Aircraft Corporation put up the toughest fight, selling more than 200 One-Elevens (an airplane slightly smaller than

AIR TRAVEL JETS INTO FASHION

When the Beatles made their first tour of the United States in 1964, they arrived on a BOAC 707. To be such a member of the **jet set** signified being not only relatively wealthy, but also fashionable as well. No movie about the rich and powerful (the James Bond movies, for instance) was complete without a shot of a jet pulling away from a runway.

Vogue noted that without steamer or railroad trunks the whole concept of travel dressing had changed: a pale gray suit and white straw hat would suffice. The stewardesses or air hostesses (people certainly never said "flight attendant" back then) wore uniforms designed by Paco Rabanne, Dior, or other top-name designers.

In 1964, *Time* reported that 86 percent of domestic air trips were taken for business reasons, and since many business travelers took multiple flights, a relatively small number of people actually accounted for most of the airline business. In 1969, it was estimated that 5 percent of passengers took 40 percent of the trips. Most of them were male.

December 19, 1957
BOAC introduces the Bristol Britannia on the London–New York route, the first transatlantic service by a turbo-prop plane.

December 20, 1957
The Boeing 707 makes its first flight.

December 28, 1957
A Cessna YH41 sets the altitude record for a helicopter at 30,335 feet.

1958
For the first time, more passengers cross the ocean by air than by sea.

January 14–20, 1958
Qantas has its first scheduled round-the-world route using Super Constellations.

January 31, 1958
Explorer I, the first U.S. artificial satellite, is launched from Cape

Canaveral. It confirms the existence of the earth's "Van Allen" radiation belts.

February 7, 1958
The Advanced Research Projects Agency (ARPA) is established, with Neil McElroy appointed as director.

February 10, 1958
The first successful radar returns from Venus.

February 28, 1958
A Douglas Thor/Lockheed Agena launch vehicle orbits *Discoverer 1*, the first photo-reconnaissance satellite.

March 17, 1958
Vanguard 1 satellite is put into orbit.

March 26, 1958
Explorer III satellite is put into orbit.

May 7, 1958
Major Howard Johnson establishes an altitude record of 91,249 feet in a Lockheed F-104.

May 15, 1958
The U.S. Air Force orders three 707-120s to transport the President and other high-ranking officials.

May 16, 1958
▶ The F-104 Starfighter sets the world's air-speed record at 1,404 miles per hour.

May 27, 1958
The McDonnell F-4 Phantom II prototype makes its first flight.

May 30, 1958
The Douglas DC-8 jet transport makes its first flight.

August 15, 1958
The Federal Aviation Agency is created.

August 15, 1958
The first 707-120 is delivered to Pan Am. Transatlantic jet services will start in October.

August 23, 1958
President Dwight Eisenhower signs the Federal Aviation Act of 1958 and revises all previous civil air law.

October 1, 1958
NASA, the National Aeronautics and Space Agency, is formed from the National Advisory Council on Aeronautics.

October 4, 1958
BOAC inaugurates transatlantic service with Comet IVs.

October 15, 1958
Three North American X-15s are rolled out.

the DC-9), but both the DC-9 and the 727 had sold several hundred copies by late 1966.

There were many reasons Boeing and Douglas led the market. One of the most important was that Boeing, Douglas, and Pratt & Whitney had developed enormous jet production capabilities on Pentagon money in the early 1950s. Even if BAC or Sud-Est Aviation had sold 1,000 airplanes, they would have had no place to make them.

The U.S. companies also proved adept at "stretching" their airplanes. The best-selling versions of the DC-9 and 727 were developments such as the DC-9-30 and 727-200, with more power and more seats. They cost slightly more to operate but could carry 20 to 30 more passengers. For the airline, the extra load was almost pure profit.

Above: The jet age caught the venerable Douglas company at a time of management and financial difficulties, and the only really successful airliner they made, beside the DC-8, was the smaller DC-9.

Right: After the debacle of the de Havilland Comet airliner, Great Britain's aerospace industry needed a shot of confidence. This was provided by the BAC One-Eleven, which featured a sleek wing and rear-mounted engines and was well liked by airlines. When production had finished in Great Britain, the production line was moved to Romania, where more One-Elevens were built.

October 26, 1958
Pan Am begins transatlantic service with 707s.

November 1, 1958
Elwood Quesada becomes the first FAA administrator.

November 17, 1958
Project Mercury is given its official name by NASA.

December 19, 1958
President Eisenhower broadcasts a message from Project SCORE satellite.

January 1, 1959
◄ USAF activates its first and only wing to use the Northrop SM-62 Snark intercontinental cruise missile.

January 2, 1959
Soviets launch *Lunik 1 (Luna 1),* which misses the moon by 3,100 miles and goes into orbit around the sun.

January 12, 1959
McDonnell Aircraft wins the contract to build the Mercury, the first U.S. crewed spacecraft.

January 25, 1959
American Airlines starts 707 service from New York to Los Angeles.

January 27, 1959
Convair 880 makes its first flight.

April 2, 1959
► The "Mercury Seven" astronauts are named.

April 13, 1959
The *Discoverer II* satellite is placed in polar orbit.

May 1, 1959
The Goddard Space Flight Center is dedicated.

AIRPORTS ENTER THE URBAN LANDSCAPE

Airports are never beautiful; they are too sprawling by nature. They did, however, acquire a certain international flavor of their own in the '60s. Some, like Los Angeles (LAX), with its UFO-like Theme Building (pictured right), were showplaces.

LAX led many trends in airport design. In the first airports, including the old mission-style Los Angeles building, passengers walked from the terminal to the airplane. As airports grew, or in places where weather was less pleasant, passengers rode buses to the airplane and boarded through mobile stairways.

At the new LAX, the airplane came to the passengers. Long piers were arranged so that airplanes could taxi to them under their own power and leave with a short push from a tug. Telescoping, movable jetways reached out like fingers to touch the airplane's door. It looked like a gimmick in the early 1960s—but it was a design that proved efficient for large, small, and growing airports and was copied worldwide.

Transportation Enters a New Era

Jets had a massive impact on transportation. They were designed for speed and comfort, but their size and speed also made them more productive. Compared to a Constellation, a 707 could carry twice as many passengers in a year. Air traffic growth was explosive. Between 1955 and 1972, the number of U.S. air travelers increased fivefold.

In the 1950s, most of the people who crossed the Atlantic had traveled on 2,000-passenger ocean liners like the *Queen Mary, Queen Elizabeth,* and *United States.* In 1967 and 1968, ten years after jets went into service on the Atlantic, the *Queen Mary* and *Queen Elizabeth* made their last scheduled crossings.

Even in the 1950s, the passenger train was still a common option for long-distance transport in the United States, and prestige trains such as the *Twentieth-Century Limited,* the *Empire Builder,* and the *City of Los Angeles* still ran daily, using modern "streamliner" locomotives and cars. In October 1970, Congress passed the act that created Amtrak, a government-funded company to salvage what was left of the train service. The trains, too, had been deposed.

On the other hand, for the airline industry, it was only the beginning. The future looked bright.

The Aerospatiale (originally Sud Est) Caravelle was the first French commercial passenger jet, and it was highly successful. It introduced the aft-mounted engines and became the first foreign jet bought by an American airline. Some 280 were built.

May 28, 1959
Able and Baker, two monkeys, are launched in the Jupiter nose cone; both will recover.

May 30, 1959
The Douglas DC-8 makes its first flight.

June 3, 1959
The FAA uses a computer for air traffic control for the first time.

June 4, 1959
Max Conrad sets a light-aircraft distance record of 7,688 miles in a Piper Comanche.

June 8, 1959
Scott Crossfield makes the first glide flight in an X-15.

June 10, 1959
The French MS-880 Rallye makes its first flight.

July 14, 1959
The Sukhoi T-431 sets the world altitude record of 94,659 feet.

August 7, 1959
The *Explorer IV* is placed in orbit.

September 12, 1959
The *Lunik II* impacts the moon. It's the first manufactured object to do so.

September 17, 1959
The North American X-15 rocket-

powered hypersonic research airplane makes its first flight.

September 18, 1959
The DC-8 enters service with United and Delta.

October 4, 1959
The *Lunik III* circumnavigates the moon and beams back television photos of its far side.

CHAPTER SIX

Aviation Experiences Some Turbulence

THE WORLD OF SUPERSONIC SPEED AND COMMERCIAL PRESSURE OPENS UP A CONFUSING TIME FOR AN AVIATION INDUSTRY TRYING TO FIND AN IDENTITY IN A NEW ECONOMY.

Playwright Marc Camoletti's farce *Boeing Boeing* opened at the Apollo Theatre in London in 1960. Bernard, the central character, somehow manages to become engaged to three air hostesses at the same time. His scheme works thanks to the Lockheed Constellation's leisurely cruising speed, which ensures that no two of his fiancées are in town at the same time. When the three women transfer to jets, however, Bernard's romantic liaisons become decidedly more difficult and confusing. Airline planners of the time could sympathize with how technology threw a confusing wrench into Bernard's life. Their professional lives were in turmoil.

Right: The Boeing 747 was a tremendous gamble by Juan Trippe of Pan American and Bill Allen of Boeing. Early problems with engines almost ended the program in disaster, but the plane soon caught on, becoming the most influential transport of the jet age.

With jets, rapid traffic growth, and elusive profits, nobody could see where the aviation industry would be in another ten years. One trend, though, had remained constant since the beginning of flight: the quest for increased speed. Consequently, most aviation workers agreed that a supersonic transport (SST) would be developed at some point, but no one was sure when or how.

The Quest for Supersonic Speed

North American Aviation was working on the Mach 3, 2,000 mile-per-hour XB-70 Valkyrie bomber, but the project had been cut back to pure research. Lockheed's Skunk Works was building a Mach 3 airplane, but very few people knew about it. The CIA had awarded Lockheed a contract to build the A-12 Blackbird spyplane in 1959, but its existence would remain secret until early 1964.

In 1961, British Aircraft Corporation (BAC) produced a design for a slender, delta-winged airplane with four jet engines that was capable of hauling 100 passengers across the Atlantic. At

the Paris air show in June 1961, Sud-Aviation showed a model of a similar airplane, the Super Caravelle.

But the technical challenges for supersonic speeds were still forbidding. A U.S. Air Force General Dynamics B-58 supersonic bomber shattered the transatlantic speed record on its way to the same show—and crashed days later in front of the crowd, killing its crew.

In November 1962, Britain and France signed a treaty under which the two countries agreed that they would cooperate to build a government-funded SST, named Concorde. It was clear that Boeing and Douglas were going to scoop the market for large subsonic jets. By starting early with an SST, Britain and France were hopeful that they could win the next round. In June 1963, Pan Am took options on three Concordes. Other airlines quickly followed.

The Kennedy administration, backed by Congress, decided to launch its own SST program. NASA and the Pentagon had expe-

The North American XB-70 was designed as a Mach 3 bomber to penetrate the defenses of the Soviet Union. However, it arrived on the scene at about the same time as effective Soviet surface-to-air missiles and was canceled.

NASA 20001   U.S. AIR FORCE

November 16, 1959
Captain Joe Kittinger bails out from 76,400 feet.

February 15, 1960
Cessna acquires 49 percent of Max Holste Aircraft so it can build Cessna aircraft in France.

April 1, 1960
The first weather satellite, *Tiros I*, is launched.

April 9, 1960
A Tupelov Tu-114 turboprop airliner sets a speed record of 540 miles per hour for propeller-driven planes.

April 13, 1960
The first experimental navigation satellite, *Transit 1B*, is launched.

May 1, 1960
Captain Francis Gary Powers is shot down in a U-2 over the USSR.

May 2, 1960
The first infrared surveillance satellite, *Midas 2*, is launched.

July 1960
The Sikorsky S-62 is used to service offshore oil rigs.

July 28, 1960
Boeing 707s evacuate Europeans from Belgian Congo.

July 29, 1960
Project Apollo is announced by NASA.

August 10, 1960
Discoverer XIII is launched into polar orbit.

August 12, 1960
USAF Major Robert White pilots an X-15 to 136,500 feet.

August 12, 1960
The first passive communications

satellite, a radio-reflective sphere called *Echo 1*, is launched.

August 19, 1960
The capsule from a KH-1-type Corona 13 reconnaissance satellite (publicly called *Discoverer XIV*) is recovered in midair by a C-119.

August 19–20, 1960
The USSR *Spacecraft II* launches with two dogs inside; both survive.

rience with managing major aerospace projects, but the administration directed the Federal Aviation Administration (FAA) to run the SST.

The FAA chose Boeing, which had never built a supersonic crewed airplane, to build the SST, rather than more experienced competitors North American and Lockheed. Boeing's design was radical. It had variable-sweep swing-wings that folded back into a low-drag position for cruising flight, measured 306 feet from nose to tail, and would fly at almost 1,800 miles per hour.

Meanwhile, the Soviet Union announced plans to build the Concorde-size Tupolev Tu-144. It was the first SST to fly, on the last day of 1968. The first Concorde flew in March 1969. Neither prototype could carry a payload across the Atlantic: Larger and heavier airplanes would be needed for airline use. The Boeing 2707 design was doing even more poorly; in December 1968, the swing-wing was abandoned in favor of a delta.

Airlines Look for Solutions

But by 1968, the development of the airliner had headed in a completely different direction. As air traffic grew, jet noise made neighborhoods around airports uninhabitable. Old air-traffic-control systems were overwhelmed, and controllers were forced to "stack" incoming flights, directing airplanes to fly in circles until cleared to land.

France desperately wanted to get back into the competition for airliners, and it succeeded admirably with the Aerospatiale Caravelle, which featured—for the first time—aft-mounted engines. The Super Caravelle was a considerably refined version of the original aircraft.

September 20, 1960
Jerrie Cobb sets an altitude record of 36,932 feet in an Aero Commander.

November 1960
▶ The first orders for the 727 are placed.

November 16, 1960
The Canadair CL-44 civil/military freighter makes its first flight.

December 1, 1960
Spacecraft III, a five-ton craft carrying a biological payload, is launched by the USSR.

December 13, 1960
USN Commander Leroy Heath sets a 91,450-foot altitude record in a North American A3-J Vigilante.

December 21, 1960
NASA selects its first "standardized" satellite design.

December 22, 1960
The nuclear submarine *Robert E. Lee* fires a Polaris IRBM.

December 31, 1960
To date, the United States has launched 31 Earth satellites and two deep-space probes; the USSR has launched seven satellites, one deep-space probe, and two lunar missions.

Convair developed a line of delta-wing aircraft, including the XF-92, Sea Dart, F-102, and F-106. None were as beautiful or as capable as its Mach 2 bomber, the B-58 Hustler. The Hustler was unusual because it carried its stores in a streamlined container that could be dropped.

the engine. These engines would be quiet and efficient and could deliver up to 40,000 pounds of thrust.

When Lockheed was selected to build the C-5A cargo plane in September 1965, Boeing and Douglas started to look at new commercial projects. Douglas had committed to a stretched version of the DC-8, with up to 250 seats. Boeing started talking to customers about a jet with four engines like those of the C-5, and more than twice the size of a 707.

With orders from Pan Am, Boeing launched the 747 in April 1966. A vast new factory was built in Everett, Washington, just north of Seattle. The 747 was more advanced than the 707, with quadruple rather than triple hydraulic systems, a new lift-boosting flap design, and a higher cruise speed. The airplane entered service on schedule in early 1970, but at a huge cost.

The 747 was followed by two smaller, nearly identical "wide-body" aircraft. In late 1966, Douglas's hopes of building a rival to the 747 had been dashed by financial problems. The company was building DC-9s as fast as it could, but production had been

The Soviet Union was anxious to beat the West to the supersonic transport and did so with the handsome Tu-144. Unfortunately, the rush to production combined with relatively inefficient engines would take the Tu-144 out of service soon after its debut.

Opposite: The supersonic Concorde was the result of an agreement between France and Great Britain. Development costs were much higher than anticipated and only 16 Concordes were purchased for passenger service. They became the true luxury liners of the air age, with seat prices twice that of a conventional first-class ticket.

What the airlines needed were larger, quieter airplanes, not faster ones. In the early 1960s, Boeing, Douglas, and Lockheed competed to build a huge military transport that could move heavy equipment from the United States to Europe. This plane would need four very powerful engines, and the USAF issued research contracts to General Electric and Pratt & Whitney for prototypes of a high-bypass-ratio turbofan: a jet engine fitted with a large, many-bladed fan on the front, driven by a turbine at the rear of

January 31, 1961
The chimpanzee "Ham" is recovered after suborbital flight in a Mercury capsule.

February 12, 1961
The Russian *Sputnik VIII* satellite releases a probe toward Venus.

February 28, 1961
The Cessna Skymaster makes its first flight.

April 12, 1961
▶ Yuri Gagarin becomes the first person in space and makes one Earth orbit in *Vostok 1*.

April 30, 1961
Eastern Airlines opens shuttle services between New York and Boston and New York and Washington. A one-way fare to Washington is $14 ($80 today).

May 1961
Sud-Aviation unveils the model of a supersonic Super Caravelle.

May 2, 1961
The Pilatus Turbo Porter plane makes its first flight.

May 5, 1961
Alan Shepard makes the first U.S. suborbital flight in the *Freedom 7* Mercury spacecraft.

May 25, 1961
President John F. Kennedy commits the United States to placing a man on the moon and returning him safely to Earth before 1970.

May 26, 1961
A Convair B-58 bomber flies from New York to Paris in 3 hours and 19 minutes. Days later, the crew is killed in an air show accident.

June 21, 1961
Freddie Laker unveils the Carvair DC-4, modified for car-ferry use.

July 1961
The Kamov Ka-25K helicopter is revealed at the Tushino air display.

July 1, 1961
The FAA begins an extensive reorganization.

July 21, 1961
Virgil "Gus" Grissom makes a suborbital flight in the Mercury *Liberty Bell 7.*

August 6–7, 1961
Major Gherman Titov makes 17 Earth orbits.

November 22, 1961
The F-4 Phantom raises the world airspeed record to 1,606 miles per hour.

December 5, 1961
The F-4 Phantom sets a sustained altitude record at 66,443 feet.

1962
Sikorsky S-61 is the first helicopter to exceed 200 miles per hour.

January 1962
Enstrom introduces the F-28 three-seat helicopter.

January 8, 1962
William Piper, called "the Henry Ford of aviation," dies at age 80.

January 10–11, 1962
A Boeing B-52H sets a nonstop distance record of 12,532 miles.

February 20, 1962
▶ John Glenn makes the first U.S. orbital flight of Earth in *Friendship 7,* completing three orbits.

PAN AM'S EFFECT ON THE 747

After looking briefly at a dual-deck design for the new Model **747,** Boeing settled on an airplane with an oval body and a single wide passenger deck, seating nine passengers abreast with two aisles. The space beneath the floor would be used for cargo stored in specially shaped containers.

At the insistence of Pan Am, which was the prime target customer, the main deck was made eight feet high to be able to accommodate two standard shipping containers next to each other. Pan Am chairman Juan Trippe believed that the new giant would be used to haul cargo after passenger traffic moved on to supersonic transport.

The 747's upper deck is there because Trippe demanded a cargo door in the nose, with the flight

deck above it. On the original design, a dome covered the cockpit, but the Boeing designers extended it into a hump to reduce the drag. Pan Am executives, doubtless with warm memories of the parties in the Stratocruiser's basement bar, suggested converting the area into a lounge for first-class passengers. In the post-1973 financial crisis, however, most airlines converted the upper deck into a passenger cabin; Boeing later stretched the upper deck to seat as many as 69 passengers.

accelerated so quickly that it was inefficient, and the company was losing money. McDonnell Aircraft of St. Louis rescued Douglas, acquiring the company in April 1967. Lockheed, meanwhile, had been eliminated from the SST contest and was doing well working on defense contracts.

Major U.S. airlines were looking for a wide-body aircraft for transcontinental flights. United's requirement to reach both coasts from mile-high Denver forced designers to use three engines. In early 1968, American and United ordered the McDonnell Douglas DC-10 with General Electric engines. TWA, Eastern, and Delta bought the Lockheed L-1011 TriStar with Rolls-Royce engines. The 250-seat jets were indistinguishable in performance and had wingspans that were identical to the inch.

The stage was set for a series of cataclysmic years in the airliner business.

The Aviation Industry Goes Off Course

The 747 arrived just as the airline industry headed into a recession. The big Boeing was too large for many routes. Airlines placed virtually no orders in 1970 and 1971 and delayed their already-ordered deliveries. In May 1971, the U.S. government canceled the SST program. Boeing was forced to lay off workers in the tens of thousands. A billboard above a highway heading out of town read: "Would the last one out of Seattle please turn out the lights?" Boeing survived by slashing costs and by selling improved versions of the 727 and 737.

Because the DC-10 and L-1011 were identical, McDonnell Douglas and Lockheed competed on price and made very little money. Rolls-Royce relied on newly invented carbon-fiber material for the L-1011 engine, but the fan blades broke up when rain and hail hit them. The cost of the redesign drove Rolls-Royce into bankruptcy. The British government rescued the company, but the engine's delivery was delayed. Losing money on the C-5 and

April 4, 1962

▶ An F-4 sets a series of time-to-climb records. At this point, the F-4 is the first airplane in history to simultaneously hold the world records for speed at high and low altitude, sustained altitude, and climbing speed.

April 26, 1962
The Lockheed A-12, the first of the Blackbird Mach 3 family, makes its first flight.

May 2, 1962
The Pentagon and CIA agree to form a National Reconnaissance Office to manage the spy satellite program.

May 24, 1962
Scott Carpenter makes a three-orbit flight in *Aurora 7.*

June 22, 1962
The last B-52 bomber is delivered.

July 10, 1962
Telstar 1, the first privately financed communications satellite, is launched.

August 11–15, 1962
Major Andrian G. Nikolayev, in *Vostok 3,* completes 64 revolutions and communicates via television with Earth, a space first.

August 12–15, 1962
Lieutenant Colonel Pavel R. Popovich

The Lockheed C-5A was born in a furious controversy over costs and performance and was badly maligned in the press and in Congress. Over the years, however, the C-5 proved to be an outstanding aircraft. It turned out to be a marvelous bargain for the taxpayer.

other projects, Lockheed had to seek out U.S. government aid in order to stay afloat.

The DC-10 fared better than the L-1011, because McDonnell Douglas developed a longer-range version for European airlines, which used it as a smaller alternative to the 747. But the parent

A MATERIAL FOR THE SPACE AGE

After its bad start on the Lockheed L-1011's engine, **carbon-fiber composite** material became very important in aviation. Developed in Britain in the 1960s, the material is made up of very strong fibers of pure carbon embedded in a tough epoxy-resin "matrix." It is stronger than steel, lighter than aluminum, and very stiff, which makes it particularly useful for wing and tail surfaces. It is, however, quite expensive to produce.

company saw commercial airplanes as money pits and would never again authorize the development of a new airliner.

Things were tough all over. Concorde was also in trouble. The complex engine inlets required a great deal of development before the plane could reach its design range. Concorde could not make money unless passengers paid fares higher than first-class levels. In 1973, Pan Am and other airlines canceled their Concorde options. Reinhardt Abraham, Lufthansa's technical director, said he wouldn't fly the airplane if St. Nicholas left one under his tree. The plane entered service in 1976, but British Airways and Air France, the builders' state-owned airlines, were its only operators.

In June 1973, a new and larger version of the Tu-144 appeared at the Paris air show. During a flying display on the last day of the show, it broke up in midair, killing its crew and several people on the ground. The project was abandoned by 1977.

in *Vostok 4* completes 48 revolutions and passes within four miles of *Vostok 3.*

August 13, 1962
The de Havilland D.H.125, an executive jet transport, flies for the first time.

September 19, 1962
The "Pregnant Guppy" conversion of the Boeing 377 makes its first flight. It

will start a trend toward carrying outsize cargo by specially modified aircraft.

October 3, 1962
Wally Schirra, in *Sigma 7*, completes six Earth revolutions.

October 29, 1962
The DC-8F Jet Trader, the first jet all-cargo transport, makes its first flight.

November 1, 1962
The Soviets launch the *Mars 1* probe spacecraft. Communication is lost a few months later, on March 21, 1963.

November 17, 1962
Dulles International Airport opens.

November 29, 1962
Britain and France sign a treaty to develop a supersonic transport (SST).

December 1962
The U.S. *Mariner 2*, the first successful probe to flyby Venus, samples the planet's atmosphere.

1963
The French Aerospatiale Alouette is the first commercial turbine-powered helicopter to operate in the United States.

1963
The Lear Jet, Aero Commander Jet

Commander, and Mitsubishi MU-2 turboprop all make their first flights.

1963
Marlon Green is the first African American hired by a major U.S. passenger airline, Continental. (Earlier African American airline pilots included August Martin and Perry Young, who flew cargo and the helicopter, respectively.)

January 13, 1963
French president Charles de Gaulle refers to the Anglo-French SST as "Concorde."

January 17, 1963
The Short Skyvan turboprop debuts.

February 9, 1963
The Boeing 727-200 debuts.

May 4, 1963
The Dassault Mystere 20 debuts.

May 15, 1963
Gordon Cooper, in *Faith 7*, completes 22 Earth orbits.

June 3, 1963
Pan Am options three Concordes.

June 5, 1963
President John F. Kennedy declares the United States will back the development of an SST.

June 16–19, 1963
Soviet Valentina Tereshkova becomes the first woman in space; she achieves 48 Earth orbits in *Vostok 6*.

August 20, 1963
▶ The British Aircraft BAC 111 twin-jet transport makes its first flight.

August 22, 1963
The North American X-15 rocket airplane reaches an altitude of

War broke out in the Middle East in October 1973. The Arab-dominated oil-exporting nations imposed an embargo on oil and boosted their prices. Environmental prophets of doom said it was only the beginning: Fuel prices would only increase as the world ran out of oil.

The Industry's Silver Linings

Despite the gloom of the early 1970s, one sector of the airline business was alive and kicking. As major airlines dumped their old propeller airplanes in the 1960s, many of them were bought by charter airlines. In the United States, they were used for charter flights for the armed forces; in Europe, they carried vacationers from cold, wet England and Scandinavia to cheap, sunny beaches in Spain.

Despite pressure from the International Air Transport Authority (IATA), charter airlines were allowed to sell seats alone, without holiday packages, starting in 1975. The IATA airlines responded with their own low fares. But two swashbuckling charter operators—World Airways' chief Ed Daly and Britain's

354,200 feet, with a speed of 4,159 miles per hour.

December 6, 1963
The Piper Cherokee makes its first flight.

December 10, 1963
The Dyna-Soar reusable spaceplane project is canceled.

December 24, 1963
The Boeing 727-100 is certificated in the United States.

January 20, 1964
The turboprop Beech King Air makes its first flight.

March–April, 1964
Jerri Mock, in a Cessna 180, becomes the first woman to fly solo around the world.

April 1964
Boeing and Lockheed are selected to continue the design for the U.S. SST.

April 6, 1964
British abandon the TSR-2 aircraft program.

May 7, 1964
The Vickers Super VC10 makes its first flight.

May 12, 1964
Joan Merriam completes the second round-the-world flight by a female pilot.

May 17, 1964
◀ British aviation pioneer John Moore, Lord Brabazon of Tara, dies.

July 28, 1964
The *Ranger 7* takes photos of the moon and impacts the lunar surface.

July 31, 1964
A. H. Parker establishes a sailplane long-distance record of 647 miles.

Right: Lockheed wanted to re-enter the passenger market and decided to do so with the wide-body L-1011 TriStar. Unfortunately, the market was not big enough for both the L-1011 and the DC-10, and the TriStar lost huge sums of money for Lockheed.

Below: The Grumman Gulfstream was a complete departure for the company, which had specialized in naval military aircraft. It proved to be a winner, starting a long line of successful executive aircraft.

Freddie Laker—wanted to go further. Both had bought cheap DC-10s in the early 1970s and planned to offer scheduled flights at low fares. Daly applied to operate transcontinental flights, and Laker wanted to fly across the Atlantic. There would be no frills and no reservations. Passengers would wait in line until seats were available.

The fight for low fares won the support of U.S. President Jimmy Carter, who was elected in 1976. Carter set about changing the airline industry. He dismantled the Civil Aeronautics Board. If your company could meet safety standards, you could start an airline and fly anywhere you wanted. Carter's transportation secretary, William Coleman, pushed other countries to open up international routes to competition. "Deregulation" would dramatically change the face of the airline industry.

September 21, 1964
The North American XB-70 Valkyrie, an experimental supersonic bomber, makes its first flight.

October 12, 1964
The *Voskhod I*, the world's first spacecraft to carry more than one person, is launched. Onboard were pilot Colonel Vladimir Komarov, scientist Konstantin Feoktistov, and physician Boris Yegorov.

November 28, 1964
NASA launches the *Mariner 4* spacecraft for a Mars flyby mission.

December 21, 1964
The Lockheed SR-71 debuts. It will be the fastest and highest-flying airplane of the 20th century.

December 21, 1964
▶ The General Dynamics F-111A, a low-altitude supersonic bomber, makes its first flight.

1965
Production on the Bell AH-1G HueyCobra begins.

1965
Female helicopter pilot Gay Maher flies solo coast to coast in a Hughes 300.

1965
Approximately 2,053 helicopters now operate in North America.

A TRAILBLAZER FOR CHEAP TRAVEL

Sir Freddie Laker was one of the pioneers of cheap air travel. A native of East London, Laker built up his aviation business by carrying cargo on surplus RAF bombers. In the 1950s, he sold airplanes and ran a maintenance and modification company. He started Laker Airways, a charter airline, in 1966.

Banned from selling tickets directly to the public, the charter airlines carried package tours, student groups, and other associations, including entirely bogus "affinity groups" that were formed to take advantage of cheap travel opportunities.

In 1974, Laker proposed to use DC-10s to operate a cheap, no-reservations service from London to Los Angeles. The British government turned him down, and Laker engaged in a bitter struggle in the courts and in the press. The Skytrain service was finally approved in 1977, but an overextended Laker Airways went bankrupt in 1982.

Below: North American used the Sabre name and the Sabre look to enhance sales of its pioneering Sabreliner, which was used by the military and by civilian firms.

On the other side of the spectrum was the new business of posh corporate jets. For the users of these crafts, the 1960s and 1970s were the start of a new era of luxury air travel aboard private jets.

Large corporate airplanes were a rarity in the 1950s. Beech continued to build the slow and elderly Model 18, and Cessna produced the faster, smaller 310. Companies that wanted fast and roomy transportation bought World War II bombers such as Lockheed PV-2 Harpoons or Douglas B-26s, which companies like Howard and On Mark modified into transports. In the early 1960s, though, the availability of small jet engines coincided with a slump in fighter deliveries, and several fighter manufacturers decided to build corporate jets.

Lockheed built the big, four-engine JetStar. North American produced the Sabreliner and sold large numbers to the USAF as trainers and light transports. Navy manufacturer Grumman built a big, turboprop corporate transport called the Gulfstream—followed in 1966 by the jet-powered Gulfstream 2—while Britain's de Havilland designed the D.H.125. Developments of the Gulfstream and the D.H.125 were still being built in 2002.

February 25, 1965
The DC-9, the first U.S. twin-jet airliner, makes its first flight.

March 18–19, 1965
Colonel Pavel Belyayev and Lieutenant Colonel Aleksey Leonov do 17 Earth orbits in *Voskhod 2*; Leonov makes the first "walk in space."

March 23, 1965
The two-person *Gemini 3* spacecraft makes its first flight. Virgil "Gus"

Grissom and John Young make three orbits in the first flight mission that moves from one orbit to another.

April 6, 1965
The first commercial communications satellite *Early Bird* is launched into a 22,300-mile synchronous orbit.

May 2, 1965
Geoffrey de Havilland, designer of many general aviation aircraft, dies.

June 3–7, 1965
James A. McDivitt and Edward White in *Gemini 4* do 62 orbits; White is the first American to walk in space.

June 16, 1965
The Antonov AN-22 Antheus, the world's largest turboprop transport, goes on display in Paris.

July 8, 1965
Stunt pilot Paul Mantz, who in 1930 set a record of 46 consecutive

outside loops, dies during filming of *Flight of the Phoenix*.

July 17, 1965
Pan Am service between New York and Prague is the first air service to the Communist bloc in 16 years.

July 17, 1965
Navy F-4s shoot down two North Vietnamese MiG-17s, the first kills in that aircraft.

July 24, 1965
A USAF F-4C becomes the first fighter to be shot down by a SAM, over North Vietnam.

September 7, 1965
The Bell 209, a prototype of the Huey-Cobra and the ancestor of all attack helicopters, makes its first flight.

November 14–17, 1965
A Boeing 707 makes the first circuit of the globe via the North and South

MAKING A BUSINESS OF CORPORATE JETS

Bill Lear was America's leading pioneer of the business jet. In the 1950s, the brilliant and tempestuous Lear made a business out of converting World War II Lockheed bombers into executive transports. He also founded a successful electronics company.

Looking for a new financial opportunity, Lear saw the business potential in the P-16, a short-take-off, 600-mile-per-hour attack fighter that had been developed in Switzerland. The fighter was canceled, but Lear obtained the rights to use its wing design in a small, sleek, fast, and relatively inexpensive business jet. The Lear Jet 23 became an instant best-seller. Lear sold his interest in the company in 1967 and went on to develop a steam-powered car and bus as well as other executive airplanes.

His last project was the Lear Fan 2100, the world's first airplane to be made entirely of carbon-fiber composite material. It was flown after Lear's death, but the Lear Fan company ran out of money before completing development.

The Lear Jet came to symbolize the executive jet aircraft to the lay public because it was associated with so many celebrities. Bill Lear brought the aircraft into being, one of his last and most important projects.

One of the most spectacular successes, however, was that of Dassault in France. This company designed a clean, sophisticated business jet and named it the Mystere 20 after their first swept-wing fighter.

Once again, it was the farsighted Pan Am Airline's Juan Trippe who saw potential in this class of airplane. Trippe intended to start up a subsidiary to sell business jet planes as well as provide training and maintenance on them, but first he needed an airplane to sell. Charles Lindbergh recommended the Dassault design. The only thing that changed was the name. Trippe guessed that American travelers would be reluctant to fly on something whose name meant "mystery" or "miracle." The airplane became the Fan Jet Falcon, and with Trippe's help, the aircraft started a dynasty.

By the mid-1970s, however, Trippe's airline was in trouble, losing money and desperately seeking government help to stay airborne. Pan Am was one of many historic names that would disappear over the next few years.

---

poles, covering a distance of 26,230 miles in 62 hours and 28 minutes.

December 6, 1965
France launches the FR-1 satellite.

December 8, 1965
The DC-9 enters service with Delta Air Lines.

January 31, 1966
Luna 9 is launched to the moon. It is the first vehicle to land on another celestial object.

March 16, 1966
Gemini VIII achieves the first space docking.

March 17, 1966
The Bell X-22A V/STOL tilt-wing makes its first flight.

April 13, 1966
Boeing announces the 747 project.

May 17, 1966
The FAA gives the Lear Jet 24 a Type Certificate.

May 26, 1966
A Lear Jet 24 completes a round-the-world flight, the first by a business jet.

August 1, 1966
The Twin Otter joins the Canadian forest service.

August 31, 1966
The Hawker Harrier makes its first hovering flight.

September 11, 1966
Tracy Barnes flies a hot-air balloon across the United States.

October 15, 1966
The Department of Transportation Act is signed.

October 20, 1966
The FAA certificates the Bell JetRanger helicopter.

October 26, 1966
The first Intelsat 2 series communications satellite is launched. The worldwide link will be completed in 1967.

December 31, 1966
Boeing is selected to design the SST.

One of France's leading pre-war firms was Marcel Bloch, which made fighters for the French Air Force. After the war, Bloch changed his name to Dassault and founded an aircraft company that has been preeminent in every field it has entered. The Dassault Falcon series of executive aircraft is prized around the world.

1967
The Sikorsky S-61 flies nonstop across the Atlantic.

January 27, 1967
▶ *Apollo 1* astronauts Virgil "Gus" Grissom, Ed White, and Roger Chaffee die in a fire during a preflight test.

February 16, 1967
The lightweight, general-purpose

helicopter Boelkow Bo.105 V-2 makes its first flight.

April 9, 1967
The Boeing 737, now the world's best-selling jetliner, makes its first flight.

April 24, 1967
Colonel Vladimir Komarov, in *Soyuz 1*, is killed on return from orbit; he is the first person to die in a space mission.

April 28, 1967
McDonnell Douglas forms by a merger of McDonnell and Douglas.

May 31–June 1, 1967
Two Sikorsky HH-3Es make the first nonstop helicopter transatlantic crossing to go to the Paris air show.

June 5, 1967
The Israeli Air Force destroys adversary forces in a surprise attack.

July 7, 1967
A Pan Am 707 makes the world's first fully automatic approach and landing by a jet transport with passengers onboard.

October 3, 1967
Major William J. Knight sets a world record of 4,534 miles per hour in a North American X-15.

CHAPTER SEVEN

Aviation Reaches for the Stars

WITH FLIGHT IN THE SKIES CONQUERED,

PEOPLE LOOK TOWARD THE HEAVENS AS THE

NEXT FRONTIER FOR AVIATION.

July 3, 1969, almost two weeks before *Apollo 11:* A giant rocket, as tall as a large high-rise building, waits on its launch-pad. Most of the rocket will be used only once and will then crash to the ground or burn up in the atmosphere once the fuel that fills its thin-walled tanks is used up. The countdown continues until...ignition!

 Flames shoot from the rocket engines in the first stage. The rocket rises as expected—but then, it falters, hesitating. Every engineer watching knows what is about to happen but is helpless to prevent it. The rocket collapses, topples, and burns up in a cloud of flame. And with it, Soviet dreams of putting a cosmonaut on the moon go up in smoke.

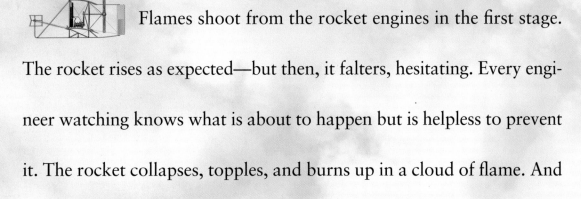

Right: The launch of the first Space Shuttle is one of the most dramatic events in history. There were hours of tension before the launch and then the terrible anxiety of the launch itself as the great rockets thundered and roared. Still today, the news that a shuttle has successfully reached orbit is always greeted by cheers.

It would be years before most people knew that the disaster had happened. In fact, there wasn't even supposed to be a Soviet attempt to put a cosmonaut on the lunar surface. Officially speaking, the program didn't exist. Unofficially and in deep secret, however, the Soviets were working furiously to put a person on the moon. The disastrous launch in July was the N-1 Moon Rocket's fourth and last failure. Two weeks later, American Neil Armstrong walked on the moon.

Much like the Schneider Trophy races during aviation's infancy, the space race was a contest that put national prestige on the line. To the victor went the bragging rights. In this case, the United States got the bragging rights. It certainly hadn't always had that luxury, though.

The Space Race Begins

When one of Sergei Korolev's R-7 rockets launched the *Sputnik* satellite on October 4, 1957, it caused near-panic in the United States. In the recriminations that followed the launch, it was easy to point out that there were three independent rocket programs

underway in the United States—the USAF, working on the Atlas and Titan ICBM projects; the Army's Jupiter; and the Navy's Vanguard—while Russia had only one. In the summer of 1958, the U.S. government transformed the National Advisory Committee for Aeronautics (NACA) into the National Aeronautics and Space Administration (NASA). It was a step of enormous importance for the American space program.

A month later, Korolev's team launched the 1,200-pound satellite *Sputnik 2* with a dog named Laika as a passenger. In December, the Navy's first Vanguard rocket exploded on its launchpad. A team led by Wernher von Braun finally launched a U.S. satellite—the tiny 30-pound *Explorer I*—at the end of January, but the Vanguard continued to fail with monotonous regularity throughout 1958. In May, Russia launched the 3,000-pound *Sputnik 3*, which was large enough to carry a person.

NASA's first major project was Mercury, which was intended to put an American astronaut into space as soon as possible. The challenge was to develop an orbital vehicle that was small enough to be launched by the Atlas, which was considerably smaller than the Soviet R-7. McDonnell Aircraft was given the contract to develop the Mercury capsule. Its modified conical shape was developed by NASA.

But it was a Russian, Yuri Gagarin, who made the first human space flight in April 1961 in the *Vostok 1* spacecraft. A month later, U.S. astronaut Alan Shepard made the first crewed U.S. space flight, but he did not go into orbit. That milestone was passed in February 1962 with John Glenn's flight.

A month after Gagarin's flight, President John F. Kennedy made a momentous promise: Before the end of the decade, the United States would place an astronaut on the moon. The project, named Apollo, would be run by NASA, and it would be the driving force behind space technology in the United States during the '60s.

The Soviet Union literally rocked the world on October 4, 1957, when the *Sputnik* began its beeping orbit. The United States public was both outraged and ashamed to have been beaten to space by the "backward" Soviet Union.

October 23, 1967
The Canadair CL-215, a firefighter water bomber, makes its first flight.

November 6, 1967
Martin Marlin makes the last U.S. Navy seaplane flight.

December 11, 1967
The Concorde prototype is rolled out.

March 17, 1968
F-111s deploy to Vietnam.

May 5, 1968
A Grumman Gulfstream II lands at London, completing the first nonstop transatlantic flight by an executive jet.

June 30, 1968
The world's largest airplane, the Lockheed C-5A Galaxy, makes its first flight.

July 15, 1968
Aeroflot and Pan Am sign an accord

for twice-weekly service between New York and Moscow.

October 11–22, 1968
Wally Schirra, Donn Eisele, and Walter Cunningham in *Apollo 7*, the first crewed Apollo mission, make 163 orbits.

December 1968
Boeing abandons the swing-wing SST design.

December 21–27, 1968
Apollo 8, with Frank Borman, James Lovell, and William Anders, orbits the moon ten times.

December 31, 1968
The Soviet Tupolev Tu-144 SST makes its first flight, becoming the world's first SST to fly.

January 14–17, 1969
Colonel V. Shatalov in *Soyuz 4* joins

with *Soyuz 5* and achieves the first docking between two piloted spacecraft.

February 9, 1969
The Boeing 747 makes its first flight.

February 24, 1969
NASA launches *Mariner 6* for a Mars flyby.

March 2, 1969
The Concorde SST makes its first flight.

The 360-foot-tall Saturn V booster, using liquid-oxygen/kerosene rockets, was to launch the Apollo craft. At the top was the command module, which would accommodate the astronauts. This was attached to the service module, containing the life-support and power systems and the rocket that would boost the spacecraft to and from the moon. The lunar lander was carried underneath the spacecraft. Once in orbit, the lander and spacecraft would separate, the spacecraft would turn 180 degrees, and the lander and command module would dock top-to-top for the trip to the moon.

The Soviet moon project was similar, but it used an even larger launcher, the N-1, with more than 30 engines. The project was delayed due to infighting among the leading rocket designers, and it was August 1964—more than three years after Kennedy's

speech—before Khrushchev even signed to authorize the project. And still, the project remained top-secret.

Although Russia launched many probes to the moon in the '60s, culminating in the robotic *Lunokhod* explorer, they were never able to catch up with the Apollo program. The N-1 rocket failed on its first launch attempt in February 1969. Two more launches would fail before the last attempt was made in July of '69.

Apollo, meanwhile, was immune to criticism because of its political backing and its association with a martyred president—but its management was far from perfect. The cost was enormous. In January 1967, astronauts Virgil Grissom, Ed White, and Roger Chaffee died in a fire during a ground test of *Apollo 1*. After a painstaking investigation—which revealed the degree to which safety

Left: The Vanguard rocket provided dismay and excitement to Americans still stunned by the Russian *Sputnik*. On its first launch on December 6, 1957, the *Vanguard TV3* blew up on the pad. Later, however, Vanguard satellites were successfully launched.

Middle: The McDonnell Douglas Delta Rocket got off to an inauspicious start on May 13, 1960, with a failed launch. Since then, it has placed many invaluable satellites into orbit.

Right: The Atlas was the first U.S. intercontinental ballistic missile. No one would have predicted its long success as a space-vehicle launcher, a career that continues to this day.

March 19, 1969
U.S. Marine Corps announces plans to buy 12 British Harrier VTOL fighters.

April 1, 1969
The first vertical-takeoff jet aircraft, the Hawker Siddeley Harrier, enters service with the RAF.

July 20, 1969
▶ In the *Apollo 11* mission, Neil Armstrong and Buzz Aldrin land on the moon.

September 15, 1969
The Cessna Citation, the first of a new family of jets, debuts.

November 26, 1969
Beech delivers the last Model 18. The first flew January 15, 1937, making it the longest production run of any aircraft at the time.

December 23, 1969
McDonnell Douglas is chosen to build the F-15 air-superiority fighter.

1970
Pratt & Whitney Canada certificates the first helicopter engine.

January 21, 1970
Boeing 747 enters service with Pan Am.

February 11, 1970
Japan launches the *Ohsumi* and becomes the fourth nation to have launched an artificial satellite.

April 11–17, 1970
Apollo 13 becomes famous by near-disaster.

April 24, 1970
The People's Republic of China launches a satellite.

May 21, 1970
President Richard Nixon signs the Airport and Airway Development Act of 1970, a piece of vitally important legislation for the future.

Satellites Change the World

While Apollo filled the headlines, uncrewed space exploration was proving commercially useful and vital to national security. In July 1962, Bell Laboratories' Telstar satellite beamed live TV pictures from the United States to Europe. The Intelsat consortium was established in 1964 to provide worldwide commercial communications via satellite. Its first satellite, *Early Bird*, was developed by Hughes Aircraft Company and was launched into a geosynchronous orbit above the Atlantic in April 1965.

Live global television quickly became routine. The 1964 Tokyo Olympics was the first sporting event that could be viewed worldwide. Intelsat completed its worldwide broadcasting link in 1967 with a satellite over the Indian Ocean, and TV networks collaborated on a live special seen by 350 million viewers. Asked by the BBC to write a song that would be understood around the world, John Lennon penned "All You Need Is Love."

While pictures were being transmitted through space, they were also being taken from space—for reasons that had little to do with love. In 1960, the Pentagon formed the National Reconnaissance Office. The NRO's existence would remain secret for more than 30 years. It was formed to settle a rivalry between the CIA and the USAF over the control of reconnaissance satellites.

Left: When the space race began, there were literally dozens of competing rockets, many derived from the German V-2 program. The Jupiter C rockets were used to test ablative warheads, in support of future intercontinental ballistic missiles.

Right: Originally designed as the most powerful ICBM in the American arsenal, the Titan was put to a peacetime use of launching satellites and was hugely successful in the role.

had been sacrificed to schedule—the first flight of *Apollo 7* took place in October 1968. *Apollo 8* orbited the moon in December, and in March *Apollo 9* demonstrated the complicated maneuvers needed in Earth orbit. On *Apollo 10* in May, the lunar module separated from the command module and entered a low orbit around the moon.

On July 20, 1969, Kennedy's pledge was realized when Neil Armstrong of *Apollo 11* became the first person to walk on the moon. More successful flights followed; the last flight in the program—*Apollo 17*—was launched at the end of 1972.

By 1972, the NRO had launched 145 Corona satellites. Built by Lockheed and launched by Douglas Thor or Convair Atlas rockets, these satellites carried high-resolution film cameras. The exposed film was wound into small recovery vehicles that descended by parachute and were caught in flight by modified transport airplanes.

After Corona, the NRO continued to produce larger and more sophisticated satellites: By the 1980s, Lockheed was building bus-size, billion-dollar spacecraft that scanned images digitally rather than using film-return capsules.

June 6, 1970
The USAF selects North American Rockwell to build the B-1A bomber.

July 16, 1970
The USAF selects Boeing to build an Airborne Warning and Control System (AWACS) radar airplane.

August 17, 1970
The Soviets launch *Venera 7*, which will later land on Venus.

August 29, 1970
The McDonnell Douglas DC-10 widebody tri-jet makes its first flight. It sets off a wide-body race with Lockheed.

September 12, 1970
Soviets launch *Luna 16*, which can return samples of lunar material to earth.

October 15, 1970
The first MiG-21 is constructed in India and handed over to the Indian Air Force.

November 10, 1970
The Soviets land the first remote-controlled moon rover, *Luna 17*.

November 16, 1970
The Lockheed L-1011 TriStar makes its first flight.

December 12, 1970
An Italian crew launches *Explorer 42* into orbit.

December 15, 1970
The Soviet *Venera 7* probe is the first confirmed landing on Venus.

December 21, 1970
The Grumman F-14 Tomcat, the first new high-agility fighter, makes its inaugural flight.

1971
The Augusta A109 twin-turbine helicopter makes its first flight.

January 31–February 9, 1971
Apollo 14 gathers 94 pounds of material from the moon.

February 4, 1971
Rolls-Royce declares bankruptcy.

March 24, 1971
The U.S. supersonic transport (SST) program is killed in Congress.

June 6–29, 1971
Soyuz 11 docks with the Soviet space

To the Heavens...and Back Again

Apollo, meanwhile, had transformed NASA into an empire of powerful dukedoms. Its major space centers—Kennedy in Florida, Marshall in Alabama, and Johnson in Texas—were big spenders in key states. NASA's budget was crucial to the prosperity of influential companies like Rockwell, which employed thousands of people. But as the Apollo project reached its end, it was clear that, unless NASA was given a new project, it would implode and take large parts of the industry with it.

The idea of a reusable spaceplane that would lift payloads into space without throwing away a rocket had been suggested in the 1950s, but it was robbed of funding during the Apollo era. The USAF's first spaceplane project, the Boeing X-20 Dyna-Soar, was scrapped in 1964.

NASA's own work on technology for reusable vehicles was fitful. Its work on creating a "lifting body" vehicle that could descend from orbit and land like an airplane had survived through the Apollo years on meager funds, and the only work it had done on a rocket engine that could be fired more than once was for a highly secret CIA program. Most people did not know the research existed at all.

President Richard Nixon gave NASA the job of developing the Space Transportation System (STS), or Space Shuttle, in January 1972. NASA wanted to use the Shuttle to support a space station, a project requiring that large loads be carried to an equatorial orbit. The Pentagon—fronting for the still-secret NRO—wanted to be able to carry a reconnaissance satellite into polar orbit and return it to Earth.

Left: The Apollo program was one of the most successful scientific efforts in American history. It built on the lessons learned in the Mercury and Gemini programs that preceded it.

Middle: *Apollo 1* became the venue for the worst tragedy of the U.S. lunar program when Edward White, Virgil "Gus" Grissom, and Roger Chaffee died in a cabin fire.

Right: One tragic lesson learned by the disastrous *Apollo 1* fire was that it was deadly to have an atmosphere of pure oxygen. Retrospectively, it seems obvious that the idea was wrong; at the time, it was a hard lesson to be learned.

station *Salyut 1*. Equipment failure causes the crew to be killed while entering the earth's atmosphere on the return trip.

June 11–August 4, 1971
Sheila Scott flies a Piper Aztec from equator to equator via the North Pole.

June 14, 1971
The U.S. KH-9 *Big Bird*, a large reconnaissance satellite, is launched.

July 26–August 7, 1971
▶ *Apollo 15* uses a lunar rover.

October 28, 1971
The United Kingdom launches a satellite.

January 1972
Development of the Space Shuttle is authorized.

March 3, 1972
Pioneer 10 makes a flyby to Jupiter

and then becomes the first artificial object to leave the solar system.

April 16–27, 1972
Apollo 16 mission sets up a lunar astronomical observatory.

April 25, 1972
A Schleicher ASQ-12 establishes the world distance record of 907.7 miles for single-seat sailplanes.

May 10, 1972
U.S. Navy fighters shoot down ten MiGs over North Vietnam.

May 10, 1972
The Fairchild A-10 makes its first flight.

May 17, 1972
The last DC-8 is delivered.

July 23, 1972
NASA launches *Landsat 1*, the earth resources technology satellite.

Right: The *Apollo 9* mission was flown by Russell "Rusty" Schweickart, James McDivitt, and David Scott. It featured a docking with a lunar module, code-named "Spider." Schweickart made an EVA, and Scott stood in the open hatch of "Gumdrop," the code name for the Apollo vehicle.

Below: The earth is seen in the distance; the gray horizon is that of the moon, and the lunar lander is as it was seen from the command module on July 21, 1969.

These performance requirements, combined with limited time and budgets, determined the design of the shuttle. The original plan was for a vehicle with two reusable stages—both rocket-powered and fueled with liquid oxygen and liquid hydrogen. To save time and money, NASA decided that the system would comprise a reusable orbiter, an expendable fuel tank, and two solid rocket boosters. NASA chose Rockwell to develop the spacecraft.

The Space Shuttle made its first orbital flight in April 1981, but, unfortunately, there were problems with the system. The shuttle's performance proved to be inadequate for the NRO mission, and the West Coast launch complex at Vandenberg Air Force Base was never finished. The four shuttles required an immense amount of maintenance. Flights also tended to fall behind schedule, and the system cost a great deal more than expendable rockets would have.

To rally the country around the program and build up public support, NASA recruited and sent non-astronauts into space,

The three crewmembers of *Apollo 11*: (left to right) Neil Armstrong, Michael Collins, and Edwin "Buzz" Aldrin, Jr.

July 26, 1972
Rockwell is selected to build the Space Shuttle.

July 27, 1972
The McDonnell Douglas F-15 Eagle makes its first flight.

September 1972
▶ Boeing chairman Bill Allen, who led the company into the jet age, retires.

October 28, 1972
The Airbus A300 makes its first flight.

December 11, 1972
Apollo 17, the last flight in the program, is launched.

December 18, 1972
Linebacker II bombing raids start, heralding the end of the U.S. involvement in Vietnam.

April 6, 1973
NASA launches *Pioneer 11* on a flyby to Jupiter and Saturn.

April 17, 1973
Federal Express starts operations. Ten years later, it will be the largest air-freight company in the world.

May 14, 1973
▶ *Skylab 1* is placed into Earth orbit, becoming the first U.S. space station.

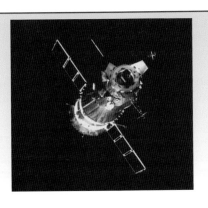

COLD WAR POWERS LAUNCH A JOINT MISSION

The seeds for 1975's Apollo-Soyuz Test Project were planted more than 15 years before, just after John Glenn's successful orbital flight in 1962. The Soviets had mocked the U.S. space program before Glenn's flight; afterward, though, Premier Nikita Khrushchev wrote a congratulatory letter to President John F. Kennedy. In it, he commented, "If our countries pooled their efforts—scientific, technical, and material—to master the universe, this would be very beneficial for the advance of science and would be joyfully acclaimed by all peoples who would like to see scientific achievements benefit man and not be used for 'cold war' purposes and the arms race." Kennedy responded, "I welcome your statement that our countries should cooperate in the exploration of space."

And so began years of delicate negotiations that alternated between hope and disillusionment. Meanwhile, the two countries continued on with their separate space programs. By 1971, the talks to create a shared mission had turned serious.

Finally, after years of discussions and planning, the Soyuz craft launched on July 15, 1975; the Apollo craft launched seven years later. The two spacecraft docked on July 17 to begin two days of joint operations. The mission was a technical success, but more important, it was a successful exercise in building trust between the two Cold War enemies.

including Utah Senator Jake Garn in 1985 and Massachusetts schoolteacher Christa McAuliffe in 1986. The public relations campaign backfired, however, ending in tragedy when the shuttle carrying McAuliffe exploded shortly after liftoff, killing her and the six others aboard.

The *Challenger* explosion left behind a stunned nation and a tarnished space program. It was three years before another Space Shuttle launch was scheduled. Since the program restarted in 1988, Shuttle missions have focused mainly on space research and exploration. Recent missions have serviced the Hubble Space Telescope and NASA's latest prestige project, the International Space Station.

Space Technology Comes Down to Earth

The important work in space relies on expendable rockets, such as the Russian Proton, Europe's Ariane, and the U.S. Atlas and Delta. By far the largest application for space technology has been communications. TV and telephone relay satellites handle hundreds of channels of traffic. Direct broadcasting system satellites deliver TV channels to satellite dishes on homes, boats, and airplanes.

Another valuable space application emerged from a 1970s Pentagon project that was originally intended to let missile-firing subs pinpoint their position instantly. The answer was a constellation of satellites that

Top left: Astronauts Neil Armstrong and Buzz Aldrin depended upon the lunar lander to set them safely on the moon and then to provide them with transport back to the orbiting command module for the return trip to Earth. Fortunately, the equipment functioned perfectly.

Left: *Sputnik*, which simply emitted beeps, kicked off a series of ever more complicated, ever more useful satellites. One of the most important of these was *Telstar 1*, built by AT&T. It established the first television link between the United States and Europe on July 10, 1962.

June 3, 1973
A production-model Tupelov Tu-144 SST crashes at the Paris air show.

August 1, 1973
The Martin Marietta X-24B lifting-body aircraft makes its first flight.

August 9, 1973
The USSR launches its *Mars 7* spacecraft.

October 6, 1973
The Yom Kippur War between Arab nations and Israel begins.

October 7, 1973
The Lear Jet Model 23 makes its first flight.

November 3, 1973
The *Mariner 10* probe is launched on a flyby of Mercury and Venus.

December 1, 1973
High fuel prices, the effect of the Arab oil embargo during the conflict in the Middle East, shock the airlines.

December 17, 1973
The crash of an Iberia Airlines DC-10 leads to the study of wind shear.

February 2, 1974
The General Dynamics (now Lockheed Martin) F-16 Fighting Falcon debuts. It is the first fly-by-wire fighter.

June 1974
The Aerospatiale AS.350/355 Ecureuil makes its first flight.

June 8, 1974
▶ The Northrop YF-17, the precursor of the F-18 Hornet, makes its first flight.

August 16, 1974
Charles Lindbergh dies at the age of 72 in Maui, Hawaii.

Above: The Space Shuttle required entirely new launching and landing techniques. The *Enterprise* was tested by carrying it aloft on a 747, casting it loose, and having it glide down to a safe landing.

Right: Once launched from Cape Canaveral, the Space Shuttle becomes a glider, as it has no engines for propulsion. This means when it is forced to land at Edwards Air Force Base in California, it has to be transported back to Florida by a specially configured Boeing 747.

November 12, 1974
For the first time in history, air traffic control instructions are given via satellite relay.

November 14, 1974
The McDonnell Douglas F-15 Eagle fighter enters the service.

December 23, 1974
The Rockwell B-1 makes its first flight.

1975
The first Robinson helicopters are launched. These lightweight, low-cost helicopters will ultimately become a success.

January 1975
The Defense Advanced Research Projects Agency issues the first contracts for a prototype "stealth" aircraft.

January 14, 1975
▶ The USAF selects the F-16 as its future Air Combat Fighter.

February 1, 1975
The McDonnell Douglas F-15 Streak Eagle sets a series of time-to-climb records.

March 18, 1975
Noted pioneer pilot Adrienne Bolland dies at age 90.

June 3, 1975
The Mitsubishi FS-T2-KAI supersonic close support fighter makes its first flight, proving the extent to which the Japanese aeronautics industry has revived.

July 15–24, 1975
The U.S. *Apollo 18* and the Soviet *Soyuz 19* launch separately and then join up in space.

transmitted coded radio signals and a computer-driven receiver that measured the distance to three satellites and used the signal from a fourth satellite to synchronize its own clock. The Global Positioning System, or GPS, became operational in the early 1990s.

What the planners had not anticipated was computing technology that made it possible to build GPS into everything from missiles and airplanes to cars and cell phones. Since the GPS receiver is passive, there's no limit to the numbers of users the system can support. Arguably, the humble, taken-for-granted GPS has had a more beneficial effect on more aspects of human life—from air travel, where it provides precision over-the-horizon guidance, to fisheries or trucking—than any NASA project in history. Whether a future world-altering NASA project will change that remains to be seen.

TRAGEDY PUTS A PROGRAM ON HOLD

NASA leaders launched a massive public relations campaign to continue the Space Shuttle program, carrying non-astronauts to show that the shuttle was safe and reliable. Senator Jake Garn of Utah flew on a Space Shuttle mission in 1985, and the agency also sought a schoolteacher to fly on the spacecraft, someone to represent the possibility of civilian space travel. With much publicity, Massachusetts science teacher Christa McAuliffe joined mission 51-L, which launched on January 28, 1986. The Shuttle *Challenger* exploded 73 seconds after liftoff. All seven on board died, and the nation reeled in shock and mourning. After an exhaustive inquiry, the accident was blamed on a faulty O-ring seal on the solid rocket fuel booster. A commission found the O-ring's manufacturer, Morton Thiokol, and NASA both responsible for the tragedy.

The *Challenger* crew: (left to right, front row) Michael J. Smith, Francis R. "Dick" Scobee, and Ronald E. McNair; (back row) Ellison S. Onizuka, Sharon Christa McAuliffe, Gregory B. Jarvis, and Judith A. Resnick.

Far left: No one ever expected the Hubble telescope to provide such an enormous amount of information. It has literally looked back to almost the beginning of time, and after its 2002 repairs, it will function for another decade.

Left: The Space Shuttle has three main engines, built by Boeing Rocketdyne. Each develops 375,000 pounds of thrust at sea level and 470,000 pounds in the vacuum of space. The fuel is a mixture of liquid hydrogen and liquid oxygen. Each engine is controlled by a throttle.

August 20, 1975
The *Viking 1* spacecraft is sent to Mars to transmit pictures from the surface.

September 1975
The Hughes AH-64A makes its first flight.

December 26, 1975
The Soviet Tu-144 supersonic transport flies from Moscow to Alma Alta, Kazakhstan.

January 21, 1976
British Airways and Air France inaugurate the first scheduled supersonic service carrying fare-paying passengers.

March 5, 1976
The new long-range Air-Launch Cruise Missile (ALCM) is test-launched.

April 1, 1976
Lockheed is selected to build the Have Blue, the first stealth aircraft.

May 19, 1976
Golfer Arnold Palmer lands his Lear Jet 36 after a record round-the-world flight.

July 28, 1976
The Lockheed SR-71 sets both speed (2,193 miles per hour) and altitude (85,069 feet) records.

September 30, 1976
Don Taylor completes the first round-the-world flight in a homebuilt craft, the Throp T-18.

December 19, 1976
The KH-11 Kennan reconnaissance satellite with digital image transmission is launched for the first time.

March 24, 1977
The first Airborne Warning and Control System (AWACS) aircraft are delivered; they revolutionize the command and control of air battle.

March 27, 1977
Two Boeing 747s collide on a runway at Tenerife in the Canary Islands. It is the world's worst aviation accident, killing 583 people.

April 1977
The British aircraft industry is nationalized and formed into a single company, British Aerospace (later BAE Systems).

CHAPTER EIGHT

Military Aviation Flies to the Forefront

PAINFUL LESSONS IN VIETNAM FORCE MILITARY AVIATION INTO A NEW, ULTRA–HIGH–TECH ERA OF STEALTH FIGHTERS AND PRECISION–GUIDED WEAPONS.

On January 15, 1991, TV news crews covered the start of an air attack on Baghdad, Iraq. It was the opening strike of a campaign aimed at removing Iraqi forces from Kuwait, the oil-rich nation that they had invaded in August 1990. The sky was on fire with anti-aircraft rounds and missile trails, but they did not seem to be tracking any visible targets. Something *was* up there, though; you could tell by the occasional flashes and explosions on the ground. Then the power went out. At the same time, U.S. Air Force planners in a bunker in Saudi Arabia let out a cheer. The power had gone out right on schedule.

Right: One of the best-kept secrets in American history, the Lockheed Martin F-117 remained under wraps for years before finally being shown to the public in 1990. Its unusual shape reflects radar beams away, giving it stealth qualities.

The Lockheed SR-71 was the fastest, highest-flying, most effective reconnaissance aircraft in the world at the time of the debut of its prototype in 1964. The Mach 3 Blackbird maintained that status throughout its long career, and no other aircraft has ever approached its performance.

Many experts, including the retired military officers hired as consultants by the media, had predicted a long and difficult war. Iraq's modern, Soviet-developed air defense system—with 600 surface-to-air missile (SAM) launchers and almost 10,000 guns—would shoot down dozens of Allied fighters. Air attacks would be indecisive, they said, and the war would be decided by massive and costly tank battles on the ground.

It never happened. Allied losses of combat aircraft never rose above a fraction of one percent of all sorties. Most of the Iraqi combat aircraft that were not destroyed on the ground fled to safety in neighboring Iran. Others were shot down in air-to-air combat. Allied aircraft could operate over most of Iraq by day and night, and this made it possible to conduct an intense bombing campaign against Iraq's ground army and the armaments and logistic infrastructure that allowed it to operate.

A ground offensive that had been expected to last for weeks was over in days, with casualty levels on the coalition side that are usually associated with mopping-up operations. The Iraqi forces were a shell; their equipment, supply lines, and morale were worn down by the bombing. A few units had one fight in them, and that was it.

The commentators were wrong because they did not appreciate that there had been a revolution in air power. It was rooted in lessons—positive and negative—learned since the 1960s.

Sowing the Seeds of Change

In commercial aviation, the 1960s saw a retreat from high speed and high altitude. The same was true on the military side. No warplane in the 1960s or 1970s was much faster than the Lockheed F-104A, which was first flown in 1956. There were two outstanding exceptions: the A-12 CIA spyplane and the fighter designed to shoot it down.

The Lockheed Skunk Works was awarded the contract to build a spyplane, also known as Project Oxcart, in 1959. The CIA's A-12 made its first flight in April 1962. It was an extraordinary achievement. Its propulsion system, essentially a turbo-ramjet, is still unique. It was not a small airplane—later versions weighed up to 140,000 pounds—and it was built almost entirely from heat-resistant titanium alloys that had never been used on such a scale before.

June 16, 1977
Rocket pioneer Wernher von Braun dies in Virginia.

June 30, 1977
President Jimmy Carter announces the cancellation of the B-1 bomber. A principal reason behind this decision—the promise of new stealth technology to come—is kept secret.

August 12, 1977
The Space Shuttle *Enterprise* makes its first free flight (glide) from a 747 carrier plane.

August 23, 1977
The *Gossamer Condor*, designed by Paul MacCready, wins the Kremer prize for a human-powered flight around a course slightly more than a mile long.

September 26, 1977
Laker Airways launches Skytrain, the first low-fare transatlantic service.

November 1, 1977
Tu-144 supersonic passenger service starts.

November 22, 1977
Concorde services start from Paris and London to New York.

December 1, 1977
The Lockheed Have Blue, the first stealth aircraft, makes its first flight.

December 10, 1977
Soviet cosmonauts join the *Salyut 6* space station and remain in orbit for 96 days.

December 13, 1977
The Airbus A300 starts trial services with Eastern Airlines.

1978
Almost 6,500 helicopters are operating in the United States.

January 10–16, 1978
The Soviets achieve the first three-spacecraft docking.

January 20, 1978
The Soviet space station *Salyut 6* is resupplied by the uncrewed cargo vehicle *Progress*.

Its full-time, computer-controlled stabilization system foreshadowed later "fly-by-wire" airplanes. The A-12 was not flyable without the computer system. Perhaps most remarkable of all, it was designed to only present a tiny image on radar. The edges of the airplane—and in some versions, the vertical tails—were constructed of a special high-temperature plastic that absorbed radar signals.

The CIA retired its flight operations, but the A-12 was so promising that the U.S. Air Force wanted to convert the design into a two-seat reconnaissance-strike aircraft. The Reconnaissance/Strike-71, or RS-71, went into development. However, when President Lyndon Johnson announced the existence of the improved airplane in late 1964, he transposed the designation to SR-71. Rather than correct the President's error, the USAF RS-71 forevermore became known as the Strategic Reconnaissance-71, or SR-71.

The SR-71 (nicknamed the Blackbird for its distinctive heat-resistant black paint) replaced the CIA's A-12s in 1968, and the Blackbird remained operational for another 23 years. The A-12 and SR-71 were fired on in battles more than 1,000 times and never got a scratch. Their speed—up to Mach 3.3, or 2,200 miles per hour in an emergency—usually turned a missile attack into a tail-chase that caused the weapon to run out of energy.

The Mikoyan MiG-25 was the Soviet answer to the A-12. It was not quite as fast, but its ability to reach Mach 2.8—1,850 miles per hour—while carrying four large air-to-air missiles was impressive nonetheless. The MiG-25's high-strength nickel-steel alloy makeup is unique. Because steel is stronger but denser than aluminum, a steel skin that is thin and light enough for airplane construction cannot be assembled with rivets; the entire airframe of the MiG-25 is welded using techniques invented for the program. Designed as an interceptor, the MiG-25 was developed into a reconnaissance-strike aircraft with an immense ventral fuel tank that gave it a respectable range at supersonic speed. In

the Gulf War in 1991, a MiG-25—then a 25-year-old design—was the only adversary airplane to shoot down a U.S. fighter.

But these two airplanes were anomalies. The most important fighters of the 1960s were the Russian MiG-21 and the U.S. McDonnell F-4 Phantom II, and the combats between these aircraft over Vietnam helped define the fighter as it is known today.

The Fighters of Vietnam

The first operational MiG-21 variant was ready in 1960. It was an extremely simple fighter, armed with two K-13A missiles—copies of the Sidewinder—and a 30-millimeter cannon. It had a

Top: When the McDonnell company originally planned the F-4 Phantom, they hoped, with luck, to sell as many as 300 aircraft to the U.S. Navy. The F-4 was also adopted by the U.S. Air Force and then sold worldwide. More than 5,000 were built.

Left: The tiny, beautiful MiG-21 was an aesthetic and performance triumph. More than 11,000 were built, and it proved to be a tough opponent in the Vietnam War. Many are still in service in air forces around the world, and some are being modernized to contemporary standards.

March 10, 1978
The Dassault Mirage 2000, the last of the Mirage line, makes its first flight.

April 6, 1978
Eastern Airlines orders 25 Airbus 300s.

June 6, 1978
Tu-144 SST services are suspended.

July 14, 1978
Boeing announces that it has launched the 767.

August 12–17, 1978
The *Double Eagle II* makes the first transatlantic balloon crossing, piloted by Ben Abruzzo, Maxie Anderson, and Larry Newman.

September 13, 1978
The Aerospatiale AS 332 Super Puma makes its first flight.

October 24, 1978
The Airline Deregulation Act is

passed. It will revolutionize air transport in the United States.

November 1978
The USAF orders the first operational stealth aircraft, the F-117, from Lockheed.

November 9, 1978
The McDonnell Douglas AV-8B Advanced Harrier makes its first flight.

February 27, 1979
McDonnell Douglas delivers the 2,960th (and last) A-4 Skyhawk after 25 years of continuous production, a combat aircraft record at the time.

May 1979
The U.S. Coast Guard buys 90 Aerospatiale Dauphins.

June 5, 1979
The first production of the Panavia Tornado is rolled out.

June 12, 1979
Paul MacCready's *Gossamer Albatross* makes the first human-powered flight across the English Channel.

August 19, 1979
Cosmonauts leave the *Salyut 6* space station after 175 days.

HELICOPTERS GO ON THE ATTACK

Another new class of military aircraft that emerged from Vietnam was the **attack helicopter.** Throughout the conflict, the U.S. Army used vast numbers of UH-1 Huey helicopters. From early days, some of these aircraft were armed with machine guns and unguided rockets.

In 1965, Bell Helicopter Corporation flew the first prototype of the Model 209. It combined the rotor and engine of the Huey with a slim, sharklike body fitted with stub wings. It had a crew of two: The pilot sat in the back seat, and the gunner was in the front controlling a Gatling-type machine gun and a grenade launcher in a nose turret. Rockets were mounted under the stub wings. It was put into production as the AH-1 HueyCobra, and it is still in production today.

UH-1 Huey

AH-1 HueyCobra

small radar that was only used for indicating the target's range; it could not search for targets. In theory, this mattered little because the Soviet air forces had developed a tight system of fighter control based on ground radar. As long as the pilots followed instructions, they would be vectored within sight of the target. However, the Soviet planners realized that the human eye becomes inadequate at closing rates of 2,000 miles per hour, and MiG-21s were soon equipped with a more useful radar to help the pilot in the last stages of an attack.

The F-4, meanwhile, was big and complicated. Designed for the U.S. Navy, it was first planned as a heavy attack airplane and then adapted as a two-seat all-weather fighter. It had a long, drooped nose thanks to a late decision to equip it with a 36-inch radar dish, which required a bigger radome. The jet exhausts were cut back, and the tail surfaces were carried on a short boom. When engineers tested models in the wind tunnel, they found

aerodynamic problems, which were quickly fixed by angling the horizontal stabilizers down and the wingtips up. "My God," one of the designers recalls thinking at the rollout in 1958, "what have we created?"

But the F-4 Phantom could carry eight air-to-air missiles (or a wide range of other weapons), and the two J79 engines—each with more power than the MiG-21's single engine—provided it with high speed and strong acceleration.

Robert McNamara, secretary of defense under Presidents John F. Kennedy and Lyndon Johnson, favored the F-111 fighter project. This big airplane with variable-sweep wings was intended to serve as a long-endurance interceptor for the Navy and as a low-altitude bomber for the USAF. In 1962, General Dynamics and Grumman were selected to build the F-111—but the project proved more difficult than expected. The USAF had ordered the F-4 as a stopgap until the F-111 arrived, so every delay in the F-111 program meant that the Navy and USAF both needed more F-4s. Eventually, more than 5,000 Phantoms were built.

In air battles over Vietnam, F-4s fought not only against MiG-21s but against MiG-17s—then regarded as obsolete machines. The fighter, which was derived from the MiG-15, didn't even have a radar. MiG-17s had proven to be surprisingly effective against F-105 bombers; the F-105 was supersonic in theory but was subsonic and unwieldy when loaded with bombs. The F-4s were used in Vietnam as the F-86 had been used in Korea—dispatched in four-plane flights to carry out combat air patrol missions above the bomber force.

The U.S. pilots and commanders learned a number of lessons in Vietnam. Designed to shoot down bombers, the radar-guided AIM-7 Sparrow missile was not very effective against fighters. The F-4's size and its smoky engines were a serious disadvantage—the "North Vietnamese" pilots (who actually hailed from

October 18, 1979
The McDonnell Douglas DC-9 Super 80, later renamed the MD-80, makes its first flight.

December 14, 1979
The Edgley EA-7 Optica, a ducted-fan observation plane, makes its first flight.

1980
Fly-by-wire control systems come into general use.

1980
Helicopters have rescued an estimated one million people since 1944.

May 8–12, 1980
Maxie and Kris Anderson, father and son, make the first nonstop transcontinental balloon flight.

August 9, 1980
Aviator and record-setter Jackie Cochran dies.

October 2, 1980
The Westland Sea King helicopter rescues 22 people from a burning ship at sea.

November 15, 1980
The Hughes 376 communications satellite, one of the first spacecraft built on a production line, is launched for the first time.

December 3, 1980
Judith Chisholm completes a solo world flight in 15 days and 22 minutes in a single-engine airplane, setting a new women's record.

December 5, 1980
Paul MacCready's *Solar Challenger* sets a solar-power endurance record of 1 hour and 32 minutes.

December 9, 1980
The 500th Boeing 747 is rolled out.

January 28, 1981
Pan Am begins a twice-weekly New York to Beijing service.

March 28, 1981
The Dornier 228 makes its first flight.

April 12–14, 1981
The Space Shuttle *Columbia* conducts its first orbital test flight.

practically every nation in the Communist bloc) almost always saw the U.S. fighters first. Nearly every combat led to what pilots called the "merge"—both sides within visual range, turning tightly to get in a position where they could fire on the enemy. This visual fight invariably took place at subsonic speed.

The original F-4 was not designed to dogfight. Flown beyond its limits, it could stall and snap into a spin from which it was very hard to recover. Also, it did not have a gun, and the MiG-17 did. After the first air battles over Vietnam, the U.S. Navy formed Top Gun, a new air warfare school that emphasized dogfighting skills. The USAF increased the emphasis on dogfight training and ordered the new F-4E, which had wing slats for better maneuverability and a gun in its nose.

Also used in Vietnam were big, low-level attack airplanes designed mainly for night and bad-weather operation. The most successful was the Navy's Grumman A-6 Intruder, a two-seat subsonic bomber with a heavy payload. With a complex radar, it could perform accurate attacks even without precision weapons. Later in the war, it became the first attack airplane to be fitted with an infrared camera for night battles.

High-Tech Missiles Enter the War

Fighters were by no means the only threat over Vietnam. The North Vietnamese forces used surface-to-air missiles (SAMs) in vast numbers. Originally designed to protect point targets from bombers, the missiles proved very dangerous, particularly when combined with radar-directed anti-aircraft artillery.

Strategic Air Command's bombers were equipped with electronic receivers to detect enemy radar as well as jamming devices to make those radars less effective, but they were not fitted to fighters. On July 24, 1965, an F-4C flying a MiGCAP (combat air patrol) mission was shot down by a Soviet-built SA-2 SAM. Three days later, anti-aircraft artillery shot down three F-105s

from a formation sent to attack the SAM sites, and two more damaged aircraft were lost in a collision on the return flight.

The United States hastily fitted its fighters with receivers and jammers. To aid in the battle against SAMs, a group of specially modified two-seat F-100 Super Sabres arrived at Korat air base in Thailand in November 1965. The aircraft—code-named Wild Weasels—were designed to locate and attack SAM sites. Five out of the first seven Wild Weasels deployed were lost in action, but they helped protect U.S. strike aircraft. Later, the F-105 was adapted for this same mission and was armed with new missiles that homed in on enemy radar.

Originally intended by Secretary of Defense Robert McNamara to be the standard fighter for all services, the General Dynamics F-111 had early problems and was not accepted by the U.S. Navy. In time, it became an extremely effective bomber, though, famous for the brilliant raid it conducted against Libya as a response to terrorism.

June 1, 1981
The Short 360 prototype makes its first flight.

June 7, 1981
In a pioneering precision-strike operation, Israeli F-16s disable Iraq's nuclear weapons plant at Osirak.

June 18, 1981
▶ The Lockheed F-117, the first operational stealth aircraft, makes its first flight.

July 7, 1981
Paul MacCready's *Solar Challenger* makes a solar-powered flight across the English Channel from Paris to England. It takes five hours and 25 minutes.

July 23, 1981
The Agusta A-109A helicopter, flown by Charles Preather, sets an altitude record of 20,000 feet.

September 3, 1981
The first British Aerospace BAe 146 Series 100 transport makes its inaugural flight.

September 7, 1981
Ed Link, the father of flight-training simulators, dies.

September 26, 1981
The Boeing 767 prototype makes it first flight. It is the first two-pilot,

wide-body airplane and the first long-range, twin-engine airliner.

October 1981
Northrop Grumman is selected to build the B-2 stealth bomber.

October 9, 1981
The *Superchicken III* makes the first nonstop balloon flight across the United States.

The MiG-17 was the first operational supersonic fighter in the world, and more than 6,000 were built. Considered obsolete at the time of the Vietnam War, it nonetheless gave a good showing, especially in turning combats.

The last of the great line of fighters from Grumman, the F-14 Tomahawk features swing-wings, blinding speed, and the Phoenix missile. It gained popular fame in the film *Top Gun*.

Before Vietnam, USAF's Tactical Air Command had trained for tactical bombing, which did not have to be accurate. The fighter pilots now found that dive-bombing was suicidal in the face of SAMs and anti-aircraft artillery, while level bombing was nowhere near accurate enough to hit difficult targets such as bridges or bunkers. Guided bombs of different types had been tested in World War II—the German Fritz-X, for example—but had been completely neglected later.

As sortie after sortie failed to damage bridges and other key targets, U.S. service laboratories and electronics companies worked on a number of different guided-bomb concepts. The most practical weapon of this kind was the laser-guided bomb (LGB), first used in 1968.

The LGB guided itself automatically toward a spot of laser light aimed at the target either from the launch aircraft or another airplane. LGBs were used to destroy the Paul Doumer and Thanh Hoa bridges during the Linebacker raids of 1972.

Vietnam was not the only tactical air war of the period. In June 1967, Egypt, Syria, and Jordan were preparing to launch an attack on Israel. Egypt's air force, equipped by the Soviet Union, was the largest in the region and included Tupolev Tu-16 medium bombers and MiG-21 supersonic fighters.

Apart from a small number of Dassault Mirage III fighters, Israel's air force was equipped with smaller, 1950s-technology airplanes. But on the first morning of the war, Israel launched a surprise air strike. The first Israeli jets carried modified bombs that cratered the Egyptian runways, and subsequent waves of attacks destroyed the airplanes on the ground. The Israeli air force was free to support its armies on the ground, driving the Egyptian forces back to the Suez Canal.

In October 1973—less than a year after the Linebacker attacks, the last major Vietnam air operations—the Arab nations attacked again. Egypt had acquired new Soviet-developed weapons, including SAMs that were a generation newer than anything encountered in Vietnam. Israel held its ground, but with very heavy fighter losses and only after new jamming equipment was delivered from the United States.

November 13, 1981
The *Double Eagle V*—piloted by Ben Abruzzo, Larry Newman, Ron Clarke, and Rocky Aoki—makes a transpacific balloon flight.

November 19, 1981
The British Aerospace Hawk is selected as a U.S. Navy trainer, indicating a step forward in international cooperation.

December 28, 1981
The Skyship 500 nonrigid airship makes its first flight.

1982
More than 900 hospitals have a heliport on their premises.

January 26, 1982
The European Space Agency approves the development of the Ariane series of launches.

February 19, 1982
The Boeing 757 prototype makes its first flight.

March 25, 1982
Beech celebrates the 35th anniversary of its Bonanza production. Almost 15,000 have been built.

April 3, 1982
The second Airbus model, the A310, makes its first flight.

April 27, 1982
The U.S. Navy purchases 18 Sikorsky SH-60B Seahawk helicopters.

May 13, 1982
Braniff International ceases operations, becoming the first major casualty of deregulation.

June 6, 1982
Israel starts operations against surface-to-air missile sites in Lebanon.

Using the F-16 and F-15 in air combat for the first time, Israel shoots down 90 Syrian MiG fighters without a loss of its own.

July 29, 1982
The *Salyut 6* space station's life is ended.

September 9, 1982
The first U.S. private venture space rocket, the *Conestoga 1*, is launched from Matagorda Island, Texas.

The Next Generation of Military Aircraft

These experiences inspired a new wave of military aircraft. After the first air combats over North Vietnam, the USAF and U.S. Navy drew up requirements for fighters that would be as fast and heavily armed as the F-4. The fighter would carry radar-jamming equipment as well as a large radar that could track many targets at the same time. It would also be agile and maneuverable at the speeds and altitudes where most dogfights take place, and it would carry an internal gun. The Navy's Grumman

F-14 Tomcat flew at the end of 1970, followed by the USAF's McDonnell Douglas F-15 Eagle in July 1972.

A group of USAF officers, Pentagon analysts, and fighter designers did not agree with the services' priorities and advocated the development of smaller, less expensive fighters. The Fighter Mafia, as they were known, won some support from Pentagon officials who saw that the F-15 and F-14 were, indeed, too costly to replace every fighter in service. Also, few foreign countries could

Left: The Republic F-105 had a troubled early career, with so many crashes that the program was threatened with termination. However, it proved itself beyond all doubt in Vietnam, where it became the principal aircraft to "go downtown" to Hanoi and Haiphong.

Right: The Grumman Intruder was designed as a night, all-weather bomber able to go in low and bomb targets when no other airplane could get through. It was a workhorse during the Vietnam War.

THE "FIGHTER MAFIA" PRODUCES AN ADAPTABLE CLASSIC

Designer **Harry Hillaker** was a founding member of the "Fighter Mafia." Talented, opinionated, and willing to go nose-to-nose with any opponent irrespective of rank, Hillaker created the General Dynamics (later, Lockheed Martin) F-16 by wrapping the smallest possible airframe around the biggest available engine (the Pratt & Whitney F100 from the F-15).

The F-16 was one of the first "fly-by-wire" airplanes. There were no rods or cables linking the pilot's control stick to the airplane's aerodynamic control surfaces; the short, side-mounted stick was actually connected to computers that in turn controlled the airplane. Other unusual features included a chin-mounted inlet and a seat that reclined by 30 degrees to improve the pilot's tolerance of the g loadings.

The YF-16 made its first flight in public at the 1975 Paris air show with an astonishing display of agility. The F-16 could clearly outmaneuver anything in the sky. Skeptics doubted whether it could carry all the equipment needed to perform a useful military mission, but the electronics revolution came to the airplane's rescue. For the next 30 years, Lockheed engineers added more and more capability to the airplane without changing its shape—replacing its radar, computers, and cockpit displays and adding new weapons under the wings. By the 1990s, the F-16 could fire long-range air-to-air missiles and deliver laser-guided bombs.

September 30, 1982
Ross Perot, Jr., and Jay Coburn complete the first circumnavigation of the earth by helicopter, a LongRanger Bell 206L-1.

December 7, 1982
The first Sikorsky UH-60A Blackhawk helicopters are received by the USAF to use for rescue work.

1983
The Space Shuttle *Columbia* flies the first flight to include a European member of the crew. It is also the first SpaceLab mission.

March 28, 1983
The first Search and Rescue Satellite Aided Tracking System (SARSAT) is launched. It is able to receive Emergency Locator Transmitters (ELT).

May 23, 1983
A Sabreliner navigates across the Atlantic entirely by Global Positioning System (GPS) and lands in Paris.

June 2, 1983
The Soviet *Venera 15* is launched to orbit Venus and map its surface by radar.

June 7, 1983
The *Venera 16* is launched to assist *Venera 15* with mapping Venus.

July 22, 1983
Dick Smith makes the first round-the-world solo helicopter flight in a Bell JetRanger III.

August 19, 1983
The last L-1011 is built; Lockheed exits the airliner business.

September 30, 1983
▶ The first production of the McDonnell Douglas (Hughes) AH-64A Apache attack helicopter is rolled out.

The McDonnell Douglas F-15 Eagle first flew on July 27, 1972, and updated versions remain the top air-superiority fighter in the world, pending the arrival of the Lockheed F-22. The F-15 has served well in all theaters of war, particularly in the Israel's air force.

generation of combat airplanes: agile, multipurpose, and heavily armed. Its peers have included the Dassault Mirage 2000 and the Russian MiG-29 as well as the F/A-18 Hornet.

Agile fighters were not the only new military airplanes to emerge from combat experience in Vietnam and the Middle East. The Egyptian-Israeli experience of October 1973, in particular, was the starting point for one of the most remarkable aerospace projects in history. The mauling of the experienced, well-trained Israeli air force was a horrible shock to the United States.

In the 1960s, the Soviet Union had steadily built up and modernized its non-nuclear forces in Europe, to the point where it seemed prepared to attack Western Europe while holding nuclear weapons in reserve. As well as building new tactical airplanes like the swing-wing Sukhoi Su-24 and the Mikoyan-Gurevich MiG-23, Soviet forces had covered Eastern Europe with a network of SAMs.

The missiles included the massive S-200 (code-named SA-5 by the West) weapons with a range of 80 miles or more; the ramjet-powered Kub (SA-6), with a 10- to 20-mile range, which were carried on a group of tracked vehicles that could accompany mobile forces; and the shoot-on-the-move Osa (SA-8), which was carried complete with its radar on an amphibious truck. The weapons were interlinked and controlled, along with fighter airplanes, by large radars and control centers in underground concrete bunkers.

afford the big fighters, so U.S. companies risked losing the export market to France's Dassault Aviation.

In 1972, the USAF asked Northrop and General Dynamics to build prototypes of a smaller fighter. Northrop's twin-engine YF-17 was later adapted by McDonnell Douglas into the Navy's F/A-18 Hornet, but it was General Dynamics' YF-16 that was chosen by the USAF at the beginning of 1975. A few months later, four European nations (Belgium, the Netherlands, Norway, and Denmark) also ordered the F-16.

The elegant F-16, with its instantly recognizable "smiley" air intake under the cockpit, has been an immense success. More than 4,000 F-16s have been built, and the fighter has defined a

NATO strategy for stopping a land invasion in Europe depended on attacking the "second-echelon" forces that would follow the first wave. This meant destroying roads, bridges, tunnels, and supply bases with air strikes. However, the strategy would fall apart if NATO air units were cut to ribbons by the SAM defenses.

Late in 1974, the Pentagon's Defense Advanced Research Projects Agency approached U.S. airplane manufacturers and asked

October 1983
The F-117 stealth fighter is declared operational.

January 21, 1984
The anti-satellite missile completes its first successful test.

February 24, 1984
The Boeing 737-300 makes its first flight. It will become Boeing's fastest-selling aircraft.

March 2, 1984
Airbus announces the go-ahead for the A320 "fly-by-wire" airliner.

June 10, 1984
The direct-hit anti-ballistic missile completes a successful test.

June 17, 1984
Captain Lynn Reippelmeyer becomes the first female captain to fly a 747 on a transatlantic run.

August 4, 1984
Ariane, the first competitive European launcher, fires off from French Guiana.

August 16, 1984
The ATR 42 makes its first flight.

December 14, 1984
The Grumman X-29 makes its first flight, marking the first flight test of the swept-forward wing.

January 7, 1985
Japan launches the *Sakigake* space-craft to flyby Halley's Comet.

January 24–27, 1985
The Space Shuttle *Discovery* conducts a defense assignment; military aviation has melded with space aviation.

April 22, 1985
Pan Am sells its Pacific routes to United, marking the end of an era.

May 29, 1985
The Soviet Union unveils the world's largest airplane, the An-124 heavy transport, at the Paris air show.

May 29, 1985
The FAA changes its regulations to allow extended-range flights for two-engine aircraft, permitting the aircraft to operate over the ocean.

them to investigate the design of an airplane that would be less visible to radar. It was not a completely new idea, but it was the first time that reduced detectability had been the top priority in the design. The study was not even classified, because nobody knew whether it was possible to produce such an airplane.

Just over a year later, the project was not merely classified: It had been declared "black," and even its existence was a secret from all but a few people who had a specific need to know about it. In tests of large-scale models, Lockheed and Northrop engineers had demonstrated that shaping and materials could reduce the size of an airplane's radar image to that of an insect. Lockheed's Skunk Works won the contract to build a pair of small proto-type airplanes called Have Blue—the first stealth airplanes.

Aviation Moves Forward With Stealth

The first Have Blue airplane flew from the secret base at Area 51 at the end of 1977. It was an outlandishly strange-looking airplane. Its shape was comprised of many flat surfaces, with not a single curve. The jet inlets were covered by knife-edged grills, and the jet exhausts were narrow slits. Even with the fly-by-wire systems from the F-16, it barely flew. Both airplanes were lost in accidents, but they did show that they could evade radar.

Above: The Lockheed Martin Fighting Falcon started off in life as General Dynamic's entry in the lightweight fighter field. First flown on February 2, 1974, the F-16 was selected by many NATO countries as their standard fighter, augmenting sales to the USAF. It has become one of the most important fighters in the world.

Left: Curiously enough, the Boeing F/A-18 started out as a loser. The Northrop XF-17 (as it was called in the lightweight fighter competition) lost out to the General Dynamics F-16. McDonnell Douglas and Northrop cooperated to create the F/A-18 for the Navy, and it has been an outstanding success.

June 29, 1985
The Rockwell B-1B, a revised version of the B-1, is delivered to the USAF.

July 2, 1985
The European Space Agency's *Giotto* spacecraft is launched to make a Halley's Comet flyby.

August 18, 1985
The Japanese *Suisei* spacecraft is launched to make a Halley's Comet flyby.

September 13, 1985
McDonnell Douglas launches an anti-satellite missile, destroying an inert satellite. The test heralds a new era of warfare.

December 17, 1985
The Douglas DC-3 celebrates its 50th birthday. There are an estimated 350 still in commercial use.

January 28, 1986
The Space Shuttle *Challenger* mission ends in disaster with an explosion after liftoff.

February 20, 1986
▶ Russia launches the first element of the Space Station *Mir*. The station will remain in orbit until March 23, 2001.

February 24, 1986
Eastern Airlines is acquired by Continental; it is later closed down.

March 13–14, 1986
The European Space Agency's *Giotto* comet probe comes within 335 miles of Halley's Comet, taking photographs.

August 11, 1986
The Westland Lynx becomes the world's fastest production helicopter, flying at 249.09 miles per hour. It features BERP III rotor blades.

The single-engine, delta-wing Mirage was conceived as the smallest possible fighter into which the SNECMA M53-5 turbofan could be placed, so that a thrust-to-weight ratio of 1:1 could be achieved. The result was a Mach 2.2 interceptor that is now used by several nations.

Meanwhile, in October 1981, Northrop won the competition to build a stealth bomber. Bomber development had never quite ended with the cancellation of the XB-70. In 1970, in fact, Rockwell (the former North American) had been chosen to build the B-1, a swing-wing bomber that was designed to fly at low altitude, under the radar horizon, like the F-111. It was still in development when it was canceled in 1977; instead, the Carter administration emphasized new long-range cruise missiles and was intrigued by the long-term potential of stealth technology.

The bomber program started secretly in 1978. A 330,000-pound, long-range airplane with a 40,000-pound bombload, the Northrop Grumman B-2 was a pure flying wing like the company's B-35 and B-49 designs from 35 years earlier. The company obtained a special security clearance so that its ailing founder, Jack Northrop, could see a model of the airplane. "Now I know," Northrop said, "why God has kept me alive this long."

By the end of 1978, Lockheed was working full speed on the F-117, an operational stealth fighter based on the Have Blue design. It was built and placed in service in secret. It could carry two laser-guided bombs. In the event of a war in Western Europe, the jets would fly undetected into Warsaw Pact territory and hit the command and communications sites that held the SAM net together. The airplane made its first flight in June 1981 and entered service in late 1983.

The Dynamics of Global Power Shift

In the late 1970s, some military professionals saw little chance of avoiding war with the Soviet Union. The USSR appeared to be continuing with a massive buildup of both conventional and nuclear forces. But within a few years, alert Soviet-watchers noticed some new trends.

Andrew Marshall, director of the Pentagon's Office of Net Assessment, estimated in the late 1980s that the Soviet defense budget was approaching 30 to 35 percent of the gross domestic product. In a revealing interview in 1984, senior Red Army commander Marshal Nikolai Ogarkov suggested the Soviet Union would have to overhaul its military once again to respond to Western technological innovations.

It never happened. Instead, the new General Secretary of the Communist Party, Mikhail Gorbachev, launched his campaign of *perestroika*, or modernization and reform. A structure so rigid,

A DESIGNER THINKS BEYOND THE CURVE

Denys Overholser, an engineer at the Lockheed Skunk Works who specialized in radome and antenna design, was off work with a broken leg when his boss asked him to work on the "stealth" project in early 1975. Overholser concluded that it was theoretically possible to make a shape that would not reflect radar signals back toward an enemy radar.

In practice, though, the task was impossibly complicated if the shape included curved surfaces, which reflect in many directions. Overholser had to design an airplane out of flat panels. He worked with mathematician Bill Schroeder on a computer program that would predict how such a shape would reflect radar. It was the key breakthrough that made the F-117 possible.

December 14–23, 1986
Burt Rutan's specially designed *Voyager*, with Dick Rutan and Jeana Yeager, makes the first nonstop, unrefueled circumnavigation of the world.

February 22, 1987
The Airbus 320, featuring a "fly-by-wire" system, makes its first flight.

March 1987
Patrice Francheske makes the first microlight round-the-world flight.

March 29, 1987
Mathias Rust lands a Cessna 172 in Red Square.

October 9, 1987
A pre-production EH 101 helicopter makes its first flight.

December 29, 1987
Russian cosmonaut Yuri Romanenko sets the space endurance record at 326 days.

January 1988
The first Low Level Wind Shear Alert System is installed.

April 29, 1988
Boeing rolls out the 747-400, the latest development of its largest aircraft.

May 23, 1988
▶ The first Bell/Boeing V-22 Osprey prototype is rolled out.

July 7, 1988
The Soviet *Phobos 1* spacecraft is launched to attempt to orbit and study Mars.

July 12, 1988
Phobos 2, the companion spacecraft, is launched to attempt to orbit and study Mars.

however, could not be reformed: The Berlin Wall came down in 1989, and the Soviet Union itself dissolved in 1991.

Meanwhile, it was the modernized U.S. Air Force that went to war with Iraq in 1991, spearheaded by the F-117 Stealth Fighters. Representing only a little more than 2 percent of the total number of fighters and bombers (shooters) available to the coalition, the F-117As attacked 31 percent of the first-day targets, including the main early-warning sites and all the downtown Baghdad targets that were hit. The latter included the main headquarters buildings, the main microwave telecommunications links, and power supplies.

F-117s and other airplanes with precision-guided weapons bombed bridges and ammunition dumps. Fighters with laser-guided bombs and infrared sensors roamed the skies around the clock, bombing Iraqi tanks. Those SAM sites that did go active were attacked by Wild Weasels and jammed by modified attack airplanes loaded with special electronics.

The conflict in Iraq introduced the Stealth Fighter to the world and proved beyond any reasonable doubt that the airplane was the decisive weapon of modern war. Something else quickly became clear in the early '90s: The Soviet Union's role in the global community had shifted forever. The Cold War was over. More important, it could even be argued that high-technology airpower had played an important role in bringing about that period's end.

Originally built by North American Rockwell (since acquired by Boeing), the B-1B has been one of the most controversial bombers in history. It has proven to be an effective weapon in the war in Afghanistan.

TANK VERSUS HELICOPTER

France was the first nation to experiment with carrying antitank missiles—originally designed for use by infantry—on helicopters. These weapons were command-guided from the helicopter, with the guidance signals carried along wires that wound out from a bobbin on the missile. In 1972, the U.S. Army evaluated a helicopter-launched version of the Hughes TOW wire-guided missile in Vietnam, with some success.

After the war, the Army launched development of a bigger, heavier **antitank helicopter,** the AH-64 Apache. Fitted with infrared viewers for the pilot and gunner, the Apache was armed with the heavy, laser-guided Hellfire missile. When the British Army ordered Apaches in the 1990s, one officer described it as the "most important innovation since the horse."

CHAPTER NINE

Flying Toward a Second Century

AFTER SURVIVING SOME LEAN YEARS, COMMERCIAL AND MILITARY AVIATION SOAR TOWARD A MURKY——AND EXCITING——FUTURE.

An era of aviation came to a close on December 4, 1991: the day Pan Am ceased taking to the skies. The death had been slow, with the airline limping along as it was buffeted by misfortune and the whims of the market, always staying just one step ahead of closing. Only the day before, a reorganization plan with Delta had seemed to give Pan Am yet another lease on life. Then, Delta abruptly pulled out, citing financial concerns. The company's last president and chief executive Russell L. Ray, Jr., sounded the death knell for the company. "Today," he said at the bankruptcy hearing, "we see the end of an airline whose name will be forever forged in American history."

Right: The Northrop B-2A Spirit uses a more modern stealth technology than that found on the earlier Lockheed Martin F-117A. Instead of angular faceted surfaces, the B-2A uses rounded surfaces to deflect radar beams. It also makes extensive use of radar-absorbent material.

Indeed, the whole airline industry had gone through wrenching changes in the early 1980s. In the United States, a number of new low-fare airlines were formed after the deregulation of U.S. air services. Most of them went bankrupt or were taken over by larger competitors.

Things were tough all over. The big airlines had shake-ups, too: Pan Am failed. TWA was acquired by American in 2001. Eastern Airlines, plagued by high costs and congested airports, vanished in the mid-1980s.

The surviving major carriers in 2002 are US Airways (assembled in the 1980s from the former Allegheny and Piedmont airlines); five long-established carriers (United, Delta, American, Northwest, and Continental); and the no-frills Southwest. The last-named remains a unique presence in the industry, with its low-key

The Boeing 737 has been continuously modified to meet market demand over the years. Its unique combination of large passenger capacity, excellent short field performance, and low operating costs have kept it competitive. Several new models of the 737 are in the planning stage.

attitude. It is also the largest airline in the world to operate one type of airplane (the Boeing 737).

Apart from Southwest, major U.S. carriers run hub-and-spoke systems in which most flights begin and end at a few airports, creating a myriad of possible connections. Consequently, U.S. airlines bought fewer large planes than anyone expected in the early 1970s. Domestic McDonnell Douglas DC-10 and Lockheed Tri-Star orders dried up. The last TriStar was built in 1983. A USAF contract for the tanker versions kept the DC-10 line going.

Smaller, narrow-body airplanes sold well, however. In 1979, McDonnell Douglas flew the DC-9 Super 80. With new, quieter engines and a stretched cabin seating 150 people, it was almost twice the size of the original DC-9. Boeing responded with the 737-300, also fitted with quieter engines. Both airplanes met new noise regulations that had been introduced in the 1970s.

With airline traffic picking up, Boeing launched two new airplanes in 1978. The 757 was a narrow-body twin-engine airplane with the same cabin cross-section as the 707, 727, and 737. It was designed as a replacement for the 727. The 767 was a twin-aisle aircraft for transcontinental flights; United was the prime sales target, and the airplane had a big, efficient wing that—for the first time—made it possible to meet United's both-coasts-out-of-Denver requirement with a twin-engine airplane.

Both the 757 and 767 were designed to be flown by two pilots. McDonnell Douglas had managed years before to get the DC-9 certificated with just a two-pilot crew rather than two pilots and a flight engineer, but all earlier Boeing jets operated with a three-person cockpit. It made the planes more expensive to operate, and the 737's sales in the United States had been weak for that reason. The new jets, however, had redesigned cockpits with TV-type displays, together with computers that monitored the operation of the engines, hydraulics, and electrical systems.

April 24, 1990
The Space Shuttle *Discovery* launches, carrying the Hubble Space Telescope.

August 2, 1990
Iraq seizes Kuwait.

September 6, 1990
▶ A 747 becomes the new Air Force One.

September 29, 1990
A prototype of the F-22A Raptor supersonic stealth fighter debuts.

October 29, 1990
Boeing gives the formal go-ahead for the 777, a twin-engine jet with a wider body than the 767. It is designed to compete with the Airbus A330 and A340.

1991
Mil-Brooke Helicopters in Miami becomes the support organization for Mil aircraft in North America.

January 17, 1991
Operation Desert Storm begins: The technology of modern warfare is unveiled.

February 13, 1991
The Swearingen SJ-30 small business jet makes its first flight.

February 27, 1991
The homebuilt Questair Venture sets three time-to-climb records.

Airbus Flies Onto the Scene

Douglas did not build an airplane comparable to the Boeing 767, but Boeing did have competition from a European newcomer: Airbus. The French and German governments founded Airbus in 1969 for the express purpose of building a twin-engine wide-body jet.

The A300 flew in 1972 and entered service in 1974. By the following year, only a handful of airplanes had been sold. Even the German state-owned airline, Lufthansa, was thinking about canceling its Airbus order and buying a new version of the 727 instead.

Airbus seemed to be headed for the same dismal fate as Concorde, but the people who started Airbus had learned from the painful lessons of the previous decade. They looked at how things had been done on Concorde and systematically did the opposite. They also unashamedly copied the U.S. manufacturers.

Unable to agree on one assembly site for Concorde, the British and French had established two assembly lines—at great cost. The German government conceded to a single Airbus flight test center and assembly line in France. To spread the work more evenly, the A300 was built in large sections—cockpit, front and rear fuselage, wing, and tail—and the sections were fitted with wiring, fuel and hydraulic lines, and many other components before they were delivered to Toulouse. As a result, there were fewer work

Above: As the market for jet air transport expanded, Boeing tailored designs to meet new market conditions. The 757 took advantage of the powerful new turbofan engines in the 37,000-pound thrust range. Designed to replace the 727, the 757 is operated by a flight crew of two.

Left: Airlines seek commonality in cockpits, so that the air crew can easily move from one series of aircraft to another. The "glass" cockpit of the 757 is highly automated, which gives the two-person crew an opportunity to watch outside the aircraft and to monitor the computer inputs.

April 23, 1991
Lockheed, Boeing, and General Dynamics are selected to build the F-22.

April 30, 1991
Boeing delivers the last 707 airframe, a Navy E-6A communications aircraft.

May 3, 1991
Robert Randolph's model airplane sets a duration record of 32 minutes and 9 seconds.

June 1991
The Soviets display the MiG-31 and the Beriev A-40 at the Paris air show.

July 1991
The Beech T-1A Jayhawk makes its first flight.

July 16, 1991
The Falcon 900 B sets a distance record of 5,012 miles, flying from Paris to Houston.

July 22, 1991
Kari Castle sets the women's hang-gliding record with a flight of 208 miles.

August 12, 1991
Delta acquires most of Pan Am's operations.

September 1991
The McDonnell Douglas C-17 makes its first flight.

October 25, 1991
The Airbus A340, the first European long-haul airliner in 30 years, makes its first flight.

December 4, 1991
Pan Am ceases operations.

December 23, 1991
The Kaman "K-Max" makes its first flight.

March 6, 1992
Virgin Atlantic launches operations.

May 12, 1992
Lockheed Martin delivers the 2,000th C-130.

September 1992
The existence of the National Reconnaissance Office is declassified.

September 25, 1992
NASA launches Mars Observer to study the Red Planet. Communication with the craft will be lost August 22, 1993.

U.S. operator, taking four airplanes on a no-cost, short-term lease. In the following year, Eastern ordered more A300s on generous terms. Boeing complained vociferously about the European company's subsidies. Airbus chairman Bernard Lathiere retorted: "I think that the Big Bad Wolf is screaming because Little Red Riding Hood has bitten him." The public relationship between the two companies went downhill from there.

By 1978, Airbus had a second product in development—the slightly smaller A310—and also had plans for an entire range of airliners, from a 150-seat, single-aisle jet to a bigger, 300-plus-seater twin and a four-engine long-haul airplane.

While the 757 retained the same relatively narrow cabin as the 727, the 767 is a wide-body aircraft. Its wings have greater sweepback than those of the 757. Powered by Pratt & Whitney turbofans of 48,000 pounds of thrust, the 767 can also use Rolls-Royce and GE engines of similar performance.

hours involved in final assembly, and the line moved smoothly. (Ironically, Airbus decided to ship all the large components by air using a Super Guppy—a converted Boeing C-97 military transport with an outsize upper fuselage—so every Airbus made its first flight on Boeing wings.)

Airbus fought desperately for survival. Lufthansa did order the airplane in 1975, and in 1977, Eastern Airlines became the first

The thought of a line of jets to rival the U.S. companies seemed a pipe dream given Europe's historic performance in that market. In March 1984, however, Airbus did indeed start work on the 150-passenger A320, challenging Boeing and McDonnell Douglas head-on in the fast-growing market for smaller jets. Three years later, Airbus announced the go-ahead for the big twin—the A330—and the four-engine A340. All the new airplanes used the same cockpit design, based on a fly-by-wire control system.

The Airbus A300 was produced by a French-German consortium, Airbus Industrie. The Airbus A300 made its first flight on October 28, 1972. The success of Airbus Industrie was assured when Eastern Airlines ordered 25 aircraft on April 6, 1978.

November 2, 1992
The Airbus A330 335-passenger twin makes its first flight.

December 9, 1992
Operation Restore Hope in Somalia begins.

December 16, 1992
The McDonnell Douglas (Boeing) C-17 sets altitude records.

March 1993
Lockheed acquires General Dynamics' Fort Worth division, the builder of the F-16.

June 8, 1993
The first Saab Grippen is handed over to the Swedish Air Force.

August 6, 1993
Sheila Widnall becomes the Secretary of the U.S. Air Force.

August 17, 1993
NASA selects Boeing as its prime contractor for the International Space Station.

December 12, 1993
▶ The Hubble's optical flaw is repaired by a shuttle crew.

January 25, 1994
The *Clementine* lunar orbiter is launched to attempt an asteroid flyby.

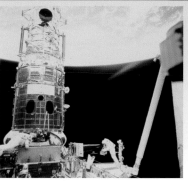

May 1994
Northrop acquires Grumman.

June 1994
The Boeing 777 makes its first flight.

December 1994
Lockheed merges with Martin-Marietta.

December 16, 1994
The Antonov AN-70 makes its first flight.

Each plane had a video-game-like sidestick instead of a two-handed yoke. A pilot could fly an A320 plane one day and an A340 aircraft the next.

The new Airbus products were the beginning of the end of the Mc-Donnell Douglas line, which looked increasingly dated. Boeing, meanwhile, was building 737s at a record pace and was pioneering the use of twin-engine planes on intercontinental routes.

Until the early '80s, no twin-engine airliner was allowed to carry passengers on a route that was more than 60 minutes' flying time from a usable airport. The rule prevented twin-engine planes from crossing oceans, but the new 767 had enough range to cross the Atlantic and was the right size to open up new air routes between smaller cities in the United States and Europe (Chicago to Munich, for instance). Engine manufacturers showed that their engines were becoming much more reliable, and governments granted permission for long-range twin-engine operations.

At the end of the 1980s, Boeing started development of a giant twin-engine jet, the 777, with two engines of 80,000 pounds thrust apiece. The long-haul airplane market—more and more

The Airbus A330 employs the same fly-by-wire control system as the innovative Airbus A320 but carries far more passengers in a high-density seating arrangement. It is powered by engines in the 65,500-pound thrust class.

1995
In one year, New York has 140,500 helicopter takeoffs/landings.

February 3–11, 1995
The Space Shuttle *Discovery* flies by *Mir* in preparation for a future docking mission.

March 31, 1995
The Cirrus SR-20 makes its first flight; it features a built-in parachute.

May 31, 1995
The FAA certifies its first aircraft from the People's Republic of China, a Model Y-12 Harbin.

June 2, 1995
Captain Scott Grady is shot down and rescued in Bosnia.

August 11, 1995
The Embraer EMB-145 makes its first flight.

November 29, 1995
The McDonnell Douglas (Boeing) Super Hornet F/A-18E makes its first flight.

1996
China invests billions of dollars in airport construction and promises a new market for vertical flight.

February 17, 1996
The U.S. *NEAR Shoemaker* craft launches to study the Eros asteroid. It will land on Eros in 2001.

February 29, 1996
European Space Agency astronaut Thomas Reiter returns after spending six months on *Mir.*

April 25, 1996
The Yak-130 two-seat trainer makes its first flight.

June 17, 1996
Burt Rutan unveils the asymmetric Boomerang.

August 6, 1996
The Kawasaki OH-X helicopter makes its first flight.

August 31, 1996
The two-seat version of the Eurofighter makes its first flight.

November 7, 1996
NASA launches the *Mars Global Surveyor* to orbit and map the Red Planet.

The computer and the aircraft came together perfectly in the Boeing 777, which was designed entirely on computers so that the very first example was not a prototype, but an actual production aircraft.

of it centered on rapidly growing air routes in and out of Asia—became a contest between Airbus and Boeing.

The Military Aviation Industry Fights to Survive

Military aviation, meanwhile, was massively affected by the end of the Cold War. In the 1980s, the Pentagon planned to rebuild much of the U.S. Air Force and Navy air fleets around stealth airplanes. More than 100 B-2 new bombers were to be followed by 750 stealthy, supersonic Advanced Tactical Fighters (ATFs) and more than 1,000 examples of the Advanced Tactical Aircraft (ATA), a bomber for the USAF and Navy.

Lockheed and Northrop flew competing prototypes of the ATF in 1990, and Lockheed's F-22 was announced as the winner of the contract in 1991, but the project has been steadily cut back and delayed over the years. The first of 300 F-22A Raptor fighters is not due to enter service until 2005, 22 years after the project started. The B-2 project was hit even harder, cut back to just 21 airplanes.

General Dynamics and McDonnell Douglas were chosen to build the flying-wing A-12 under the ATA program, but the project was canceled in 1991. There was no direct replacement. Instead, the Pentagon decided in 1995 to develop a single airplane—the Joint Strike Fighter (JSF)—which will replace most of the fighters in its inventory.

The JSF will be available in three versions. The Air Force version will be armed almost solely with guided weapons. Infrared cameras will be installed all around the airplane, feeding images to a display mounted on the pilot's helmet. Even at night, the pilot will be able to see clearly all around the airplane and will be able to aim a weapon at a target simply by looking at it. The USAF plans to buy more than 1,700 planes.

The Navy version will operate from carriers. Since the '50s, when the U.S. Navy built carriers for nuclear bombers, the service has continued to build ever larger and more powerful ships. Eventually, each of these huge ships will carry up to 36 JSFs.

November 16, 1996
Russia's *Mars 96* probe is launched.

November 16, 1996
Boeing and Lockheed Martin are chosen to build prototypes of the multiservice Joint Strike Fighter.

December 6, 1996
Rockwell Aerospace and Defense, formerly known as North American Aviation, is acquired by Boeing.

December 15, 1996
Boeing makes plans to buy McDonnell Douglas.

December 26, 1996
The Chinese Jingdezhen Z-11 helicopter makes its first flight.

1997
Eurocopter twice raises the production rates on the EC-135 helicopter.

May 17, 1997
The McDonnell Douglas X-36 tailless fighter makes its first flight.

June 25, 1997
The *Progress*, a Russian supply ship, collides with the *Mir* space station during a training exercise.

August 1, 1997
Boeing officially merges with McDonnell Douglas.

September 25, 1997
The Sukhoi S-37 Berkut advanced-technology fighter makes its first flight.

October 12, 1997
Singer John Denver dies when his experimental single-engine Rutan Long EZ plane crashes.

October 15, 1997
NASA launches *Cassini*. The robotic craft is designed to journey to Saturn and then study that planet.

October 15, 1997
The European Space Agency launches the *Huygens* probe, designed to research Saturn's Titan moon.

December 24, 1997
The *Asiasat 3* communications satellite is launched. The manufacturer, Hughes Global Services, will buy back the spacecraft from insurers when the craft fails to orbit properly. Renamed the *HGS-1*, the satellite performs two lunar flybys.

The third JSF version will be a short takeoff, vertical landing (STOVL) fighter for the Marine Corps and Britain's Royal Navy.

With only one fighter project after the year 2000, the U.S. industry was forced to undergo massive consolidations to survive the '90s. Lockheed bought General Dynamics' fighter division, which makes the F-16, in 1994 and then merged with Martin-Marietta to form Lockheed Martin. Northrop acquired Grumman in 1995. After McDonnell Douglas was eliminated from the JSF competition in late 1996, the company agreed to merge with Boeing. Lockheed Martin won the contract to build the JSF in late 2001, and the plane should enter service in 2008.

Pilotless military airplanes are assuming greater importance. In the war against the Taliban in 2001, the United States launched dozens of uncrewed combat air vehicles (UCAVs) on reconnaissance and attack missions. Most of them were RQ-1 Predators, built by General Atomics. Powered by an 80-horsepower Rotax piston engine, the one-ton Predator carries day and night TV cameras in a stabilized turret, a laser designator, and a satellite data link, which allows it to be controlled from anywhere in the world. Some Predators carry a pair of Hellfire antitank missiles.

A larger UCAV is the Northrop Grumman Global Hawk, with the wingspan of a 737. Using cameras and radar, it can map 40,000 square miles of territory (roughly the size of Ohio) in a day. It's already started to prove its chops: In early 2001, a Global Hawk flew to Australia from Edwards Air Force Base in California, the longest oceanic flight by a UCAV. The Global Hawk also was used experimentally in Afghanistan in late 2001.

Armed UCAVs may replace piloted fighter jets for hazardous missions like suppressing enemy air defenses, the type of mission that cost five of the first seven Wild Weasels in Vietnam. A prototype armed UCAV, the Boeing X-45, is expected to be flight-tested throughout 2002.

POWERING HIS WAY INTO THE MARKET

Mention small turbine engines, and you have to mention **Dr. Sam Williams.** As a young engineer with Chrysler in the 1940s, Williams worked on a Navy turboprop engine. He left Chrysler in 1954 to start his own company, with a single, clear intention: to design small, efficient, and inexpensive turbine engines.

Williams Research—later Williams International—was ready in 1975 when the Pentagon wanted engines for small, long-range, jet-powered cruise missiles. The company produced thousands of such engines. In the 1990s, Williams International became the first company in 30 years to break into the commercial engine business, and in 2002, the company was well into developing the revolutionary low-cost EJ22 small jet engine.

The costly Concorde made it unlikely that there would ever be another supersonic transport. However, new technology may permit the elimination of the sonic boom. This, combined with more environmentally friendly engines, has brought the idea of the SST back into prominence.

The Next 100 Years of Flight

The surviving mega-companies operate global businesses. Britain's BAE Systems has large operations in the United States and is a big partner in the Joint Strike Fighter program. Major pieces of the Boeing 777 are built in Japan and other countries and shipped to Everett, Washington, for final assembly. Boeing has an engineering office in Moscow, which is staffed by engineers rendered unemployed by the collapse of the Soviet industry.

The rivalry between Airbus and Boeing continues. In 2000, Airbus started development of the A380, a 600-seat, dual-deck giant that will compete with the Boeing 747. It will enter service in 2005. Boeing, meanwhile, has announced plans to develop a smaller jet, the Sonic Cruiser, which will fly higher and faster than today's airliners—just below the speed of sound.

The Wrights, de Havillands, and Kelly Johnsons of aviation's next century have new tools at their disposal, many of them

After one of the most closely contested—and closely observed—fighter competitions in history, the Lockheed Martin F-35 Joint Strike Fighter won over the competing Boeing contender. The competition was for the most lucrative aircraft contract in history: The F-35 will replace F-16s in overseas markets.

THE RISE AND FALL (AND RISE AGAIN) OF PRIVATE AIRPLANES

Small **private airplanes** have gone through a boom and a slump like no other part of the industry. The popularity of private flying soared in the 1950s and 1960s, driven by economic prosperity, a large population of war-trained pilots, and the advent of relatively cheap, reliable, low-maintenance airplane designs from manufacturers such as Cessna, Beech, and Piper.

In 1978, the U.S. lightplane industry delivered 18,000 private aircraft, including 14,400 single-propeller airplanes—and then the market imploded. In 1987, the industry shipped a mere 600 single-engine airplanes.

Production has picked up a little since then, but the sector is still not very active. One reason: The industry developed almost no new technology after the 1940s. The 2001-model Cessna 172 has no basic features that were not on many World War II aircraft.

On the other hand, the market for self-built airplanes has grown. The first homebuilts in the 1950s were made from plans and took a great deal of skill to put together. Since then, it's gotten easier—more and more people have learned to build their own airplanes, and the kits have gotten simpler to put together. By the 1980s, airplanes such as the Glasair and Lancair—four-seat, high-performance aircraft—could be bought as complete kits, avoiding complex metal fabrication tasks.

September 1998
Galileo spots the sources of Jupiter's rings.

September 6, 1998
The Fuji Blimp sets the duration record for covering a television event: 14 hours and 9 minutes at the U.S. Open Tennis Tournament.

September 24, 1998
The Beriev Be 200 fire-fighting flying boat makes its first flight.

October 10, 1998
The F-22 goes supersonic for the first time.

October 24, 1998
NASA launches *Deep Space 1* to explore deep space, including asteroids and comets.

October 29, 1998
▶ Space Shuttle *Discovery* launches with 77-year-old John Glenn as part of its crew.

November 20, 1998
The first module of the International Space Station is launched by a Russian expendable rocket.

December 11, 1998
NASA launches the *Mars Climate Orbiter.*

December 22, 1998
The Spanish CASA C 295 transport makes its first flight.

1999
Sikorsky and partners fly the first prototype of the S-92 Helibus.

January 3, 1999
NASA launches the *Mars Polar Lander* to land on and explore Mars. Contact will be lost as it descends toward the planet almost a year later.

January 24, 1999
The Ariane 42L puts the Galaxy XR satellite into orbit.

based on computers. Computers helped to model the radar reflections from the first stealth aircraft through techniques such as computational fluid dynamics (CFD). CFD allows designers to see how air will flow around a new design before they build a wind-tunnel model. CFD also lets designers solve aerodynamic problems in more efficient but untried ways, rather than choosing a less efficient approach because it is known to work.

Some major challenges could be overcome in the early-to-mid 2000s. The sale of small private airplanes slumped and stagnated after the boom of the 1970s because their old-style piston engines are heavy and noisy, but turbine engines were too expensive for the market. In 2002, a new-start company called Eclipse Aviation expects to fly a small, six-place jet with two new-technology Williams turbofan engines and a price tag less than $900,000.

Small airplanes could also become easier and safer to fly. New electronics technology makes it possible to combine an autopilot and navigation system in one small, affordable box. In a dire emergency, such a unit could land an airplane automatically. In

The Lockheed Martin F-22 Raptor is the most advanced fighter in the world and will be the U.S. air-superiority fighter for most of the 21st century. Stealthy, with supercruise performance and high maneuverability, the Raptor will absolutely dominate all opposing fighters.

Above: The Global Hawk uncrewed aerial vehicle is shown returning to land at Edwards Air Force Base, California. The Global Hawk is the harbinger of a whole new world of remote-controlled war vehicles.

Near right: The General Atomics RQ-1 Predator made history when it fired a Hellfire missile at al Qaeda troops in Afghanistan, becoming the first UAV in history to engage in independent combat operations.

Right: The U.S. Air Force wants an aircraft that is maneuverable in space and not confined to orbital flights. The time frame has not been established, but it probably will not be in the first half of the 21st century.

the late 1990s, companies started using laptop computer screens as the basis for the kind of large-format, easy-to-read cockpit displays that commercial pilots now take for granted.

At the opposite end of the size scale, the airship may be making a comeback. In 2001, the CargoLifter company built a giant hangar near Berlin, where it plans to assemble an airship bigger

than the *Hindenburg*. With its envelope made of modern synthetic fabrics and the latest in flight-control technology, the CargoLifter is designed to transport huge pieces of machinery, like construction and power-generating equipment—the sort of equipment that today travels on ships and in road convoys.

One of the most exciting new projects is the Defense Advanced Research Projects Agency's Quiet Supersonic Platform (QSP), a supersonic-cruise airplane that leaves no sonic boom behind it. The QSP should cruise at 1,600 miles per hour—almost three times as fast as most airplanes today—with the same level of efficiency as subsonic airplanes. A prototype could fly by 2007.

But it is still essential, once in a while, to take a break from the technology and join the late July pilgrimage to a wide-open air-

July 2000
Raytheon delivers the first Beech/Pilatus PC-9 to the Greek Air Force.

July 2000
The first missile firing is conducted for the F-22 (AIM-9).

July 2000
The Westland WAH-64 Apache makes its first flight.

August 2000
The first V-22 Osprey is delivered to the USAF.

August 2000
Aviastar starts deliveries of the upgraded An-124s.

September 18, 2000
The Boeing X-32 Joint Strike Fighter prototype makes its first flight.

October 24, 2000
The Lockheed X-35 Joint Strike Fighter prototype makes its first flight.

November 2, 2000
A joint United States-Russian crew takes up residence in the International Space Station.

December 19, 2000
Airbus launches the A380 giant airliner to compete with Boeing's 747.

February 2, 2001
The Predator B 001 Drone with a turboprop makes its first flight.

February 12, 2001
The *NEAR (Near Earth Asteroid Rendezvous) Shoemaker* probe lands on the asteroid Eros, taking pictures on the way down and transmitting data after it has landed.

February 20, 2001
The Russian SS-25 ICBM launches the Swedish *Odin* spacecraft.

February 21, 2001
The Bombardier CRJ900 makes its first flight.

March 14, 2001
The Boeing X-40A RLV makes its inaugural flight.

field in Oshkosh, Wisconsin. In terms of number of airplanes, the annual get-together of the Experimental Aircraft Association (EAA) there is the biggest air show in the world.

The organization's members, guests, and affiliates bring in almost everything that flies—in fact, almost everything that has ever flown without feathers. You can see a virtually perfect reproduction of a Sikorsky S-38 flying-boat; some sleek, efficient composite homebuilt airplanes; the long lines of immaculately restored P-51s, F4Us, and other warbirds; and even modern classics like the F-104.

Snowmobile-engine-powered ultralights take to the air in the mornings and evenings, flying low lazy circles—as slow, skinny, and insect-like as the Antoinettes and Bleriots that flew at Rheims in 1909.

Oshkosh reminds us that aviation isn't just about the developments in technology or the records that are broken. What Oshkosh is really about is the dream of flight—the dream that first became reality for two French papermakers in 1783.

Left: Paul Poberezny founded the Experimental Aircraft Association in 1953. One has only to attend an EAA Fly-In at Oshkosh to know that it is, indeed, "the greatest show on earth." In all truth, EAA saved general aviation.

Below left: The Lockheed X-33 Venture Star was intended as a vehicle that could take off from a conventional runway, fly into orbit, then descend, and land just as a conventional aircraft does. Structural complications with its fuel tank have sidelined the X-33, at least for the time being.

A VISIONARY OF TODAY . . . AND FOR TOMORROW

One of the most controversial and visionary figures in aviation for the last 25 years has been **Burt Rutan.** After serving as an engineer with the U.S. Air Force, Rutan set up shop in Mojave, California, and started to design airplanes that people could build in their garages. Rutan believes that easy-to-fly, jet-powered personal aircraft will eventually render commercial airlines as obsolete as buses.

Lacking access to a wind tunnel, Rutan would attach wing sections to the roof of his Buick and race along the Mojave runway. In the mid-1970s, Rutan published plans for the elegant, tail-first Vari-Eze, one of the first homebuilts to outperform factory-built aircraft, and then formed the Scaled Composites company to build prototypes for other companies.

The low point of the 1980s was the Starship, designed for Beech Aircraft, which took much longer than expected to build and sold poorly. The high point was the December 1986 circumnavigation of the world by Rutan's specially built Voyager, flown by the designer's brother, Dick Rutan, and Jeana Yeager. The nonstop, unfueled flight took nine days.

March 29, 2001
Boeing announces the Sonic Cruiser as the next airliner.

April 23, 2001
The Airbus Industrie A-340-600 makes its first flight.

April 23, 2001
The Global Hawk makes a 23-hour flight to Australia.

April 28, 2001
▶ American millionaire Dennis Tito becomes the first space tourist, paying $20 million to join a Russian flight to the International Space Station.

May 7, 2001
The Antonov An-225 Mriya super-heavy transport is test-flown.

May 10, 2001
China launches the Long March 4B.

July–August 2001
Lockheed Martin and Boeing Joint Strike Fighter prototypes become the first practical supersonic fighters to demonstrate a vertical landing.

July 2, 2001
The Zeppelin NT begins making operating flights over Lake Constance.

August 13, 2001
The solar-powered Helios sets an altitude record of 96,500 feet.

September 11, 2001
Terrorists hijack three U.S. passenger airliners and strike New York and the Pentagon. A fourth hijacked plane crashes in Pennsylvania.

October 2001
Uncrewed Predator aircrafts launch weapons in combat in Afghanistan.

October 29, 2001
The Lockheed Martin X-35 wins the Joint Strike Fighter competition.

Index